Gordon S. Miko

With Piety and Learning

*To Jack,
with deep respect
and fondness.

Rich*

International Practical Theology

edited by

Prof. Dr. Chris Hermans (Nijmegen),
Prof. Dr. Maureen Junker-Kenny (Dublin),
Prof. Dr. Richard Osmer (Princeton),
Prof. Dr. Friedrich Schweitzer (Tübingen),
Prof. Dr. Hans-Georg Ziebertz (Würzburg)

in cooperation with the
International Academy of Practical Theology (IAPT),

represented by

Bonnie Miller-McLemore (President)
and Jean-Guy Nadeau (Vice President)

Volume 11

LIT

Gordon S. Mikoski, Richard R. Osmer

With Piety and Learning

The History of Practical Theology
at Princeton Theological Seminary
1812 – 2012

Gedruckt auf alterungsbeständigem Werkdruckpapier entsprechend
ANSI Z3948 DIN ISO 9706

Bibliographic information published by the Deutsche Nationalbibliothek
The Deutsche Nationalbibliothek lists this publication in the Deutsche
Nationalbibliografie; detailed bibliographic data are available in the Internet at
http://dnb.d-nb.de.

ISBN 978-3-643-90106-4

A catalogue record for this book is available from the British Library

©LIT VERLAG GmbH & Co. KG Wien,
Zweigniederlassung Zürich 2011
Klosbachstr. 107
CH-8032 Zürich
Tel. +41 (0) 44-251 75 05
Fax +41 (0) 44-251 75 06
e-Mail: zuerich@lit-verlag.ch
http://www.lit-verlag.ch

LIT VERLAG Dr. W. Hopf
Berlin 2011
Fresnostr. 2
D-48159 Münster
Tel. +49 (0) 2 51-620 320
Fax +49 (0) 2 51-922 60 99
e-Mail: lit@lit-verlag.de
http://www.lit-verlag.de

Distribution:
In Germany: LIT Verlag Fresnostr. 2, D-48159 Münster
Tel. +49 (0) 2 51-620 32 22, Fax +49 (0) 2 51-922 60 99, e-mail: vertrieb@lit-verlag.de

In Austria: Medienlogistik Pichler-ÖBZ, e-mail: mlo@medien-logistik.at

In the UK: Global Book Marketing, e-mail: mo@centralbooks.com

To our colleagues in the department of practical theology
May the conversation continue

Contents

	Acknowledgments	ix
	Introduction	xi
Chapter 1	*An Able and Faithful Ministry*	1
Chapter 2	*Honoring the Patriarchs: Technical Elaboration of Original Vision*	31
Chapter 3	*Practical Theology and the Reorganization of the Seminary*	73
Chapter 4	*Reformed and Ecumenical: Practical Theology and New Currents of Theology*	103
Chapter 5	*The Flowering of Practical Theology during the McCord and Gillespie Years*	133
Chapter 6	*A Continuing Conversation*	177
	Epilogue	203
	Bibliography	213
	Index	225

Acknowledgements

A book that traces the history of practical theology at Princeton Theological Seminary over a span of two hundred years could not have been completed without the help of many colleagues. We are deeply grateful to those who have provided assistance along the way. We give special thanks to Kenneth Henke, reference archivist, and Kate Skrebutenas, reference librarian, of Princeton Theological Seminary, and to their wonderful staffs. We are also grateful for the assistance of the staff at The Presbyterian Historical Society. Special thanks also is offered to president Iain Torrance and the Board of Trustees of the seminary, who granted Rick Osmer a sabbatical leave during which much of his research and writing for this project was carried out. Many colleagues offered insights into the story told here. Thanks especially to James Lapsley, J. Randall Nichols, Geddes Hanson, Karlfried Froelich, Charles Bartow, Freda Gardner, Craig Dykstra, Rodney Hunter, Dana Wright, Thomas Hastings, Chip Dobbs Allsopp, Katharine Sakenfeld, Barbara Chaapel, Herbert Anderson, Keith Drury, Duncan Ferguson, James Kay, James Moorhead, Kenda Creasy Dean, Sally Brown, Nancy Lammers Gross, and Deborah Hunsinger. Various students have played important roles along the way. Here we thank Emily Cain, Campbell Hackett, Blair Bertrand, Chananporn "Oan" Jaisaodee, Marcus Hong and Christiane Lang Hearlson. Margo Dudak, program assistant for Education and Formation, has facilitated our communication and resources in numerous ways. Thank you, Margo.

Every academic project of this sort is both a joy and a burden to a scholar's family. We offer our deepest gratitude to our children and to our wives, Nancy Mikoski and Sally Osmer. You are our partners in love and life. This book could not have been completed without your loving support.

This project is the outcome of numerous conversations between the authors. Repeatedly, we have read and commented on one another's work. The task of research and writing the first two chapters, covering the nineteenth century, fell to Gordon Mikoski. The task of covering the twentieth century in the three chapters that follow fell to Rick Osmer. The Introduction, Chapter Six, and the Epilogue were joint efforts.

Gordon S. Mikoski and Richard R. Osmer
March, 2011
Princeton Theological Seminary.

Introduction

Why this book?
    This book arose out of a convergence of several intersecting lines of interest. In 2012, Princeton Theological Seminary will celebrate its bicentennial. This approaching milestone has provided the immediate impetus for various efforts to reflect upon and assess the seminary's contributions to the church, theological inquiry, theological education, and wider society. As PTS moves toward its grand birthday celebration, it does so with reverence for its past and a resolute commitment to address creatively the challenges of the present as well as the possibilities of the future. This book seeks to contribute to conversations about the history and significance of PTS by exploring the distinctive ways that the seminary has embodied and understood practical theology throughout its history.
    This study also seeks to contribute something of value to the ongoing and widely differentiated conversation that is the field of practical theology. This robust, multifaceted, and contested field of theological study today includes normative and methodological perspectives from practical theologians working in such countries as Australia, the Netherlands, Canada, Germany, the United Kingdom, France, India, South Africa, and the United States. Engaging in this dynamic intellectual conversation today means taking a seat around a very diverse table. New voices and views have valued places alongside those that have been participants in the conversation since the days of the German Enlightenment. PTS occupies one of the long established seats at the practical theology roundtable. This book aims to give some account of the interests and norms associated with practical theology at PTS as a

way to enrich and further develop the wider conversation. While practical theology at PTS has been and continues to be enriched by the ever growing range of Protestant and Catholic voices in practical theology, we hope to contribute something of value to others out of the storehouse of our particular memories and commitments.

At a more personal level, this book provides a vehicle for its two authors to answer the question, "What is distinctive about practical theology at PTS?" When working with colleagues in practical theology in national and international contexts, we have often had the sense that the way we engage in thinking about and practicing the theory and practice of practical theology has some distinctive features and commitments that are related to our institutional home. Our doctoral students often press us to define both what we share with other practical theologians from a wide range of contexts and what is distinctive about how we do practical theology. Even if this work does not provide a complete answer to such questions, it has at the very least helped us to clarify what it means to be a practical theologian from Princeton Seminary.

This book also seeks to make a contribution to the history of practical theology, a significantly underdeveloped dimension of the wider field. By virtue of its aims, subject matter, and methods, the field of practical theology tends to focus on the present in service to changes toward a more desirable future. Dynamic interpretations of present issues and creative proposals for future interventions related to church and society often result in neglect of the importance of memory in practical theology. We offer this history of practical theology at PTS, in part, as a way to encourage the development of historical studies by others in the wider field. A rich array of textured historical studies of institutions, movements, paradigms, and figures in practical theology might help each new generation of practical theologians to avoid having to reinvent or rediscover the field. A collection of such historical studies might also provide some disciplinary anchors sufficient to address the concerns of many outside the field who wonder if such a thing as practical theology even exists or whether it might simply be a curricular convenience for housing the faculty and courses that do not fit anywhere else in a theological school.

What is this book?

Essentially, this project is an extended historical case study of the character and forms of practical theology at one established mainline theological seminary in the North America context from the beginning of the nineteenth century through the beginning of the twenty-first century.

This book will attend to internal developments as well as to how those developments sought to respond to or even to shape changes taking place in the larger cultural context. Examining the features of practical theology at PTS across the course of two hundred years will bring to light practical theological themes and issues that persist in the PTS context as well as ways in which several key assumptions and practices have fundamentally changed or been rejected. The historical case study approach will sift out the strengths, limitations, complexities and tensions of practical theology in the oldest Presbyterian seminary in the United States of America.

This project aims to illuminate one case. While it does not make a large claim that PTS is somehow representative or exemplary of the whole class of theological schools in which practical theology holds a curricular place, this study does seek to offer some insight into issues relevant to both the theory and the practice of "theory and practice" in other contexts. Doubtless, some features of practical theology as instantiated in various periods at PTS are unique if not singular or even quirky. Yet, some dimensions of the unfolding PTS narrative will likely resonate with the ways in which practical theology has been understood and practiced in several other contexts. For this reason, this extended historical case study seeks neither to be representative in a hegemonic manner nor to be unique in a way that is utterly idiosyncratic; rather, it seeks to illuminate both its own inner logic and key issues that are frequently if not perpetually at play in the wider field of practical theology.

Because this book traces the features, developments, and problems of practical theology as played out in the PTS context over the course of twenty decades, some problems with terminology inevitably arise. As will become clear in the first chapter, during the nineteenth century the entirety of the theological curriculum was assumed to have a practical character and, within that larger framework, it was also assumed that a particular part of the curricular whole should focus on the duties and skills of pastoral leaders. When dealing with the more narrow aspect of the curriculum, the predominant term was "pastoral theology." The term "practical theology" was introduced explicitly at PTS in the inaugural address of Alexander Taggart McGill in 1854, and his professorial chair incorporated this term for one academic year.[1] For reasons not entirely

---

[1] Alexander T. McGill, "Practical Theology: An Inaugural Discourse," in *Discourses at the Inauguration of the Rev. Alexander T. McGill, D.D., as Professor of Pastoral Theology* [sic], *Church Government, and the Composition and Delivery of Sermons in the Theological Seminary at Princeton, N.J., Delivered at Princeton, September 12, 1854, Before the Directors of the Seminary*, (Philadelphia: C. Sherman, 1854), 35-60.

clear in the historical record, McGill and the seminary as a whole reverted to the term "pastoral theology" and continued to use that term until the middle part of the first decade of the twentieth century, at which point the terminology shifted from "pastoral theology" to "practical theology." When looking back at the term "pastoral theology" through the lenses of contemporary practical theology, it becomes clear that this term referred to that part of theological wisdom that pertained to the frameworks, practices, habits of mind, and skills associated with clerical leadership as a whole. The term did not mean primarily what it often does today: theological reflection on the ministry of pastoral care and counseling. Neither did the term "pastoral theology" in the nineteenth century simply reduce down to a treatment of ministerial skills (as if it were Exhibit A for Edward Farley's much discussed "clerical paradigm").[2] This term, as used at PTS in the nineteenth century actually included much more than tips and techniques for pastors, though, to be sure, those sorts of things were also included.

How Does this Book Tell the Story of Practical Theology at PTS?

One of the most difficult challenges we faced in writing this book was to limit the scope of our research and writing. Early on in our conceptualization of this project, we decided to focus primarily on pastoral and practical theology at Princeton Theological Seminary. This story is complex in its own right. Yet we came to believe that this story could not be told unless it was placed in several contexts: the history of conflict and change at the seminary, the larger story of practical theology in the United States, and the broader social context of American history. In the chapters that follow attention is thus given to matters like the influence of Scottish Common Sense Realism in nineteenth century American higher education, the Religious Education Movement, and the Clinical Pastoral Education Movement. The distinctive character of pastoral and practical theology at PTS only becomes clear when placed in the context of these trends and movements.

We also decided to focus on representative figures in this story. Rather than sharing briefly about many faculty members in practical theology, we decided to explore extensively the work of a few key persons. We are painfully aware that many people who have taught in the area of practical theology are not covered in this book. The discourse

---

[2] Edward Farley, *Theologia: The Fragmentation and Unity of Theological Education* (Philadelphia: Fortress, 1983), 85-8.

of pastoral and practical theology at PTS is an ongoing conversation, one far richer and more complex than the story narrated here. Our story is told by exploring the thinking and practice of representative figures.

In making the decision to focus on certain people, we have been guided by four criteria. First, the person must have primary responsibility for teaching in the area of pastoral or practical theology. Only gradually, over many years did pastoral and practical theology become a distinct subject area or department in the curriculum. In the seminary's earliest years, Archibald Alexander and Samuel Miller, for example, taught courses in pastoral theology along with courses in other areas. We decided to focus on them and only briefly mention Charles Hodge because pastoral theology was among their primary teaching responsibilities.

Second, we selected representative figures based upon their identifiable impact on the area of practical theology and on the seminary as a whole. Charles Erdman, for example, was appointed to a new chair in practical theology in 1906, created by the Board of Directors to bring greater balance to a curriculum heavily weighted toward specialized, academic studies. Erdman was at the epicenter of the struggle to reform the curriculum during this period. Elmer Homrighausen, likewise, was a seminal figure at the seminary. He was the Thomas Synott Professor of Christian Education and, later, the first appointment to the newly created position of Charles R. Erdman Professor of Pastoral Theology. He was the chair of the department for seven years and the dean of the faculty for ten.

Third, all of the figures were chosen because they wrote explicitly out of a practical theological perspective. Even early figures such as Alexander and Miller acknowledged that there is something distinctive about what they called "pastoral theology" at that time. In their course lectures and published writings, they drew attention to the combination of theological reflection, wisdom, learning, and experience that pastors must possess. As we drew closer to the present, this third criteria guided our decision to focus on a representative figure in each area of the department: pastoral care, Christian education, and preaching, speech communication in ministry, and worship.[3] We chose Seward Hiltner, James Loder, and Charles Bartow because each explicitly wrote from the perspective of practical theology and articulated a larger vision of the field.

Finally, several of these figures deserve to be better known. They not only anticipated issues with which the field of practical theology continues

---

[3] Official departmental nomenclature and organizational patterns have changed across the years. These terms point to important subject areas in the department.

to struggle, but also provided living options for addressing these issues. John Breckinridge, for example, was Professor of Pastoral Theology and Missionary Instruction for only two years. Yet his vision of the church as a mission society is relevant to the contemporary discussion of the missional church. As the first English translator and personal friend of Karl Barth, Elmer Homrighausen articulated a theory of Christian *paideia* that remains unique in American Protestantism. While better known, Seward Hiltner and James Loder articulated models of practical theology that deserve more serious study today. One of the themes to emerge over the course of our story is the prominent place granted the *theological* dimension of practical theology by the figures examined. Sometimes, this placed them at odds with perspectives that were prominent in the guilds and movements of their day. It is worth taking a second look at their thinking, for practical theology continues to struggle to define its constructive task and its contribution to the larger theological enterprise as a whole.

An Overview of the Book

A brief overview of chapters will provide readers with a sense of the whole as they begin to engage this text. Chapter 1 begins the story with the founding of Princeton Theological Seminary in 1812. It examines the way pastoral theology was conceptualized and taught within the broader parameters of a curriculum committed to a classical humanistic education grounded in orthodox Reformed theology. While *all* of theology was viewed as practical, pastoral theology had a special role to play in the curriculum. Here, we grant pride of place to the founding "patriarchs" of PTS, Archibald Alexander and Samuel Miller, and also examine John Breckinridge's short tenure at PTS.

Chapter 2 traces the continuing influence of the original "paradigm" established by Alexander and Miller on the people who taught pastoral and practical theology during the second half of the nineteenth century. During this period, the duties of the pastor, sacred rhetoric, and ecclesiastical governance became special subject areas, assigned to faculty appointed to teach exclusively in these areas. Pastoral and practical theology also became more technical and specialized. Here, we examine James Alexander, Alexander McGill, and William Paxton.

Chapter 3 follows the story into the first decades of the twentieth century, a time of considerable conflict and tension at PTS. Charles Erdman's inaugural lecture, "Modern Practical Theology," marks a turning point in the history of pastoral and practical theology at PTS, and he is the representative figure examined from this period. We highlight the distinctiveness of Erdman's understanding of theological education and practical theology by comparing him to Gresham Machen, who argued vehemently for continuing the traditions of "Old Princeton" at the seminary. Machen would leave PTS to establish Westminster Theological Seminary in Philadelphia, taking other faculty and students with him.

Chapter 4 focuses on changes that took place at PTS under the leadership of the new president, John Mackay. During this period, PTS moved toward patterns of theological education that sought to cultivate a Reformed identity that was more ecumenical and missional. Elmer Homrighausen is the representative figure treated in this chapter. In dialogue with Karl Barth's theology, Homrighausen signaled the new currents of theology flowing into PTS during the Mackay era and articulated a new theological foundation for practical theology.

Chapter 5 explores the emergence of a new level of shared responsibilities, a common discourse, and overlapping pedagogies across the specialized areas in the department of practical theology. We examine a figure from each area who wrote explicitly from the perspective of practical theology: Seward Hiltner, James Loder, and Charles Bartow. These figures highlight the diversity of the discussion of practical theology at PTS and the tension between specialized areas and a shared language and pedagogies that continues to characterize practical theology today.

Chapter 6 brings the story into the present, noting the arrival of the first woman and first African Americans in the department, Freda Gardner, Edler Hawkins, and Geddes Hanson. It also provides insight into the current discussion of practical theology at PTS through a transcript of a focus group of four tenured women in the practical theology department. The title of this chapter, "A Continuing Conversation," identifies a central lesson that emerged from our story. As the student body and faculty have become more diverse, it has become more important to acknowledge the varied ways practical theology is carried out at PTS and in the field. If Archibald Alexander and Samuel Miller could conceptualize the "duties" of the pastor in terms of a single denomination, gender, and cultural context, this is emphatically not the case today.

The Epilogue is both retrospective and prospective. It asks two questions: What have we learned form this project? What might this project contribute to the future of practical theology? The story we tell in the pages that follow is only one strand of the intricate story of practical theology in North America. It represents one set of voices in a larger conversation. We can only hope that it will contribute to a continuing conversation about what this field has been and what it might become in the future.

Chapter 1
An Able and Faithful Ministry

Day One

On August 12, 1812, several ecclesiastical dignitaries, a number of students from the College of New Jersey, and a tiny cohort of seminary students gathered in the sanctuary of the Presbyterian Church in Princeton, New Jersey to mark the inauguration of "The Theological Seminary" of the Presbyterian Church. That day represented the culmination of several years' worth of efforts by many—including those who addressed the gathered company on this occasion—to persuade the General Assembly that a school designated solely for the purpose of preparing clergy and other church leaders was a pressing and justifiable necessity. Samuel Miller, a prominent Presbyterian pastor in New York City, preached a sermon on the elements of an "able and faithful ministry." Archibald Alexander, a distinguished pastor who had only recently been appointed by the General Assembly to serve as the initial and sole member of the faculty, offered an inaugural speech on the central importance of biblical knowledge in the theological education of pastors. Philip Milledoler, a German Reformed pastor serving a Dutch Reformed church in New York City—who was soon to become president of Queen's College (later known as Rutgers) in New Brunswick, New Jersey—delivered the charge to the professor and the students. This momentous event marked the opening of a theological school that put into practice a vision for the vital conjunction of piety and learning among its graduates. The themes sounded on this day resonated in the halls and classrooms of this school down through the decades of the nineteenth century and beyond. In several key respects, the messages delivered at the opening of Princeton Theological Seminary bore witness to a vision and a set of values that would shape the ethos of the seminary into a long and distinguished future that its founders could scarcely imagine.

Samuel Miller (1769-1850), a child of the manse, was born and raised in Delaware. After graduating from the University of Pennsylvania in 1788, he prepared for ordination as a Presbyterian minister by studying with his father and with the Scottish Presbyterian divine Charles Nesbit, first president of Dickinson College. From 1793 until 1801, Miller acted as an associate pastor at the First Presbyterian Church in New York City. He was called to serve as pastor for the Wall Street Presbyterian Church in 1801 and as moderator of the General Assembly in 1806. He resigned from his pastorate in 1813 in order to become the second professor at PTS. For thirty-six years, he taught church history, church government, and the preparation and delivery of sermons. A highly productive author, Miller wrote several important works on Presbyterian polity as well as the highly acclaimed *A Brief Retrospect of the Eighteenth Century*.

Miller's sermon, "The Duty of the Church to Take Measures for Providing an Able and Faithful Ministry," marked out much of the intellectual territory in which the seminary would function for the next two hundred years.[1] While the profound internal disruptions that surfaced over the interpretation of the Bible in the 1920s would lead to a significant reorganization of the seminary in 1929, the underlying vision for a pious and learned ministry articulated in Miller's sermon continued to exert influence throughout the twentieth century and into the present.

According to Miller, an able and faithful ministry is composed of four elements: piety, talents, learning, and diligence.[2] He considered piety the most important, the foundation that conditions the coordination and use of the other three elements. Harkening back both to Gilbert Tennent's warnings about the dangers of an unconverted ministry and John Witherspoon's condemnation of learning without piety, Miller asked:

---

[1] Samuel Miller, "The Sermon Delivered at the Inauguration of the Rev. Archibald Alexander, D.D. as Professor of Didactic and Polemic Theology in the Theological Seminary of the Presbyterian Church in the United States of America. To which are Added the Professor's Inaugural Address and the Charge to the Professor and Students" (New York: Whiting and Watson, 1812), 12. Hereafter, Miller's contribution will be referred to as "Sermon," Alexander's address as "Inaugural Discourse" and Milledoler's speech as "Charge."

[2] Miller, "Sermon," 12.

> How can a man who knows only the theory of religion, undertake to be a practical guide in spiritual things? How can he adapt his instructions to all the varieties of Christian experience? How can he direct the awakened, the inquiring, the tempted, and the doubting? How can he feed the sheep and the lambs of Christ? How can he sympathize with mourners in Zion? How can he comfort others with those consolations wherewith he himself has never been comforted of God? He cannot possibly perform, as he ought, any of these duties, and they are the most precious and interesting parts of the ministerial work. However gigantic his intellectual powers; however deep, and various, and accurate his learning, he is not *able*, in relation to any of these points, to *teach others*, seeing [as] he is not taught himself. If he make the attempt, it will be *the blind leading the blind*; and of this, unerring wisdom has told the consequence.[3]

For Miller and the other PTS professors of the nineteenth century, the differentiated unity among the four elements of an "able and faithful ministry" was asymmetrical: a vital, personal, and transforming relationship with Jesus Christ through the power of the Holy Spirit served as the cornerstone of normative pastoral ministry and the theological education appropriate to it.

While native gifts and a persevering attitude were key elements in an able and faithful ministry, the church through its theological seminary could do little to inculcate them. Requisite talents—practical wisdom and sound judgment chief among them—and appropriate moral character were gifts of divine grace that had to be in place prior to formal theological education and formation for ministry. At most, a theological school could only encourage the proper use and development of these gifts.

---

[3] Ibid., 13-4, emphasis in original. For Tennent's sermon see Gilbert Tennent, "On the Dangers of an Unconverted Ministry," *Sermons of the Log College* (Ligonier, PA: Soli Deo Gloria, 1993), 375-404. For Witherspoon's statement, see Miller, "Sermon," 17-8. Miller quoted Witherspoon directly: "Accursed be all that learning which sets itself in opposition to the cross of Christ! Accursed be all that learning which disguises or is ashamed of the cross of Christ! Accursed by all that learning which fills the room that is due to the cross of Christ! And once more, accursed be all that learning which is not made subservient to the honor and glory of the cross of Christ!" John Witherspoon, "Glorying in the Cross," *The Works of the Rev. John Witherspoon*, vol. 1 (Philadelphia: William Woodward, 1800), 531.

The church could, however, do something more directly about learning. Theological education for ministry would focus primarily on the cultivation of learning appropriate to the ministerial vocation. Miller held that without adequate learning, "Both piety and talents united are inadequate to the official work."[4] Worse, learning without piety could and probably would lead to active harm to the church. The range of learning that Miller envisioned for future ministers was to be both deep and wide:

> [The minister] is, then, to be ready, on all occasions, to explain the Scriptures. This is his first and chief work. That is not merely to state and support the more simple and elementary doctrine of the gospel; but also to elucidate with clearness the various parts of the sacred volume, whether doctrinal, historical, typical, prophetic, or practical. He is to be ready to rectify erroneous translations of sacred Scripture; to reconcile seeming contradictions; to clear up real obscurities; to illustrate the force and beauty of allusions to ancient customs and manners; and, in general, to explain the Word of God, as one who has made it the object of his deep and successful study. He is *set for the defence* [sic] *of the gospel*; and, therefore, must be qualified to answer the objections of infidels; to repel the insinuations and cavils of skeptics; to detect, expose, and refute the ever varying forms of heresy; and to give notice, and *stand in the breach*, when men ever so covertly or artfully, depart from *the faith once delivered to the saints*. He is to be ready to solve the doubts, and satisfy the scruples of conscientious believers; to give instruction to the numerous classes of respectful and serious inquirers; to *reprove, rebuke, and exhort, with all long suffering and doctrine*. He is to preach the gospel with plainness, dignity, clearness, force, and solemnity. And, finally, he is to perform his part in the judicatories of the church, where candidates for the holy ministry are examined and their qualifications ascertained; where a constant inspection is maintained over the faith and order of the church; where the general interests of Zion are discussed and decided; and in conducting the affairs of which,

---

[4] Miller, "Sermon," 21.

legislative, judicial, and executive proceedings are all combined.[5]

The learning appropriate to ministry had to be deeply anchored in the study and use of Scripture. It had to include knowledge of people in various spiritual conditions. It also had to prepare pastoral leaders to make appropriate and contextual ecclesial judgments of various kinds. Drawing from the General Assembly's plan for the seminary, Miller envisioned a curriculum of biblical exegesis and hermeneutics, theology (in its didactic, polemical, and "casuistic" or practical modes), church history, the duties of the pastoral office (especially preaching and church government or polity), and moral philosophy. Additionally, the seminary's curriculum should include such auxiliary subjects as "Logic, Metaphysics, Natural Philosophy, Mathematical Science, Geography, Natural History, and polite [sic] Literature."[6] This formidable curriculum would be the "result of combined wisdom, learning, and experience"—particularly of its professors.[7] Taken as a whole, Miller's vision of theological education in its entirety was classically Reformed, broadly humanist, and thoroughly practical.

In his charge to Archibald Alexander and to the first class of students, Philip Milledoler echoed in all essentials Miller's main themes. He called for a "learned, orthodox, pious, and evangelical Ministry."[8] On the subject of the importance of a learned ministry, Milledoler added the conviction that "true learning has never injured the church, and never will. Such is the harmony subsisting between the works and word of God, that discoveries in the former will never cease to promote our regard for the latter."[9] In harmony with both Witherspoon and Miller, he warned against learning without piety in the church and extolled the importance of a theological curriculum that plumbed the depths of theological knowledge, the "spoils of science," and "almost every department of literature."[10] Milledoler further urged that the seminary curriculum ought to place a premium on teaching the Westminster Confession of Faith and "the form of government connected with it."[11]

---

[5] Ibid., 23-5, emphasis in original.
[6] Ibid., 25-6.
[7] Ibid., 37.
[8] Milledoler, "Charge," 108.
[9] Ibid.
[10] Ibid.
[11] Ibid., 113.

Reiterating the inherently practical character of the entire curriculum of the new seminary, Milledoler wistfully offered the hope that "the time is far distant, when our churches will be satisfied with mere exhibitions of learning, or eloquence, or with the substitution of dry moral lectures for the preaching of the cross."[12]

Archibald Alexander (1772-1851) came from the rough hewn frontier of Virginia. He received his theological education by tutorial and independent study. Upon ordination to the Presbyterian ministry, he briefly shepherded a small congregation in rural Virginia and in 1797 was elected president of Hampton-Sydney College. After four years as the college's president, he was called to serve as pastor of Pine Street Presbyterian Church in Philadelphia. The General Assembly of the Presbyterian Church elected him moderator in 1807 and he played a key role in convincing that body to establish a theological seminary. In 1812, he was appointed as the first, and for a time only, professor at PTS. He taught everything from Bible to theology to pastoral theology for thirty-nine years. A prolific writer, he was one of the most widely regarded theologians in the early part of the nineteenth century.

Alexander's inaugural lecture focused on the importance of informed and thorough biblical knowledge in the curriculum of the theological seminary. In typical Reformed fashion, Alexander emphasized that the only reliable and useful knowledge of God derives from a discerning grasp of knowledge of Scripture. The Bible functions as "a guide to man in matters of religion; a rule of faith and practice."[13] Consequently, biblical study should serve as the anchor for all pious learning in the theological school. It would include knowledge of the text in its original languages and in various translations. It would also involve familiarity with the social, historical, and cultural contexts that shaped its writings. Reliable principles for exegesis and hermeneutics in addition to a robust theological account of the inspiration and authority of Scripture would be essential to the enterprise. In concert with the vision articulated by both Miller and Milledoler, Alexander called for a broad knowledge of subject areas beyond the strictly theological as resources for interpreting Scripture:

> Indeed, to speak the truth, there is scarcely any science or branch of knowledge, which may not be made subservient to theology. Natural history, chemistry, and geology, have

---

[12] Ibid., 115.
[13] Alexander, "Inaugural Discourse," 73.

sometimes been of important service, in assisting the Biblical student to solve difficulties contained in the Scripture; or in enabling him to repel the assaults of adversaries, which were made under cover of these sciences. A general acquaintance with the whole circle of science is of more consequence to the Theologian, than at first sight appears. Not to mention the intimate connexion [sic] which subsists between all the parts of truth, in consequence of which important light may be collected from the remotest quarters; it may be observed, that the state of learning in the world requires the advocate of the Bible, to attend to many things which may not in themselves be absolutely necessary. He must maintain his standing as a man of learning. He must be able to converse on the various topics of learning with other literary men; otherwise the due respect will not be paid to him; and his sacred office may suffer contempt, in consequence of his appearing to be ignorant of what is expected all learned men should be acquainted with.[14]

It should be kept in mind that the breadth of learning called for by Alexander aimed at the practical purposes of furthering the gospel, defending biblical faith to critics and skeptics, and building up the church. Alexander gave no thought to the study of the Bible for its own sake or as a merely literary phenomenon; his sole interest was promoting the practical purpose of helping people and communities to come to faith, grow in faith, and live out faith in Jesus Christ.

Alexander emphasized the superiority of divine revelation to human reason. This emphasis had two dimensions. First, utilizing subtle allusions to Paul's meditation on the superiority of divine wisdom to human knowledge in the opening chapters of 1 Corinthians, Alexander argued forcefully that revealed knowledge exceeded the knowledge attained or manufactured by even the best of human reason.[15] Second, he brought into bold relief the necessity of divine illumination in the eminently practical task of studying Scripture:

> A proud and self-sufficient person, however endowed with acuteness of intellect, and furnished with stores of literature,

---

[14] Ibid., 84-5.
[15] Ibid., 75.

is continually prone to fall into pernicious error; whilst the humble man occupies a station from which truth may be viewed to advantage. Prejudice, proceeding from education or passion, blinds the mind, and warps the judgment; but the sincere and ardent love of truth disposes us to view the whole evidence, and impartially to weigh the arguments on both sides of any question. As much therefore depends upon preserving our own minds in a proper state, as upon the diligent use of external means of information. The conclusion from these premises is, that the student of sacred literature should be possessed of sincere and ardent piety. He should be a man 'taught by God,' conscious of his own insufficiency, but confident of the help of the Almighty. Indeed, when we consider the weakness of the human intellect, and the various prejudices and false impressions to which it is constantly liable, we must be convinced, that without divine assistance, there is little hope of arriving at the knowledge of the truth, or preserving it when acquired.[16]

This second dimension lays bare another core relation between piety and learning: proper knowledge and use of Scripture. Only through active faith and the practice of prayer can theological students come to the kind of scriptural proficiency that will serve a properly evangelical and ecclesiastical purpose. According to Alexander, God plays an active and explicit role in the theological education of future pastors. Only divine illumination can enable future leaders of the church to come to right knowledge of God, the origin of evil, the divine plan of redemption, the work of the Holy Spirit, the will of God for Christian living, and the ultimate future of humanity.[17] In the study of Scripture—as in the entirety of theological study—reason has to be supplemented and suffused with divine illumination if learning is to guide the church as the "pillar of cloud and of fire, did the Israelites."[18]

A Time of Rapid Expansion and Growing Tension

Miller, Milledoler and Alexander lived through the decades following the ratification of the American Constitution, a time when major

---

[16] Ibid., 90-2.
[17] Ibid., 96-101.
[18] Ibid., 194.

challenges emerged for the fledgling United States. The country had to work out how to function as a whole and not simply as a confederation of semi-autonomous parts. The nation's judicial system and financial structures and institutions had to be developed. Confronted by roiling international conflicts, the new government had to carefully manage diplomacy and foreign policy in order to avoid becoming entangled in wars that could bankrupt the country or destroy its independence.

Nevertheless, the period of the early republic was marked by crisis and tension. The War of 1812—"the Second Anglo-American war"—rocked the nation and threatened its independence.[19] This war bankrupted the federal government.[20] The United States went to war with Mexico in 1846-8 and, consequently, annexed vast territories in the southwest, from Texas to California.

The physical size of the country more than doubled during the early republic. The Louisiana Purchase opened up vast new spaces for enterprising and hardy settlers, many of whom were immigrants. A dramatic rise in US population during the first half of the nineteenth century accompanied the geographic expansion. Among other pressing demands, these changes resulted in a massive shortage of ministers to serve churches in frontier areas.

With the construction of water powered textile mills in the 1790s, the Industrial Revolution arrived in the United States.[21] It sparked a rapid expansion of industrial technologies and enterprises that lasted throughout the nineteenth century. This expansion heralded a great shift in American life from rural agriculture to urban industrialization, a shift that would not be fully accomplished until the middle part of the twentieth century.

Schooling and the modern classroom-based American educational system grew out of the rise of industrialization.[22] Education as apprenticeship was gradually replaced by education as schooling in the first half of the nineteenth century. The identification of education with schooling was not limited to children and youth; it also encompassed

---

[19] William Earl Weeks, "War of 1812," in *Oxford Companion to United States History*, ed. Paul S. Boyer (New York: Oxford, 2001), 814-5.
[20] Ibid.
[21] Gordon S. Wood, *Empire of Liberty: A History of the Early Republic, 1789-1815* (New York: Oxford, 2009), 702-4.
[22] Allen Collins and Richard Halverson, *Rethinking Education in the Age of Technology: The Digital Revolution and Schooling in America* (New York: Teachers College Press, 2009), 54-5 and 91-104.

professional education for adults. Many American colleges and universities trace their founding to the era of the early republic. The shift from apprenticeship to schooling also affected the way churches prepared men for pastoral ministry. Though schools like Harvard, Yale, and Princeton had been originally founded for the purpose of training Protestant clergy, by the early decades of the nineteenth century many colleges and universities had expanded their missions well beyond their original clerical purpose. As a result, many denominations started theological schools specifically devoted to the purpose of ministerial education. In most Protestant denominations in America, preparation for ministerial service increasingly required attendance at a theological school.

The early 1800s also witnessed a dramatic change in modes of transportation and communication in America. Ambitious, labor-intensive canal building in several areas was displaced by railroads almost as soon as the first rails were laid. The first long distance railroad in America was operational by 1833.[23] Throughout the rest of the nineteenth century, the railroad system would expand exponentially. Even though ordinary citizens continued to travel by horseback, boat, and foot, by 1900, every corner of the nation had been interconnected with railroad lines.[24] Samuel F. B. Morse and Alfred Vail developed a plan for a telegraph system in 1832.[25] In the following two decades, telegraph lines would connect all major American cities.[26] Faster transport of people and goods coupled with more expedient communication set in motion transformations that would permanently alter the rate of change in both the country and the world.

The most significant internal tension in the country in the first half of the nineteenth century focused on the institution of slavery. As early as the revolutionary period, many in America recognized the contradictions inherent in the proclamation of universal freedom and human rights on the one hand and chattel slavery of millions of black people on the other. Many in the early 1800s believed that the institution of slavery was dying and would soon come to a natural end.[27] This group tended to support a growing colonization movement in which freed slaves—now converted to Christianity—would be sent to what eventually became Liberia to reestablish their lives on the continent of Africa while spreading the gospel

---

[23] Colleen A. Dunlavy, "Railroads," in *Oxford Companion*, 648.
[24] Ibid.
[25] Paul Israel, "Telegraph," in *Oxford Companion*, 768-9.
[26] Ibid.
[27] Wood, *Empire of Liberty*, 518-9.

message to indigenous "heathens." Others came to the conclusion that slavery would not go away in the natural course of things and began to organize concentrated and sustained efforts aimed at more immediate elimination of this social evil. Still others, mainly slaveholders, saw no reason for the elimination of such a lucrative economic enterprise. The rise of abolitionism increased tensions between Northerners and Southerners, fueled the fires of sectionalism, and set the stage for what would eventually become the bloodiest war in American history. No more contentious issue would divide Americans during the years before the Civil War than slavery. When brewing tensions erupted into widespread carnage, families, churches, and the country itself were torn in two.

From this brief consideration of some of the key developments in the American experiment during the first half of the nineteenth century, it becomes clear that PTS opened in the midst of a period of intense societal change and upheaval. The early professors at the seminary responded to issues in their social context though their teaching in both implicit and explicit ways.

The Shape of Practical Theology: Practical, Humanist, Reformed
Pedagogical Philosophy

The term "practical theology" proper appears for the first time at PTS only in 1854 with the inaugural lecture of Alexander Taggart McGill to the chair of Pastoral Theology, Church Government, and the Composition and Delivery of Sermons. Prior to and often subsequent to that occasion, the preferred term used by the board and the faculty for the practical dimension of the seminary's curriculum in the nineteenth century was "pastoral theology." This more prevalent term focused on the theory and practice of the work of the pastor. It would be a mistake, however, to reduce practical theology at PTS in the nineteenth century to the so called clerical paradigm.[28] While pastoral theology at the seminary was not less than the clerical paradigm, it was actually a good bit more.

The entire study of theology in the seminary was understood to be nothing other than practical theology. In the opening lecture of his

---

[28] Farley, *Theologia*, 85-8. This way of organizing practical theology focuses on the work of pastors as congregational leaders, applies theological theory to situations of practice, and provides little room for the complex ways in which varied and changing contexts may influence or reconstruct theological reflection. It specializes in the study of role of the minister as well as ministerial tasks and techniques. While all of these descriptors were characteristic of practical theology at PTS during the period of the patriarchs, they do not tell the whole story.

"Pastoral Theology" course for third year students, Archibald Alexander observed, "pastoral theology includes the whole of the practical and consequently all theology. Taken in a more limited sense for the practical use of theological learning this examines how the office of pastor is discharged."[29] Showing little interest in speculative or idealistic theological reflection, Alexander and Miller and their successors in the nineteenth century taught PTS students that:

> General principles derived from experiences cannot but be very useful to those who are commencing a new pursuit. Every person who has traversed a particular road is qualified to give some advice to those who are about to go the same way. The very mistakes into which he has fallen will enable him to warn others of their danger.[30]

The practical character of the entirety of the seminary's curriculum arose as much if not more from the extensive pastoral experience of the professors than from theories derived from theological textbooks. Alexander and Miller—as well as John Breckinridge, James Waddell Alexander, Alexander Taggart McGill, and William Miller Paxton (the professors of practical theology at the seminary in the nineteenth century)—offered theoretical perspectives and tools as ways to make their pastoral experience intelligible and transferable. Theoretical material was always disciplined by theological wisdom born of reflection upon considerable pastoral experience.

Similarly, Samuel Miller understood that the entire scope of the theological curriculum was thoroughly practical in character. In one of his standard introductory lectures, Miller insisted to seminarians:

> After all, young gentlemen, it is my earnest desire that both you and I may constantly bear in mind that knowledge [is] in order to practice; and that all our knowledge, in especial manner, is to be consecrated to the service and glory of Jesus Christ – unsanctified knowledge in any man is a curse; but in a minister it is a double, 10 fold curse!...What will it avail

---

[29] Archibald Alexander, "Lectures on Pastoral Theology," student notes of Thomas B. Markham, 1850, The Archibald Alexander Manuscript Collection, Special Collections, Princeton Theological Seminary Library, box 5, file 3, 1.

[30] Archibald Alexander, "Lectures on Pastoral Theology," Archibald Alexander Manuscript Collection, Special Collections, Princeton Theological Seminary Library, box 7, file 3.

you, my young friends, when you come to die to recollect that you have read many books, that you have attended many learned lectures; and that you are at home in all the erudition of ancient and modern times? It will avail you nothing! …One simple, humble exercise of faith in a living redeemer – one blessed ray of the hope that maketh not ashamed, is worth them all! – Let me, then, solemnly warn you about contenting yourselves with mere speculative and unsanctified learning. – While it is granted that piety without learning can never form an able minister; and while it is equally certain that no man ever despised books or learning who knew anything about either – yet beware, I repeat it, beware of imagining that mere learning will qualify any man to be an ambassador of Christ. – It is an awful thought, but I am persuaded, nevertheless, true, that the more brilliant your talent and the more various and profound your erudition – if they are not sanctified by the grace of God – the more dreadful, in all probability will be your curse, both to the church and to yourselves!....

Let all your studies be attended with much prayer! Depend on it, without prayer your most painful labours [sic] will all be idleness and worse than idleness.[31]

According to Miller, all the subjects covered in the theological school curriculum were in service to the practice of deep faith in Jesus Christ, lived out in the context of the life and work of the church. Church history, for example, was not to be taught solely for its own sake, but always with an eye toward its "practical results."[32]

This did not mean that Miller rejected a distinction between theoretical and practical knowledge. In a sermon delivered at the opening of the Presbyterian General Assembly on May 21, 1807—six years prior to taking up his post as professor at PTS—he argued that the common distinction between "doctrinal" and "experimental" knowledge that pertains to all fields of knowledge ought also to apply to religion.[33] In the

---

[31] Samuel Miller, "Introductory Lecture," Samuel Miller Manuscript Collection, Special Collections, Princeton Theological Seminary Library, box 2, file 1, 19-21.
[32] Samuel Miller, "Lectures on Ecclesiastical History," Samuel Miller Manuscript Collection, Special Collections, Princeton Theological Seminary Library, box 2, file 10.
[33] Samuel Miller, "Sermon at the Opening of General Assembly, May 21, 1807," Samuel Miller Manuscript Collection, Special Collections, Princeton Theological Seminary

context of Christian faith, doctrinal knowledge pertained to the divinity of Jesus Christ and the character of God. It also addressed the divine plan of salvation culminating in the death and resurrection of Jesus Christ. Such knowledge, while crucial, is insufficient because it is objective and potentially abstracted from actual human experience. Mere knowledge about the identity and work of Jesus Christ lodged in the head and sealed off from the heart is a most pitiable thing. Such doctrinal knowledge must be supplemented and fulfilled with "practical experimental knowledge."[34] This latter kind of knowledge Miller described as having

> ...its seat in the heart as well as the head of the Christian; and it consists in perceiving the loveliness, and relishing the excellence of the object in general – and especially of him who is the chiefest among 10,000 and this knowledge, in short, makes an essential part of that living faith and of that holy love which distinguishes and adorns the discipline of Christ...Doctrinal knowledge may be imparted to man by his fellow man; but this knowledge is the work of the Holy Spirit.[35]

Practical or experimental knowledge of Jesus Christ comes about as the result of divine pedagogy. It cannot be imparted directly from one human being to another. Further, such practical or experimental knowledge has moral and spiritual valence. It is a "moral principle" that stimulates "holy taste for holy objects."[36] This holy, practical knowledge leads to inner transformation of the believer and outer witness to Jesus Christ in acts of obedient discipleship in church and society. Miller had this understanding of practical knowledge in mind when he, like Archibald Alexander, understood the entire curriculum of the theological school to be of a practical theological nature.

In his inaugural lecture delivered on November 7, 1828, Charles Hodge, Alexander's protégé and the seminary's third professor, reinforced his elders' views with respect to the pervasively practical character of the whole sweep of theological studies as he dismissed the German critical approaches to Bible and theology he had recently encountered. The decline in "vital religion" in German speaking lands

---

Library, box 12, file 8. Miller preached this sermon in various settings and at the seminary in 1815, 1817, 1821, 1833, and 1834.

[34] Ibid. The term "experimental" was used in this period to mean "experiential."
[35] Ibid.
[36] Ibid.

had led to the ordination of pastors who lacked "practical religion" and who were "little distinguished for piety."[37] Biblical critics like Johann Semler "had no inward necessity for believing" and consequently eroded the authority and even the canonical shape of Scripture.[38] New and barren systems of philosophical religion had led the masses of German speaking Christians away from authentic Christian faith—at least until crises at the national and personal levels brought about a return to biblical orthodoxy and the "revival of [authentic] religion."[39] Hodge held that the whole sweep of German church history from the Reformation until the middle of the second decade of the nineteenth century taught with great clarity the "vital connexion [sic] between piety and truth."[40] In a theological call to arms, Hodge maintained that vital and orthodox Protestant piety would function as a bulwark against the onslaughts of rationalists, pantheists, and "self-idolaters" that were only too evident in contemporaneous German theological scholarship.[41] The critical and speculative developments in contemporary German theological circles were to be guarded against:

> …Beware of any course of life or study, which has a tendency to harden your hearts, and deaden the delicate sensibility of the soul to moral truth and beauty….
> As far as my observation extends, it is the uniform tendency of such speculations to deaden the moral sensibility of the soul. Beware then of unhallowed speculations on sacred objects. Bring all your doctrines to the test of God's word and of holiness….When men forsake the word of God, and profess to be wise above that which is written, they inevitably and universally lose themselves in vain speculations. Look at the state of things, when every man is following the light of his own reason. Each boasts that he alone has the truth, and yet each is often a miracle of folly to every man but himself. True, such men are often men of great

---

[37] Charles Hodge, "Introductory Lecture, Delivered in the Theological Seminary, Princeton, N.J. Nov. 7, 1828," *Biblical Repertory: A Journal of Biblical Literature and Theological Science, Conducted by an Association of Gentlemen*, New Series, 5:1, (1829), 93.
[38] Ibid., 94.
[39] Ibid.
[40] Ibid.
[41] Ibid.

intellect; but can mere intellect perceive moral truth? Can man by wisdom find out God? Can he find out the Almighty unto perfection? No man knoweth the Father but the Son and he to whom the Son shall reveal him. Submit yourselves, therefore, to the teaching of him, in whom "are all the treasures of wisdom and knowledge." It is only when thus taught, that you will be able to teach others also.

One more word—keep as you would your hold on heaven your reverence for Jesus Christ. Reverence for the Redeemer of sinners, is the very last feeling which deserts a falling Christian, or a sinking church. When all other evidence, and all other arguments for the Bible had lost their force, this solitary feeling has held up the soul from sinking into infidelity and thence into perdition. When this is lost, all is lost. The soul that is insensible to the glory of the Son of God, is "as a tree twice dead and plucked up by the roots."[42]

While Hodge's courses focused on biblical backgrounds and content during the initial phase of his very long faculty tenure at PTS, his teaching—like that of Alexander and Miller—aimed to function as a form of practical theology broadly conceived.

Hodge demonstrated his commitment to theological reflection that was thoroughly practical in character even while he travelled abroad in German speaking lands. This can be seen in the short preface to his translated and excerpted version of Stapfer's *The Life of Kant*, which was published in the *Biblical Repertory* in 1828. In addition to claiming that Kant's system "now lies in ruins" in the German speaking areas of Europe, he saw little likelihood that any significant challenge to pious learning would arise in the American context.[43]

Hodge's "introductory remarks" on Stapfer's work treated Kant's critical philosophy and its subsequent effects in biblical studies, theology, and German Idealism as an utterly failed project. His considered dismissal of the Kantian revolution and its aftermath seems to be have been based in large measure on the Scottish Common Sense philosophy that undergirded the entire vision of practical theology (in both the more encompassing and the more narrow sense of the term) at

---

[42] Ibid., 96-8.
[43] Charles Hodge, "Introductory Remarks on *The Life of Kant* by Professor Stapfer of Paris, Translated from the French by the Editor," *Biblical Repertory, A Collection of Tracts in Biblical Literature*, 4:3 (1828), 299.

PTS during the entire course of the nineteenth century. As articulated by such leading lights as Thomas Reid and Dugald Stewart, the Scottish response to the radical implications of Humean skepticism sought to provide a defense of both conventional morality and Protestant faith. It insisted that, "perception involves both sensations and certain intuitively known general truths or principles that together yield knowledge of external objects."[44] In this view, such knowledge included the foundations for Christian moral principles and Protestant beliefs.

Hodge's practical theological assessment is important to note for several reasons. It marked one of the earliest, if not the first, serious engagement with Kant and German critical thought at PTS.[45] It also provided a glimpse into the deeper intellectual structure of practical theology—built upon Scottish Common Sense philosophy—at the seminary during the nineteenth century. Further, it foreshadowed the issues at stake in the seminary's internal battle during the 1920s.[46]

One of Archibald Alexander's most widely read works, *Evidences of the Christian Religion*, gave classic expression to the linkage between lived experience and the truths of revelation. This linkage was made possible by Scottish philosophy, which understood the order of creation to be resonant with revealed religion in its key features. In short, the preferred philosophy of the seminary's patriarchs established a durable epistemological bridge between revelation and human experience. While the bridge essentially only carried one way traffic from revelation to experience, lived human realities could and did legitimize revelation's claims. No serious thought was given to anything like the possibility of reconstructing theological norms in light of human experience. Within this framework, the contours of human experience could only support,

---

[44] Jerome B. Schneewind, "Scottish Common Sense Philosophy," in *The Cambridge Dictionary of Philosophy*, 2nd ed., edited by Robert Audi (New York:Cambridge, 1999), 822-3.

[45] Archibald Alexander mentioned Kant in his "Compend of Didactic Theology Lectures" of 1822. The Archibald Alexander Manuscript Collection, box 2, file 3, 6.

[46] The version of the fundamentalist-modernist controversy that engulfed PTS during the decade of the 1920s was philosophically a struggle between Scottish and German trajectories of response to the radical skepticism introduced by David Hume. The party that withdrew from PTS and went on to found Westminster Theological Seminary and the Orthodox Presbyterian Church sought to maintain continuity with the Scottish Common Sense philosophical tradition that had undergirded the vision of (practical) theology at PTS for a little more than a hundred years. The party that remained at PTS and participated in its rebuilding believed that German critical scholarship in theological fields could be faithfully and judiciously appropriated for authentic Christian belief and practice.

reinforce, verify, or buttress doctrinal insights derived ultimately from scriptural revelation. This principle also applied to the use of the early professors' own experience as pastors who had served congregations prior to joining the faculty. They often drew upon their pastoral experiences to flesh out a practical principle of ministry—but only if that principle had first been determined to be derived from or resonant with Scripture.

The Princeton patriarchs also articulated very clear limits for the role of experience in authentic piety and theological reflection.[47] Alexander and Miller were both wary of the excesses of revivalism, particularly with respect to its tilt toward human experience as the index of authentic faith. Taken to an extreme, religious fervor could undermine sound theological principles derived from careful study of Scripture. They were equally concerned about Deism and its cold ethical rationalism.

Pedagogical Practice

Practical theology during the period of the patriarchs operated pedagogically within the framework of clericalism. While it would be reductionist to claim—particularly in light of the foregoing—that their work was limited solely to applying biblical insights to pastoral practice, the courses most directly related to practical theology taught by Alexander, Miller, and, later, John Breckinridge, did have the character of theological theory applied to pastoral technique, but tempered and fleshed out by considerable pastoral experience. A brief look at some of their core courses will elucidate this dimension of their work.

Even though Alexander had a practical and clerical purpose in mind for all of his classes, his capstone course on "Pastoral Theology" for third year students made clear his understanding of the field known today as practical theology. After focusing on biblical history and exegesis for first year students and various modes of doing theology for second year students, Alexander taught the principles and techniques of pastoral ministry. In the opening lecture of this course, Alexander made clear that the term "pastoral theology" had both a larger, more encompassing sense and a more specific, technical sense: "Pastoral theology includes the whole of the practical and, consequently, all [of] theology. Taken in a more limited sense for the practical use of theological learning, this

---

[47] Lefferts A. Loetscher makes the case that PTS was founded in part to counter the threats posed by the distortions of revivalism (emotionalism) on the one side and the distortions of Deism on the other (rationalism). See Lefferts A. Loetscher, *Facing the Enlightenment and Pietism: Archibald Alexander and the Founding of Princeton Theological Seminary* (Westport, CT: Greenwood, 1983), 16-7.

examines how the office of pastor is to be discharged."[48] While it is clear that Alexander viewed the entirety of the seminary's curriculum as an expression of pastoral theology, this third year course provided a careful examination of the calling to and key functions of the pastoral office.

Alexander began the course with a detailed consideration of both God's call to pastoral ministry and the qualifications necessary to undertake this call (natural abilities, learning, and eloquence).[49] Natural abilities include good judgment, the ability to speak well and with sufficient volume to be heard in (unamplified) worship spaces, good physical health, lively imagination, and accurate memory. Among other spiritual and moral qualities, future pastors should have a heart for the glory and cause of God, fidelity, compassion, willingness to labor and suffer, humility, temperance in all things, moderation in the enjoyment of creature comforts, patience, circumspection, and, above all, piety.[50] Yet these qualities—admirable and necessary as they are for pastoral ministry—are insufficient. Good pastors also need to have a classically liberal education that strengthens the mind and furnishes it with broad knowledge that can be drawn upon in the practice of ministry.[51] Most centrally, pastoral ministry requires deep and articulate knowledge of Scripture.

Alexander also emphasized the importance of contextual awareness in pastoral ministry. In providing guidance to future pastors on how to enter into leadership in a new congregational context, Alexander compared pastors to farmers coming to a new farm.[52] They need to tend to the good things that are already in place and to remove any "thorns and encumbrances."[53] In order to provide leadership conducive to growth, pastors should heed this advice:

> Calling of elders should be made by the new Pastor [to] learn the conditions of the people and former history. Learn how elders and deacons have performed [their] duty. Make a list of

---

[48] Alexander, "Pastoral Theology," Markham notes, box 5, file 3, 1.
[49] Archibald Alexander, "Lectures on Pastoral Theology," according to student notes by J. Peter Lesley, 1843-4, The Archibald Alexander Manuscript Collection, box 3, file 25, 1-40.
[50] Archibald Alexander, "Questions on Theology," Lesley notes, and "Lectures on Pastoral Theology," lecture notes according to Allen H. Brown, 1841-2, The Archibald Alexander Manuscript Collection, Special Collections, Princeton Theological Seminary Library, box 3, file 5, single sheet and box 4, file 3, 31-46.
[51] Ibid.
[52] Ibid., box 3, file 25, 46 and box 4, file 3, 73.
[53] Ibid.

members and families in [a] blank book with remarks in ciphers. List of [the] baptized not in Communion should be made.[54]

Alexander further counseled that, while changes and innovations should be made early in a pastorate, they should be introduced only after paving the way by "private influence" of key leaders in the congregation who might take the lead in initiating changes. Further, new pastors should befriend the former pastor and use him as a counselor— particularly if he still lives in the area and worships in the congregation.[55] In purveying such sound principles of contextually oriented leadership, we can see Alexander's more deductive practical theological impulses tempered or even completed by his attentiveness to the conditions of local context.

Following general admonitions about pastoral ministry, Alexander offered guidance about specific duties of pastoral ministry. Among the various tasks of ministry, he deemed preaching and teaching deemed to be the most important by far. Both must grow out of disciplined engagement with Scripture and should eschew self interest, personal gain, and abstract philosophical investigations.[56] "Christ crucified" should be at the center of all preaching. According to Alexander, "[The] preacher must love the doctrine of the cross and glory in it." In order to serve that homiletical core, classic Reformed themes should be sounded: particularly the pervasiveness of sin, the centrality of grace in Jesus Christ's death and resurrection, and the necessity of spiritual regeneration. The particular order of subjects selected for preaching "will depend on circumstances, [that is] knowledge of the flock." Future preachers should be aware that "the people are more ignorant than is commonly supposed" about the gospel message and the core elements of orthodox Reformed belief.[57]

The manner of preaching should serve the hearer. It should be systematic, clear, and audible. Plain English—not academic jargon— should be used at all times. Sermons should be delivered "with affection" and not with coldness or needless rhetorical flourish. Preaching should be done impartially, comprehensively, and harmoniously. Moreover, preaching ought also to bear in mind differences among hearers—

---

[54] Ibid.
[55] Ibid.
[56] The Archibald Alexander Manuscript Collection, box 7, file, 3, 3.
[57] Ibid.

particularly when dealing with elders or young people, with private or public sins.[58]

Next in order of importance comes teaching or "catechizing." The teaching ministry of the church should seek, among other things, to provide the rudiments of Christian understanding necessary to make the preaching of the gospel intelligible. Parents and guardians have primary responsibility for laying down such primary tracks of belief and practice. Those who teach in elementary schools and academies should be under the watchful care of pastors and elders to ensure that they teach the basics of religion properly. Pastors are responsible for visiting homes in order to check on catechetical progress and to provide exhortation. Once or twice a year, all parents and children should be gathered together in order for the pastor to provide instruction and exhortation. Catechizing children, youth, and pagan adults requires a joint effort by pastors and catechists; pastors cannot do the entire work of catechizing alone. Alexander affirmed the importance of congregational Sabbath schools and urged pastors and elders to exercise careful oversight of them, noting that these schools do not take the place of ministerial and parental catechizing.[59]

In Alexander's vision, all religious instruction should pay attention to the capacities and prior knowledge of learners.[60] New learning should be incremental and scaled to the attention span and memory capacities of each learner. Basic facts needed to be understood before moving to doctrines. The emphasis should always be on spiritual exhortation and practical matters of faith and practice.

Alexander believed that the aim of all catechizing and religious instruction is evangelical commitment to Jesus Christ. Practical doctrines based on solid biblical facts have a high likelihood of leading people to repentance and faith. Essential biblical facts and doctrines can be taught with the aid of printed catechisms—particularly the Westminster catechisms.[61]

Not every graduate of the seminary became a congregational pastor. From its very earliest days, PTS has always produced a certain number of teachers, professors, and leaders for academies, classical schools, colleges, universities, and seminaries across the country. Alexander's lectures on the teaching dimension of ministry acknowledged the

---

[58] Ibid.
[59] Ibid.
[60] Ibid.
[61] While Alexander thought that the Heidelberg Catechism could serve a useful purpose, the Westminster Larger Catechism was "the best body of divinity of its size that exists." Ibid.

importance of these other forms of pedagogical service to the church. Because the center of gravity lay with pastoral ministry in congregational settings and because academic leaders and school presidents in the Presbyterian ethos during the first half of the nineteenth century were almost invariably ordained ministers, Alexander apparently did not develop a special set of lectures covering these other forms of pedagogical leadership—though he was well aware that some of his students would pursue such forms of ministry.

Alexander's course on pastoral theology covered a range of other essential pastoral duties. He provided basic principles and tips—though not nearly as elaborate as was the case for preaching and teaching—for visiting the sick, dealing with poverty and immigration, leadership during spiritual awakenings and revivals, evangelism, church unity, public worship, and mission work. In this material, he enumerated, for example, criteria for discriminating between true and false revivals, as well as the duties of pastors in relation to both the unconverted and the newly converted. He also supplied extensive statistics about mission fields around the world and gave detailed information on various missionary societies. He offered an exhortation to students to listen carefully for God's call to domestic and foreign mission work.

Samuel Miller also taught courses resonant with practical theology, particularly classes in church history, church government, and the preparation and delivery of sermons. Miller sounded many of the same themes that Alexander touched upon, including the practical character of the entirety of theological education, the importance of broad Christian humanistic learning, a decided priority given to deductive principles derived from scriptural revelation and theological reflection of a Westminster kind, and the crucial importance of context and contextual judgments. Miller's teaching in the area of church history, for example, went beyond analysis and description to include extensive practical implications for ministry in contemporary churches, implications that were based on gleanings from various periods in the long sweep of church history. His teaching in the area of ecclesiastical government or polity provided biblically based, theologically attuned, and historically informed principles for effective pastoral leadership at all levels of church life, from the local congregation to the General Assembly. While Miller was capable of historical analysis of a more disinterested kind—he had, in fact, written the first serious American analysis of intellectual developments during the eighteenth century Enlightenment—he believed that all areas of the theological curriculum ought to have a practical character.[62] The seminary's primary aim—preparing future pastors for the church—conditioned the way in which he appropriated and taught material from historical and practical ecclesiology.

The Church as Missionary Society

As the seminary found its footing and developed, a need to expand the faculty arose. In 1835, the Presbyterian General Assembly voted to increase the size of the faculty from three to five. The Assembly acceded to the request of the existing seminary faculty and boards to appoint John Breckinridge to the position of Professor of Pastoral Theology and Missionary Instruction. Breckinridge's appointment allowed Alexander to concentrate more fully on the various dimensions of and approaches to the study of theology by freeing him up from responsibility for the course in pastoral theology. It also had the added benefit of further developing the curriculum by adding explicit courses on the theory and practice of mission in domestic and foreign contexts.

At the time he was called to join the faculty of PTS, John Breckinridge was one of the Presbyterian Church's shining stars. Hailing from the prominent Breckinridges of Kentucky, he had studied at both the College of New Jersey and PTS. He had occasionally been called upon to fill in for Samuel Miller for preaching engagements when the latter took ill. Breckinridge married Miller's daughter and with her moved to Kentucky and Baltimore to serve Presbyterian churches. The combination of his compelling vision of the church as primarily a mission society and his phenomenal preaching abilities resulted in appointment to the position of General Secretary for the Board of Christian Education in Philadelphia. Breckinridge's leadership in fundraising for indigent theological students and for the cause of missions was equaled by the quality of his articulate defense of Protestantism in a running dialogue with a Roman Catholic priest about the nature and purpose of the church.[63] After having served for three years on the seminary's board of directors, he was everyone's first and

---

[62] Samuel Miller, *A Brief Retrospect of the Eighteenth Century*, vol. 1 and 2 (Bristol, England: Thoemmes, 2001).

[63] This dialogue was first published in the Philadelphia newspapers and later as a substantial book. John Breckinridge, *Controversy between the Rev. John Hughes, of the Roman Catholic Church, and the Rev. John Breckinridge, of the Presbyterian Church: relative to the existing differences in the Roman Catholic and Protestant religions* (Philadelphia, PA: Joseph Whetham, 1833).

most obvious choice to fill the seminary's newly established position in pastoral theology and missionary instruction.

Breckinridge moved with his wife and children to Princeton and took up his teaching duties in 1836. He took over Alexander's pastoral theology course for third year students and developed his own course for second year students on missionary theory and practice. His teaching was shaped by his particular understanding of the nature of the church and the character of the Christian life, which he had articulated in his 1832 Spruce Street Lectures when speaking about the human response to grace:

> …This love God-ward is not a vague and heartless theism, but a supreme, intelligent, commanding, and practical affection for the God of the Bible—God in Christ. And this love of man is not a vain sentiment, or a wild spirit of religious knight errantry; but a wise, dutiful, and disinterested love which seeks to do good to all men….The church of God is essentially in its organization, and in the purpose of God, a Missionary institution….It is then apparent, that the very constitution of the Christian character, is missionary in its nature, and that what makes a man a Christian, endows him in the same measure with the spirit and influence of missions.[64]

Such passionate articulation of mission-oriented theology exerted significant influence well beyond the students at the seminary. His appeals to take up and support the cause of mission in order to rescue "the heathen" from darkness, death, and eternal ruin provided a major stimulus to the cause of domestic and foreign mission work by Presbyterians more broadly.[65] Breckinridge's practical theology was oriented primarily toward making the message of the gospel clear and compelling to people in the pews so that they, in turn, would find true happiness and motivation for reaching out to others in the name of Jesus Christ.

Breckinridge's tenure on the seminary faculty lasted for nearly three years. Always active in fundraising both for the seminary and for the cause of missions, Breckinridge appears to have been perpetually pulled in three directions: teaching, fundraising, and missionary activism. When

---

[64] John Breckinridge, "Lecture X, May 13, 1832," *Spruce Street Lectures by several clergymen. Delivered during the years 1831-32. To which is added a lecture on the importance of creeds and confessions by Samuel Miller,* (Philadelphia: Presbyterian Board of Publications, 1840), 261-5.
[65] Ibid., 297.

not in the classroom, he travelled nonstop in order to raise money for the seminary and for the great missionary enterprise to which he was indefatigably committed.

He probably could have kept up this grueling pace of life for some considerable time if his wife had not died. Margaret Miller Breckinridge died after an increasingly desperate struggle with a wasting disease in 1838—a mere two years after the Breckinridges' return to Princeton. The pious Mrs. Breckinridge's tragic death shook the seminary and the entire Princeton community.

A year later, Breckinridge was instrumental in the publication of a commemorative volume in her memory.[66] He himself contributed a pious biography of his beloved wife in the first section of the book. Archibald Alexander's sermon at her funeral was included as the second part. A series of touching letters on Christian education and formation by Samuel Miller to his three surviving grandchildren comprised the final section of the little volume. This commemorative work gave dense expression to the practical theology operative at PTS in its early decades.

With particular poignancy, Archibald Alexander brought to bear the essence of early Princeton practical theology on the sad occasion. Noting that the tragic death of a loved one brought the difference between abstract theology and practical religion at the point of divine providence into sharp relief, Alexander observed:

> On this subject, we all can teach and inculcate what is right; but when it becomes necessary to practise [sic] our own lessons, we experience a sad deficiency. This [i.e. death] is a school in which sooner or later, we must all be learners; and it behooves us to use all diligence in preparing ourselves to endure trials with fortitude, and cheerfully to acquiesce in those painful events which we cannot avoid....There is but one effectual remedy for the evils which man is heir, while on his earthly pilgrimage; and that is RELIGION—true religion, not merely apprehended and approved in its theory, but deeply felt, and cordially embraced in the inmost soul. This is the only principle of sufficient potency to tranquillize the perturbations of the soul when deeply afflicted. This only can sustain the mind, ready to sink into despair. This furnishes the only medicine which heals the anguish of the broken heart;

---

[66] *A Memorial of Mrs. Margaret Breckinridge* (Philadelphia, PA: W.C. Martien, 1839).

the only balm which relieves the wounds made in the spirit by painful bereavements....These blessed effects of genuine piety are not produced by any irrational process, or blind impulse; but by contemplation of truths adapted to the end. Consolations which do not rest on this firm foundation, will ever be found precarious, and commonly evanescent. Buoyant hope and cheerful resignation must have the solid pillar of truth on which to repose.[67]

Alexander's functional practical theology—here in the mode of pastoral care—was heartily, if tearfully, affirmed by professors Miller, Hodge, J.A. Alexander, and Breckinridge.

The death of his wife, combined with a growing sense of call to serve the cause of mission in a more direct way, led John Breckinridge to resign his faculty position and to accept the post of General Agent of the Board of Foreign Missions of the Presbyterian Church in late 1838. For a time, some thought that he might be able to keep his teaching post while working as the leader of the denomination's mission agency. That thought turned out to be more pious hope than workable reality. By 1840 Archibald Alexander had resumed the teaching of pastoral theology and his title was changed to "Professor of Pastoral and Polemical Theology." John Breckinridge continued to travel to inspire and support the vision of the church as a society of mission until his own untimely death in 1841.

Tragic death was not the only crisis to lay bare the essential character of practical theology at PTS during the period of the patriarchs. The growing schism in church and society over slavery also disclosed the contours of the seminary's practical theology from its founding until the Civil War.

Practical Theological Reflections on Slavery and the Church's Responsibility

The shape of practical theology at PTS during its early decades cannot be fully perceived only through the lens of the dynamics of Christian experience and pastoral ministry. It must also be seen in relation to the way in which Alexander and Miller engaged the deepening national divide over slavery. The institution of slavery provides an acid test for the nascent practical theology operative at PTS.

---

[67] Ibid., 75-6.

It shows both the strengths and the limitations of the seminary's early formulation of practical theology.

At the outset, it must be said that the members of the seminary's faculty were all fundamentally opposed to slavery, despite the fact that they likely owned slaves themselves, according to American church historian, James H. Moorhead. "Evidence suggests that Alexander, Miller, and Hodge all were slaveholders at some point in their lives. Apparently through his marriage to Janetta Waddell, Alexander acquired at least one slave. Miller, too, according to his son, came from a Delaware slaveholding family and used slave labor on occasion while in Princeton."[68] They believed that this evil and terrible blight upon human society should eventually be eliminated. With many people in the antebellum period, the faculty of the seminary sincerely believed that the institution of slavery would decline over time and come to a natural end in the imaginable future. They were not supporters of slavery. Yet, they could not bring themselves to oppose it publically and aggressively.

The faculty's commitment to scriptural revelation as the final arbiter of all truth and the ultimate judge of human experience made it impossible for them to join forces with the abolitionist movement—in point of fact, they actively opposed abolitionism. Because slavery was assumed by and not opposed in the New Testament (particularly in the Pauline epistles), they were unable to conclude that slavery was fundamentally against the will of God. In addition to this exegetical struggle, they also worried deeply that aggressive measures to end slavery too quickly would result in schism in the church and terrible division in the country. In the decade following the deaths of Alexander and Miller, their worst fears were realized as horrifying facts on the ground.

---

[68] James H. Moorhead, personal correspondence with authors. Moorhead also notes, "For a revealing episode indicating the family's paternalistic understanding of their engagement with slavery, see J.W. Alexander's *Life of Archibald Alexander* (Harrisonburg, VA: Sprinkle, 1991), 280-2. See also Samuel Miller, *Life of Samuel Miller* vol. 2 (Philadelphia: Claxton, Remsen, and Haffelfinger, 1869), 300. On Hodge, see the essay by Allen Guelzo, "Charles Hodge's Antislavery Moment," in the book *Charles Hodge Revisited: A Critical Appraisal of his Life and Work*, ed. by John W. Stewart and James H. Moorhead (Grand Rapids: Eerdmans, 2002), 299-325. Slavery in New Jersey still existed prior to the Civil War. In 1804, a law decreed that all persons born to slaves after July 4 of that year would be free people; however, they remained bound to serve their mother's owner until adulthood—men until twenty-five years of age, women until twenty-one. Those already in bondage in 1804 remained so until their deaths. When the state decided in 1846 to abolish slavery in name, those still in bondage remained permanent 'apprentices.'"

The seminary faculty embraced a practical theological strategy for dealing with slavery that included three elements: teaching and evangelism of slaves, pastoral role limitation, and support for African colonization. Alexander's pedagogical vision included provision for teaching slaves. He noted that only about 10% of slaves were literate and that teaching them to read might prove impossible or difficult.[69] Nonetheless, pastors should turn their pedagogical attention to them if opportunity permitted. In a set of undated lectures—though presumably from later in his career—Alexander expounded on the need for teaching slaves by means of plantation Sunday Schools.[70] Pastors in contexts where there were illiterate slaves should attempt to teach them to read by using key passages of Scripture. They should be taught the gospel message, with a specific focus on the basics of the story of redemption, the doctrine of justification, and their Christian duties.[71]

Alexander and Miller both emphasized the limits of the pastoral role when lecturing to future pastors about their responsibility in relation to the slavery crisis. Alexander argued, "It is absolutely necessary…that you avoid meddling directly or indirectly with the subject of slavery."[72] Because the political aspects of the problem were so dangerously divisive, he counseled that such matters should be left solely to politicians. Preachers of the gospel should have nothing to do with politics; it is their duty, he argued, not to change society, but to teach the way to heaven.[73]

Under the surface, there may have been some differences of perspective. Though Miller echoed these sentiments from his colleague from Virginia, he may have held a slightly more progressive view on the matter. In his meticulously kept records of sermons, weddings, and funerals, one can find instances in which Miller preached in the "African

---

[69] Alexander, "Pastoral Theology," Brown notes, box 4, file 3, 215.

[70] Alexander, "Pastoral Duty to the Colored Race," The Archibald Alexander Manuscript Collection, Special Collections, Princeton Theological Seminary Library, box 12, file 55.

[71] Alexander, "Colored Race." "In present circumstances, the only effectual method of instructing the slaves is by Sunday Schools on the plantations to which they are attached or by collecting them from several contiguous plantations."

[72] Ibid.

[73] Ibid. According to James Moorhead, "As for the support of colonization, Alexander wrote his longest book on the subject, and the work makes clear that, while he wished the end of slavery and a better lot for blacks, he could not imagine black and white living together on an egalitarian basis in the USA." Personal correspondence with authors. See Archibald Alexander, *A History of Colonization on the Western Coast of Africa*, (Philadelphia: William S. Martien, 1846).

Church" in Princeton and also numerous occasions on which he performed weddings and funerals for black families in New York City and in the Princeton area.[74] It is also interesting to note that at least some PTS graduates did not heed their professors' warnings and subsequently became leaders in the cause of abolitionism. Included in that number are John Finley Crow, John Montieth and Elijah Parish Lovejoy.[75]

The third element of the Princeton practical theologians' strategy for dealing with the slavery crisis involved vigorous and public support for the African colonization movement. Alexander, Miller, and Breckinridge all supported the effort to send freed and converted slaves to Liberia. They composed elaborate theological and practical arguments in support of the colonization effort as a way to both address the problem of integrating former slaves into American society and contribute to the evangelization of the African continent. Speeches, publications, and financial contributions by the PTS faculty contributed significantly to widespread support in American Protestantism for these colonization efforts.

Summary and Concluding Reflections

Practical theology—more properly, "pastoral theology"—during the period of the patriarchs at PTS encompassed all of theology and had the character of an evangelical Christian humanism.

Practical theology in this period of the seminary's life exhibited many strengths. While differentiated in an asymmetrical manner, piety and learning were understood as a unity absolutely necessary for faithfully effective pastoral ministry. The warmth of intimate, personal knowledge of Jesus Christ through faith had to be integrated with and articulated through deep knowledge of biblical revelation. To have one without the other would lead to a dangerous imbalance (e.g. revivalistic excess and emotion on the one hand or deistic reductionism of faith in the direction of rationalism on the other).[76]

The seminary's budding understanding of practical theology during this period also demonstrated a deep commitment to biblical revelation.

---

[74] These sermons can be found in the Miller Manuscript Collection.

[75] Crow ran an abolitionist press before being run out of town and subsequently founding both Hanover College and what became McCormick Theological Seminary. Montieth provided strong leadership for the abolitionist cause (even in the face of strong objections of his congregation and his family) and eventually co-founded the University of Michigan. Lovejoy was America's first martyr for the freedom of the press. He was killed defending his abolitionist press from an angry mob on November 7, 1837 in Alton, Illinois.

[76] See Loetscher, *Enlightenment and Pietism*.

The theological dimension of practical theology was funded by a classical Protestant commitment to the priority of Scripture in the formulation of belief and practice. Archibald Alexander, Samuel Miller, and John Breckinridge all strongly emphasized the normative aspects of practical theology. Further, they worked out the implications of biblically shaped practical theological norms for ecclesiology, ministerial practice, and Christian life.

The primacy of place accorded to biblical revelation—particularly with little explicit awareness of the cultural frameworks of texts and interpreters—also stands as one of the chief vulnerabilities of the Princeton perspective on practical theology at this time. Practical theology understood primarily as a one-way mechanism for applying the truths of revelation to the challenges of contemporary society resulted in rather tortured and not entirely credible strategies for responding to the ecclesial and societal challenges posed by the institution of slavery. While the early practical theologians at PTS, to a person, opposed slavery and saw it as a terrible blight upon society, they were unable to condemn it publically because the Bible did not explicitly condemn it. As a result, the earliest practical theologians at PTS advocated a gradualist and colonialist strategy for the end of slavery while rejecting the more radical, direct, and prophetic strategies associated with abolitionism. Their evangelical Christian humanism had definite and deeply problematic limits.

Chapter 2
Honoring the Patriarchs:
Technical Elaboration of the Original Vision

Sinful but Not Forsaken

On Sunday, January 4, 1861—a fortnight after South Carolina seceded from the Union and five days before the secession of Mississippi—Princeton Theological Seminary professor of ecclesial history and church government Alexander Taggart McGill preached a notable sermon entitled "Sinful but Not Forsaken" at the Fifth Avenue Presbyterian Church in New York City.[1] Preaching at one of the most prominent Presbyterian pulpits on a "Day of National Fasting," McGill sought to provide a practical theological interpretation of the rapidly deepening crisis in American national life. In the midst of what appeared to be an apocalyptic unfolding of events, McGill strove to answer the question, "Where is our God?" In the sermon's four movements—the nature of the nation's sins, the character of divine punishment, evidence for divine engagement amid the crisis, and reasons for hope in divine clemency—McGill offered a sober and encouraging practical theological answer to the most pressing question of the day.[2]

---

[1] Alexander T. McGill, "Sinful but Not Forsaken: A Sermon Preached in the Presbyterian Church, Fifth Avenue and Nineteenth Street, New York on the Day of National Fasting, January 4, 1861" (New York: Fifth Avenue Presbyterian Church, 1861).
[2] Ibid., 4-5.

McGill accounted for the emerging national cataclysm by naming the defining sins of nation, sections, families, and individuals. As a nation, Americans committed the cardinal sin of pride:

> ...We are a nation of "boasters." There is not one of us, probably, whose soul has not been lifted up with pride for the greatness of our country, in every particular, which constitutes true national grandeur. Her traditions, her immunities, her extent of territory, her advancement in resources of moral and intellectual power, as well as material greatness, have filled her sons and daughters everywhere, and especially when abroad, with inexpressible pride and exultation.[3]

Such a pervasive lack of gratitude, held McGill, gave rise to acts of divine punishment upon the nation as a whole. Yet, pride and ingratitude did not exhaust the catalogue of America's sins for which divine punishment was being administered. The nation had also been so greedy and infatuated with the accumulation of material wealth that divine wrath against such covetous idolatry was as deserved as it was inevitable. The avenues of commerce had been used habitually to break the Sabbath, to cheat others in business, and to defraud thousands out of their savings.[4] Elected leaders from every political party were subject to terrible disrespect and abuse by the populace.[5] Families, which were supposed to be "nurseries of piety and fraternal love," had become incubators of political strife and discord.[6] The devastating factionalism in contemporary society could, in fact, be traced back to a pervasive failure to teach the basics of Christian piety and neighbor love in the nation's homes. In thundering criticism concerning the abdication of parental responsibilities for Christian nurture, McGill scornfully observed that it was "no wonder [that] fanaticism has left the cloisters of religious bigotry to seize on politicians, North and South, East and West, until it now rides on the whirlwind of passions, which have had a life-long ferment in the animosities of party."[7] While each section of the country had its own particular sins, the aggregated totality of American sin had risen up to heaven.

---

[3] Ibid., 5-6.
[4] Ibid., 9.
[5] Ibid., 10.
[6] Ibid., 11-2.
[7] Ibid., 12.

As a result of such deep and pervasive sin, God had begun to act in terrible judgment against the nation. All voices of reason and conciliation had disappeared from the scene and only the fanatical voices from the North and the South were left on the public stage. The fraternal battle that was to ensue would be an epic struggle fanned into a raging inferno by those who had given themselves over to ideological madness.

Amid such ominous signs of the times, McGill asked if there might be any hope at all for the nation. With only one state having declared secession at the time of the sermon, it was possible to imagine that God might intervene to pull the nation back from the brink of bloodshed if sufficient and widespread repentance occurred. Perhaps family ties across the yawning divide between North and South would make it possible for cooler heads to prevail. With more than a little ecclesiastical messianism, McGill expressed a hope that God might use the united Presbyterian Church of the Old School persuasion to heal the nation of its crisis and to bring an end to the terribly divisive issue of slavery:

> Who knows but that it may be the glorious mission of the Presbyterian Church, in these last and perilous days, to wipe out the scandal which has rested on visible Christianity ever since the days of the apostles; and instead of civil power interposing to heal divisions in the Church, the Church will come, with plastic hand, to bind a shattered confederacy in better union than ever?[8]

The divinely inspired religious revivals of the nation's past had had a salutary effect on the well being of the whole American enterprise. Perhaps God would bring about another such revival of vital religion through the agency of the Presbyterian Church and so change the course of the nation's history for the better. After all, McGill reasoned, God had done something similar in the British Empire only a few years earlier. The possibility of divine correction through religious revival was all the greater in the current crisis because Christians in England and in the United States had begun of late to work together to spread the gospel message to the entire world.[9]

According to McGill, the deepest reasons for hope amid bleak and rapidly deteriorating circumstances lay in Scripture's promise of divine

---

[8] Ibid., 16.
[9] Ibid., 18.

providence. That people had gathered in divinely inspired prayer and repentance in places across the land indicated that God had not ultimately forsaken the nation. With the exhaustion of hope in human beings, Scripture's promises about divine mercy provided the last and best hope.[10] The biblical witness to the unchanging character of God as both righteous and merciful served as the last resort. When all else fails—and all else had failed—McGill exhorted the faithful to fervent repentance from sin and to humble hope in God's merciful and mighty providence in history.

In this sermon, delivered in the midst of intense national crisis, we can see something of the character of practical theology at PTS in the generations following the death of the patriarchs. McGill sought to engage the pressing issues of the day in terms of the judging and merciful actions of the sovereign God who acts in history. Shaped by a reading of Scripture through the lens of Westminster orthodoxy and his adherence to the somewhat reticent gradualism of Alexander and Miller on the question of slavery, McGill could only obliquely address the issues of slavery and race. To deal with these issues in a more vocal and direct way would have meant identifying with and giving support to the often religiously critical voices of the abolitionists. That McGill would not and did not do. Instead, he called for widespread engagement in evangelical practices of prayer and repentance, hoping that such engagement would lead to a national religious revival that could pull the nation back from the brink of disaster.

From Civil War to Industrial Behemoth

The United States lived through tremendous change in the half century between 1850 and 1900. In these fifty years, the country convulsed at increasingly sharp sectional tensions, staggered through a bloody and apocalyptic Civil War, groped through a complicated period of Reconstruction, and grew into an industrial behemoth in the Gilded Age. Richard R. Osmer and Friedrich Schweitzer aptly summarize some of the dizzying transformations of this period:

> This period marks the transition of the United States to an industrialized, urban society, a process that began in earnest in the last three decades of the nineteenth century, following the American Civil War (1861-1865). Although the war had

---

[10] Ibid., 20.

left all parts of the country depleted, it served as a spur to manufacturing, especially in the North. By the late 1870s, the postwar economy had entered a period of growth. During the final two decades of the century, the volume of industrial production, the number of workers employed in industry, and the number of manufacturing plants all doubled. The aggregate annual value of all manufacturing goods increased from $5.4 billion in 1879 to $13 billion in 1899. A series of inventions during this period—the telephone, typewriter, linotype, phonograph, electric light, cash register, air brake, refrigerator car, and automobile—became the basis of new industries. Corporate forms of business organization also began to emerge, marking the shift to a national economy based on large-scale financing and the marketing of goods across regional lines. The woeful conditions of many workers led to the formation of labor unions, such as the Knights of Labor in 1869 and the American Federation of Labor in 1881. Accompanying these developments was a steady process of urbanization. Most plants were located in or near urban areas and agriculture in general became less important. In 1860, it represented 50 percent of the total national wealth; in 1900, it represented only 20 percent.[11]

In addition to these massive changes, the country abolished the institution of slavery and struggled—by and large, unsuccessfully—to resolve longstanding and deep seated issues about race. Westward expansion continued at a brisk pace. By the turn of the century, the country was comprised of forty-five states—nine of which were added after the Civil War. As a consequence of westward expansion or "manifest destiny," Native Americans were pushed off of their ancestral lands and moved onto reservations. This forced exit was accompanied by a flood of European and Chinese immigrants.

Recent thought about globalization, by theorists such as William Sheuerman, points to the origins of this phenomenon in the nineteenth

---

[11] Richard R. Osmer and Friedrich Schweizer, *Religious Education between Modernization and Globalization: New Perspectives on the United States and Germany* (Grand Rapids: Eerdmans, 2003), 91-2.

century.[12] Sheuerman's three key markers of globalization—deterritorialization, interconnectedness, and social acceleration—began in the nineteenth century with such revolutionary technological developments as railroads and the telegraph.[13] In the latter half of the nineteenth century, perceptions about and actual experiences of time and space began to change dramatically.

Princeton Practical Theologians in the Latter Half of the Nineteenth Century

The era of the PTS patriarchs came to a close with the death of Archibald Alexander in 1851. Samuel Miller had died the previous year. From the end of the patriarchal period until the calling of Charles R. Erdman to the faculty in 1906, practical theology at PTS remained tethered to the foundations laid by Miller and Alexander and became increasingly technical and calcified. The three practical theologians who served on the faculty in the second half of the nineteenth century—James Waddell Alexander (1849-51), Alexander Taggart McGill (1854-83), and William Miller Paxton (1883-1902)—assumed the practical theological vision established by Alexander and Miller while developing and articulating it in terms of technical rationality, especially in relation to the practices of sacred rhetoric and church government.

Some aspects of this continuity with the seminary's original vision of practical theology come to light through consideration of the social connections that J.W. Alexander, McGill, and Paxton had with the generation of the patriarchs. J.W. Alexander, Archibald Alexander's eldest son, grew to maturity in Princeton and knew Miller well. When John Breckinridge resigned from his teaching post in order to pursue his calling as General Secretary of the Board of Missions of the national Presbyterian church, J.W. Alexander purchased his house and agreed to serve as private tutor for his son.[14] Even though McGill had been a part of the Associate Reformed Presbyterian Church and had attended one of that

---

[12] William Scheuerman, "Globalization," *The Stanford Encyclopedia of Philosophy (Summer 2010 Edition)*, Edward N. Zalta (ed.), URL = http://plato.stanford.edu/archives/sum2010/entries/globalization/, 1. Accessed June 26, 2011.
[13] Ibid.
[14] It is interesting to note, in passing, that the son whom J.W. Alexander tutored was named Samuel Miller Breckinridge. This arrangement—wherein J.W. Alexander lived in Breckinridge's house in exchange for his tutoring services—was worked out in July of 1838 and signed subsequent to the death of Breckinridge's wife (Samuel Miller's eldest daughter).

denomination's seminary, he strongly identified with the patriarchal legacy and sought to carry forward the fruits of that legacy. After his first wife died, McGill was grafted into the PTS patriarchal family through his marriage to Charles Hodge's daughter. Upon McGill's retirement, William Paxton was appointed to take his place. Paxton, who graduated from PTS in 1848, was the last member of the PTS faculty ever to have studied directly under Alexander and Miller. Each of these three PTS practical theologians understood their scholarship and teaching as both a continuation and a further refinement of the practical theological vision framed by Alexander and Miller in the early decades of the seminary's life.

James Waddell Alexander

In 1849, James Waddell Alexander was called by the seminary and the General Assembly of the Presbyterian Church to serve as Samuel Miller's permanent replacement as Professor of Ecclesiastical History and Church Government.[15] A child of both the manse and the professor's study, he grew up in Virginia, Philadelphia, and Princeton. He graduated from the College of New Jersey and PTS and was ordained as pastor in the Presbyterian Church in 1827. Having served as pastor for a Presbyterian church in Charlotte County, Virginia and in Trenton, New Jersey for several years, he was appointed Professor of Rhetoric and Belles-Lettres at the College of New Jersey in 1833. He held that post for eleven years, for much of that time also serving as the pastor for the black Witherspoon Street Presbyterian Church in Princeton and preaching there and elsewhere sixty to a hundred times per year.[16] Alexander accepted a call to the Duane Street Presbyterian Church in New York City in 1844 and served that congregation until he was called to join the faculty of the seminary in 1849. Apparently quite unsettled in the role of professor at the seminary, he resigned his post after only two years in order to return to his heartfelt calling as pastor of the Duane Street Church (eventually to become the

---

[15] The faculty position occupied by both Miller and J.W. Alexander also included the responsibility to teach "the preparation and delivery of sermons."

[16] Founded in 1837 and originally named the First Presbyterian Church of Color of Princeton, the name of the church was changed in 1848 to the Witherspoon Street Presbyterian Church. For Alexander's pastoral leadership of the Witherspoon Street Presbyterian Church and his frequency of preaching while serving as professor, see David B. Calhoun, *Princeton Seminary: Volume 1: Faith and Learning, 1812-1868* (Carlisle, PA: Banner of Truth Trust, 1994), 287. For a record of the number of sermons preached for the years 1844-9, see n1. James W. Alexander, *Forty Years' Familiar Letters*, ed. by John Hall, vols. 1 and 2 (New York: Scribner, 1860), 2:106.

Fifth Avenue Presbyterian Church).[17] During his second tenure as pastor of that church, he preached effectively, wrote copiously, and, according to Charles Hodge, "His pastoral duties wore out his constitution."[18] In addition to his preaching and teaching duties, J.W. Alexander wrote several books and many periodical articles, while also contributing a long list of articles and reviews to the seminary's quarterly journal, *The Biblical Repertory and Princeton Review*. His published books include a biography of his father, a prayer book for soldiers and sailors, a book on the importance and practices of family worship, various collections of sermons, two volumes of collected correspondence, and over thirty books for the American Sunday School Union.[19]

J.W. Alexander's understanding of practical theology was deeply informed by the vision forged by his father and Samuel Miller. Upon assuming the post of professor at the seminary, he delivered an inaugural address entitled "The Value of Church History for the Theologian of our Day." In it, he emphasized his continuity with the generation of the patriarchs by approaching the study of church history with a primary interest in its practical implications for ministry in contemporary churches.[20] Church history, in other words, was to serve as a fund of cases which bear witness to the unfolding of divine providence in church

---

[17] Soon after making the transition from pastor of the Duane Street Church to professor at the seminary, Alexander complained of sorely missing pastoral ministry in a letter dated November 8, 1849: "I did not leave pastoral life willingly; I foresaw the very evils I begin to feel; they distress me more than I reckoned for. I miss my old women; and especially my weekly catechumens, my sick-rooms, my rapid walks, and my nights of right-down fatigue." *Familiar Letters*, 2:107. In a letter written to a friend on Christmas day one year later, Alexander gave expression to his deep wrestling with a call to return to the Duane Street Church: "What moves me somewhat is, (1,) I do not feel a special quality for teaching: (2,) I greatly miss pulpit and pastoral work. Yet when I think of tearing up again—it seems next to impossible. I am much concerned, and in real trouble of mind, and I shall profit by any unprejudiced thoughts you have." *Familiar Letters*, 2:128.

[18] "The Late Dr. Alexander," *New York Times*, August 5, 1859, 4.

[19] Note on the American Sunday School Union publications taken from "The Late Dr. Alexander," *New York Times*, August 5, 1849.

[20] Of Samuel Miller, his immediate predecessor, James Alexander remarked in a letter dated December 30, 1843, "I think him one of the most conscientious and pious men I ever knew." *Familiar Letters*, 1:386-7. James Alexander's respect and appreciation for his father was duly expressed in the biography he wrote of the latter, *The Life of Archibald Alexander, D.D., First Professor in the Theological Seminary at Princeton, New Jersey* (New York: Scribner, 1854).

and society.[21] Church history is "a record, not of bare events...but of the progress of revealed knowledge. Here our topic is nothing less than the perpetual struggle of truth against error."[22] The past is replete with lessons and with perennial insights that can aid in contemporary battles over orthodox faith. More than that, church history bears witness to evangelical faith through the ages:

> For what is the intimate and essential treasure of Christian history, and of the Church, if it is not Christ's religion, or the life of God among men? Leave this out, and you may have prosperous and adverse events, creeds and canons, enlargements and contractions, rites and ceremonies, developments of dogma, and suppression of heresy, but these are as cheerless as Egyptian temples, or sculptured cenotaphs....It is the life which once dwelt in these piles after which we are seeking; and the search cannot be unedifying, for this is God's work among men.[23]

Church history, in his view, provides ample and detailed knowledge in service to vital piety. Conceived of in this way, this field of study functions as a form of practical theology, the guiding principle of which is the "laws of gracious operation" of the Holy Spirit in relation to the death of Jesus Christ in the experience of individuals and communities.[24] Consequently, the study of church history is also the study of Christian missions and missionary practice because it "teaches us how truly Christian faith and love work towards the evangelizing of the nations. It teaches the modern missionary how the ancient missionary went to work, in circumstances often precisely similar."[25] Finally, the study of church history can fund the pastor's imagination of the future by providing perspective on the ways in which prophetic promises have been fulfilled by divine action in later periods. In this respect, "The history of the past is auxiliary to the history of the future."[26]

---

[21] James Waddell Alexander, "The Value of Church History to the Theologians of our Day: An Inaugural Discourse," *Discourses at the inauguration of the Rev. James W. Alexander ... as professor of ecclesiastical history and church government in the Theological Seminary at Princeton: delivered at Princeton November 20, 1849 before the Directors of the Seminary* (New York: Robert Carter and Brothers, 1850), 71.
[22] Ibid., 72.
[23] Ibid., 80-1.
[24] Ibid., 83.
[25] Ibid., 87.
[26] Ibid., 92.

James Alexander's inaugural address concluded by sounding themes resonant with his father and Samuel Miller's practical theological vision. Contrary to the predictions of the elder Alexander, Miller and Charles Hodge, the perils of German Protestant thought—as symbolized by the writings of Kant, Hegel, and the German Idealists—had not faded from the American religious scene. James Alexander warned his hearers:

> By a slow but inevitable process the distillations of the German alembic are coming to tincture the theology of Britain and America. The most alarming latitude widens around us; and heresies which all the Confessions of all the Reformed Churches, without a single exception, agree in denouncing, and at which even Rome revolts, are declared by ministers of religion not to touch the foundation. In such warfare it is well to have daylight, and to know the dogmas which are our enemies; for which purpose we cannot too sedulously study their portraits in the great gallery of ages."[27]

In this call to arms, Alexander reaffirmed the practical theological synthesis provided by the welding together of Westminster orthodoxy and Scottish Common Sense philosophy. In order to conquer the ideological enemies of the gospel, the next generation of pastors would have to redouble their efforts to hold together genuine piety and deep learning, particularly in the act of preaching. The future leaders of the church should not separate piety and learning; nor should they allow themselves to be fooled into playing one off the other.[28] While they should be joined together, their union was asymmetrical. Perhaps unsurprisingly, piety was the real center of gravity at PTS in the nineteenth century:

---

[27] Ibid., 94. Note: the term "alembic" refers to an apparatus used in the process of distillation. Published a year before his death, Alexander continued to rail against contemporary German Protestant theology: "In our times, if one country more than another has the boast of learning, it is Germany; and there, if anywhere, Infidelity has made its wildest ravages….The metaphysical reasoners, one after another, have spiderlike, spun a thread out of their bowels, wherewith to entangle and crush the doctrines of the Gospel." James W. Alexander, *Discourses on Common Topics of Christian Faith and Practice* (New York: Scribner, 1858), 18.

[28] Alexander, *Inaugural Discourse*, 95.

> Wherever vital piety decays, [evangelical Christianity] decays. It takes its flight long before the alteration of creeds or the denial of doctrines; for there may be an age of cold orthodoxy unenlivened by one beam of love to the Redeemer. But when this affection has fled, sound doctrine soon prepares to spread its wings likewise. For a time there may be accurate metaphysical discussion, controversy about tenets, and even persecution for differences. But by degrees the Cross is thrust into a corner; and at length the propitiatory work of Christ is extenuated or forgotten. The Atonement being tarnished or exploded, the Godhead of Christ is soon found to be superfluous. There is no need of a divine Redeemer under that easy system of liberal Christianity in which every man is his own savior. This may account for the known fact, that among those who reject the Trinity, small account is made of personal love towards the Lord Jesus Christ. The too frequent allusion to his double nature and to his redeeming blood becomes offensive, and the people are in a fair way to forget that there ever were such spots as Gethsemane or Golgotha. Whereas, in direct opposition to this, whenever vital piety revives, there is a marked revival of love to Jesus Christ.[29]

Only with the spiritual strength that arises from the joint embrace of piety and learning—with piety as the anchor—will leaders of the church withstand the corrosive assaults launched by the pantheistic ways of German Idealism and all other heresies of the day.

These concluding sentiments bear witness to a growing apprehension about and defensiveness against the more liberal waves of contemporary German Protestant theological thought that continued to exert influence on mid-century American Protestant thought. For the PTS faculty, much more than the character of (practical) theology was at stake; the integrity of the gospel itself and the vitality of the churches were perceived to be at risk.

Alexander Taggart McGill

Alexander Taggart McGill (1807-89) was born in central Pennsylvania and had studied for the bar and worked briefly as a

---

[29] Ibid., 123.

surveyor in northern Georgia before entering the ministry. He had served as a pastor of three small Presbyterian congregations in Carlisle, Pennsylvania before he became a minister member of the Old School Presbyterians, serving as the pastor of the Second Presbyterian Church in Carlisle.[30] After eight years of congregational ministry, he was appointed to teach church history at Western Theological Seminary in Allegheny, Pennsylvania. While serving as faculty member in church history there, he was elected Moderator of the Old School Presbyterian General Assembly in 1848. Through his friendship with southern Presbyterian leader James Henley Thornwell, he served quite briefly on the faculty of Columbia Theological Seminary in 1852 (when it was still located in South Carolina) before joining the PTS faculty in 1854. For more than half of his PTS tenure he also served as the primary officer for government and discipline at the national church level. He served as permanent clerk of the General Assembly from 1850 to 1862 and stated clerk for that same body from 1852 to 1870, while teaching full time.[31] In 1857, he was appointed, along with Charles Hodge, to serve on the General Assembly committee charged with the task of revising the *Book of Discipline*.[32] W. Henry Green, one of McGill's PTS colleagues, noted in his address at McGill's funeral:

> From the time of his election in 1854 until the spring of 1883, when he withdrew from active service, Dr. McGill continued to perform the full duties of a professor in this Seminary, duties which were varied during two years, 1859 and 1860, by his giving instruction in Church History, which had belonged to his professorship in Allegheny, but during most of the time he was occupied in training the students in Practical Theology, that is to say, in preaching, pastoral care and in church government, in each of which he was assiduous and enthusiastic. His known familiarity with ecclesiastical questions led to his being consulted constantly by his former students and by others in the perplexities which arose in the course of their actual experience, the lectures and instructions

---

[30] "McGill, Alexander Taggart," in *The National Cyclopædia of American Biography*, no author provided (New York: James T. White, 1904), 364.
[31] Ibid.
[32] W. Henry Green, "Address at the Funeral of Rev. Alexander Taggart McGill, D.D., LL.D., In Princeton, Jan. 16, 1889" (n.p., 1889), 13.

of the class room [sic] being thus supplemented largely by subsequent correspondence.[33]

For decades, McGill was the leading Presbyterian authority on matters of polity. His correspondence bears ample witness to the ways in which Presbyterians sought out his sage advice on matters of practical ecclesiology.

McGill laid out his vision of practical theology in his inaugural address of 1854. As the new professor of "Pastoral Theology, Church Government, and the Composition and Delivery of Sermons," he sought to carry on the formidable patriarchal legacy established by Archibald Alexander and Samuel Miller. McGill's position combined elements of the teaching portfolios of both Alexander and Miller, and he sought to integrate these elements under the rubric "practical theology." McGill's inaugural address provides the first written attestation to the term "practical theology" at PTS. He saw himself, "standing in a place already built by others—and more than built—adorned, with living talent, which enlightened Christendom confesses, and with festooned memories…"[34]

McGill distinguished practical theology from various forms of merely theoretical theology.[35] Under the influence of the fourfold pattern of theological school curriculum, McGill saw practical theology as:

> …The complement of that perfect cycle, in which exegetic, systematic, and historic theology, are primary and main departments, in theological training. It is necessary to these, as art is to science, as speech is to thought, as action is to life and vigour [sic]: sharing with them, also, difficult investigations, which demand the highest culture and discipline of mind.[36]

---

[33] Green, 12.
[34] Alexander T. McGill, "Practical Theology: An Inaugural Discourse," in *Discourses at the Inauguration of the Rev. Alexander T. McGill, D.D., as Professor of Pastoral Theology* [sic], *Church Government, and the Composition and Delivery of Sermons, in the Theological Seminary at Princeton, N.J., Delivered at Princeton, September 12, 1854, Before the Directors of the Seminary* (Philadelphia: C. Sherman, 1854), 57. Note that the publisher used the term "Pastoral Theology" in the title of the publication, whereas McGill explicitly used the term "Practical Theology."
[35] Ibid., 37.
[36] Ibid. For a discussion of the development of the fourfold pattern in theological education, see Farley, *Theologia,* 110-6.

The practical area of the theological school curriculum functioned for McGill as the realization of theory in practice and as a bridge between the seminary and the life of the church in society. While it definitely had the character of "applied science," it was by no means any less intellectually rigorous or challenging than the other three areas of the curriculum.[37]

In his analysis of the history of revelation and of the various periods of church history, McGill argued that practical theology had always been present and had, in key eras, been primary. His most forceful and compelling argument on this score came in relation to the ministry and teachings of Jesus Christ:

> The Great Teacher himself, within his college of disciples, dwelt mostly on themes of Pastoral Theology and Church Government; on a call to ministry, and its qualifications, its cross, and its crown; on the nature of his kingdom, its separation from the state, its parity of ministers, its bench of elders, and even its method of process for the exercise of discipline; not omitting, by any means, important hints in his own example and precept, for the composition and delivery of sermons.[38]

To McGill's mind, Jesus Christ was primarily a practical theologian. Likewise, the apostles and the various epistolary material in the New Testament bear witness to the primacy of practical theology in the life of the church. The early church leaders mainly wrote practical theological literature. The middle ages also produced significant material of a practical nature. McGill criticized Luther and Calvin for their comparative neglect of practical theology, but justified their behavior as a response to the distortion of the gospel in a practical (presumably Aristotelian) direction in the medieval era. The seventeenth century stood out for McGill as the golden age of practical theology, particularly evident in the work of the Westminster divines.[39] The establishment by the General Assembly of his new chair was a momentous occasion in the history of Presbyterian practical theology in that, for the very first time, all the components of practical theology had been brought together into a single chair.[40]

---

[37] McGill, *Inaugural Discourse*, 48.
[38] Ibid., 50.
[39] Ibid., 52.
[40] Ibid., 53.

McGill used the term "pastoral theology" in a specific and restricted sense as that knowledge pertaining to the calling, role, and responsibilities of the pastoral leader. He used the term "practical theology" as a larger, more encompassing category that included subjects like homiletics, liturgics, catechetics, ecclesiology, and polity. McGill understood his chair in practical theology to encompass six discreet subject areas. *Pastoral theology* would deal with the calling, role, and work of the pastor. *Homiletics*, understood as sacred rhetoric, would draw from both theological and secular sources to focus on development, criticism, and performance of preaching—particularly in relation to evangelical conversion. *Catechetics* would focus on instructing young and new congregants in Christian beliefs and practices not already addressed through preaching. Like homiletics, it would also engage broader discussions about pedagogical theory and practice. It would also provide future missionaries with skills for "imparting elementary instruction, dealing with superstitions of the heathen, and managing the education of their children."[41] McGill further envisioned teaching about church school leadership, methods for conducting Bible studies, principles for home visitation (for the purpose of accountability in domestic religious education), and the preparation and oversight of public school teachers. *Liturgics* would deal with anything having to do with corporate worship (including prayer, music, the proper administration of the sacraments, oral performance of Bible readings, and stewardship). McGill's fifth division, on *the Church*, would effectively teach the theory and practice of ecclesiology. Special attention would be given to general matters of polity, church officers, and connectionalism.[42] In this area, McGill intended to expand upon the foundations laid by Samuel Miller and to promulgate Miller's understanding of practical theology.[43] *Ecclesiastical Law and Discipline* would deal with "the diacritical power and practice of the Church."[44]

Each of these subject areas would have a biblical foundation. As with the other three divisions of the theological school curriculum, practical theology and its subareas should use the Bible "as a textbook."[45] Exegetical study of Scripture would yield useful and necessary insights for practical theology. While the entire seminary

---

[41] Ibid., 41.
[42] Ibid., 44.
[43] Ibid.
[44] Ibid., 45.
[45] Ibid., 46.

faculty ought to attend to the biblical insights offered by each of the theological areas, certain biblical topics or passages would be handled best by the professor of practical theology.

McGill's approach to practical theology was not narrowly biblicist. He advocated a robust interdisciplinary engagement with fields of study that might shed light on theory and practice in certain areas of practical theology. For example, "spiritual anthropology" could shed useful light on human nature, pagan rhetoric could illuminate the nature of preaching, and secular pedagogical theory could enliven and inform catechetic endeavors.[46] Studies in practical theology and its constituent areas should not focus solely on the church; such research and teaching should also "attempt to explain the contact and confluence of religion with civilization."[47] Practical theology should also concern itself with matters pertaining to the public good and with "the welfare of our nation."[48]

Due to the complexity, range, and theoretical sophistication needed in practical theology, McGill argued forcefully that it should neither be left to students' own emerging pastoral imagination nor left to excellent practitioners. Students need instruction in principles and intellectual frameworks. Skilled practitioners often cannot explain why they do what they do:

> …The man of right conduct for himself, is not always the man to explain even his own conduct, for the benefit of others. In daily intercourse, we often find an incapacity of practical men to give intelligible reasons for the success with which they direct their own business, and meet the changes and emergencies of life; and in the most elevated spheres of magisterial vocation, the same ineptitude has been frequent and striking…While, therefore, we bow to the practical pastor, as the noblest of human characters, and eagerly seek, at all times, to learn from his lips, the art of caring for souls, there may be an extravagant estimate of practice alone, as a qualification for teaching the rising ministry, to the disadvantage of any department; and especially those great theoretic departments, which demand the studies of a lifetime, intensely given, to furnish a proper defence [sic] of

---

[46] Ibid., 47.
[47] Ibid.
[48] Ibid.

> the gospel, against the erudite and subtle enemies, which now "come in like a flood." Yet, in this particular Chair, though its themes might well demand illimitable stores of erudition, and cannot be handled by merely empirical tact, experience is indispensable; experience of the world, of the pastor's office, and the teacher's art. Without having had a fair and full experiment with the pastoral life, and surpassing fondness for all its duties, along with previous training of many a kind in common life, which brings a man most fully into contact with human nature, as well as fits him somewhat for the last two branches here detailed, my own consent to adventure to this high office could not have been obtained.[49]

According to McGill, there are actually two dangers that can threaten research and teaching in practical theology. Excellent practitioners who lack theoretical frameworks for understanding and articulating the principles of excellent practice do a disservice to the next generation of pastoral leaders because they cannot provide those principles and frameworks that enable transfer of learning to a range of contexts. Conversely, academic practical theologians who lack sufficient experience in the full range of pastoral leadership do not know how to assess and deploy theoretical frameworks in the practice of ministry.

Of the six members of the PTS faculty who taught in the area of practical theology during the nineteenth century, McGill had the most developed and explicitly articulated understanding of practical theology. Building on the foundations laid by Alexander and Miller, McGill assembled the parts of the field into an integrated whole under the category of practical theology. He sought to integrate theory and practice by applying theory to the practices of the church with overt concern for the wider good of society. His understanding of practical theology was deeply grounded in Scripture and robustly interdisciplinary. He provided convincing rationale for the claim that the teacher of practical theology should integrate theoretical frameworks and pastoral experience, eschewing alike excellent practitioners who lacked theoretical frameworks and erudite academics who lacked significant pastoral experience. McGill built upon and affirmed the broad Christian humanism at the heart of the vision for PTS established by Alexander

---

[49] Ibid., 55-6.

and Miller. In many respects, McGill made contributions relevant for his own time while anticipating by as much as a century themes and issues that would characterize practical theology at PTS in the latter half of the twentieth century.

William Miller Paxton

William Miller Paxton (1824-1904), like his immediate predecessor, hailed from central Pennsylvania. After studying law for a time, he turned his sights toward pastoral ministry and was one of the last students of Archibald Alexander and Samuel Miller at PTS.[50] He served pastorates in Greencastle, Pennsylvania, Pittsburgh, and New York City. During the second half of his fifteen year pastorate in Pittsburgh, he also filled the chair of sacred rhetoric at Western Theological Seminary in Allegheny, Pennsylvania, where McGill had taught church history in an earlier era. For three of Paxton's eighteen years of service as pastor of First Presbyterian Church in New York City, he also served as lecturer in sacred rhetoric at Union Theological Seminary. In 1880, Paxton was elected moderator of the Presbyterian General Assembly. From 1883 until 1902, he served on the PTS faculty as professor of Ecclesiastical, Homiletic, and Pastoral Theology.

Beyond a handful of sermons, Paxton's publications were few—chiefly a small handbook on types of preaching published by PTS the year of his death.[51] Paxton functioned more as a powerful practitioner and teacher of homiletics than as a published scholar. The seminary catalogues during the last two decades of the nineteenth century provide witness to Paxton's power as a master teacher of sacred rhetoric. In addition to the general course of study (including the optional fourth "graduate" year), the catalogues list students engaged in a variety of specialized studies at the seminary that were over and above the basic curriculum. Paxton's special course in sacred rhetoric grew steadily until well over thirty students regularly enrolled in it. For several years, his

---

[50] John DeWitt, "Discourse at the Funeral Service, in the First Presbyterian Church, Princeton, New Jersey, November the Thirtieth, 1904," in *In Memoriam: William Miller Paxton, D.D., LL.D., 1824-1904: Funeral and Memorial Discourses with Appendixes and Notes* (New York: n.p., 1905), 11.

[51] The book had been developed by Paxton for use in his lectures on homiletics and was originally printed up solely for distribution in his classes. William M. Paxton, *Homiletics: Classification of Divisions* (Princeton, NJ: Princeton Theological Seminary, 1904). The PTS archives contain several boxes of Paxton's unpublished, handwritten sermons.

concentration had the largest number of students enrolled of any of the special supra-curricular offerings.[52]

In marked contrast to McGill, Paxton showed little interest in intellectual frameworks for understanding practical theology or for working out the architecture of the field. More of a technician than a theorist, Paxton excelled in mentoring and molding future preachers. He had a knack for developing excellent homiletic practitioners. B.B. Warfield noted that in Paxton's early teaching of preaching at Western Seminary in Allegheny:

> He saw in the task that had come to him unsought an opportunity, not to philosophize upon the principles that underlie the homiletical art, nor to discuss the nature of preaching as a literary form, but simply to show the young men gathered in the seminary how to do it....His main characteristic as a teacher of homiletic springs at once into its fullest manifestation. I mean his intense practicality. The lectures are analytical and precise: the entire subject of sacred rhetoric is developed in them with formal completeness: but the whole tone and effect are those of a master-workman training his apprentices in the practice of an art. It is perfectly clear that Dr. Paxton is simply showing his pupils how to do what he himself has been accustomed to do with so great success; taking them into his confidence, so to speak, and making them free of the secrets of the trade. And this effect is powerfully reinforced by another striking element in his teaching—what we may call its empirical basis. Discarding all *a priori* theorizing as to what a sermon ought to be, he had set himself to make a survey of the existing sermonic literature with a view to ascertaining what, as an actual fact, good sermons are. His enunciations of the principles of sermon-building [sic] had in them, therefore, the vitality that comes from touch with the real.[53]

---

[52] For example, see *Catalogue 1898-1899* (Princeton, NJ: C.S. Robinson and Co., 1989), 15-6.

[53] Benjamin Breckinridge Warfield, "Memorial Discourse, Delivered by Appointment of the Faculty of Princeton Theological Seminary, in Miller Chapel, on the Twenty-Fourth of February, 1905, by the Rev. Benjamin B. Warfield," in *In Memorium: William Miller Paxton, D.D., LL.D, 1824-1904: Funeral and Memorial Discourses with Appendixes and Notes* (New York: n.p., 1905), 32-3.

This apt observation captured Paxton's approach to practical theology—particularly in the mode of homiletics—at Western, Union (New York), and Princeton seminaries. Whether reflecting on his own practice or conducting focused empirical research on published sermons, Paxton sought to identify and teach best practices of the art of preaching.

Paxton's emphasis on effective technique assumed a norm of devotional piety articulated by his own seminary teachers Alexander and Miller. He held that ministers should have both vital piety and deep learning. As with the patriarchs, he made a strong case for the primacy of piety. In the charge he gave to his friend Archibald Alexander Hodge on the occasion of the latter's inauguration as professor at the seminary, Paxton gave fiery expression to the relation between piety and learning that Alexander and Miller would have both recognized and applauded:

> There stands that venerable institution [i.e. PTS]. What does it mean? What is the idea it expresses?...Is it a place where young men get a profession by which they are to make their living? Is it a school in which a company of educated young men are gathered to grind out theology, to dig Hebrew roots, to read patristic literature, to become proficients in ecclesiastical dialectics, to master the mystic technics of the schoolmen, and to debate about fate, free-will, and the divine decrees? If this be its purpose, or its chief purpose, then bring the torch and burn it!...We do not in any way depreciate a learned ministry. We must have learning...But whenever in a theological seminary learning takes the precedence, it covers as with an icicle the very truths which God designed to warm and melt the hearts of men...No, no, this is not the meaning of a theological seminary...It is a school of learning, but it is also a cradle of piety.[54]

Echoing the patriarchs, Paxton insisted that theological learning without genuine piety does a positive disservice to the church. Only with piety comes the discernment necessary to put learning in biblical studies, theology, and church history to work for the transformation of lives by the gospel and the edification of the church.

---

[54] As quoted by B.B. Warfield, "Memorial Discourse," 44-5.

Paxton represents an approach to practical theology characterized by technical elaboration of the charismatic vision developed by the patriarchs. He assumed the inherent worth of their vision and sought only to work it out and carry it forward in relation to ever more precisely honed homiletical technique.

The Late Nineteenth Century PTS Practical Theology Curriculum
Sacred Rhetoric

No area of practical theology in the nineteenth century at PTS received more attention and priority than preaching. Every member of the faculty who taught in the area of practical theology made the theory and practice of preaching a hallmark of their teaching. J.W. Alexander, Miller's supposed replacement, loved the practice of preaching so much that he returned to his pulpit after only two academic cycles. Alexander McGill was an able preacher and taught the art of preaching with competence. William Paxton lived and breathed preaching; it was his burning pastoral and professorial passion. The seminary catalogues for the latter part of the nineteenth century bear witness to a comprehensive and pervasive pattern of education in the art of sacred rhetoric. Oral proclamation of the gospel was the primary expression of practical theology in its more narrow, technical sense. The other dimensions of practical theology at PTS during the nineteenth century—polity, mission, the theory and practice of pastoral ministry, catechetics, and pastoral care—all took a back seat to sacred rhetoric.

Analysis of the seminary's catalogues provides further insight into the importance and the shape of teaching about preaching and speech during the entirety of the nineteenth century. In the curricular vision implemented by Archibald Alexander and Samuel Miller, teaching about preaching and speech appears to have served as a capstone or integrating function for the whole curriculum. Approximately half of Alexander's Pastoral Theology course for third year students focused on the dynamics of effective oral communication and best practices of preaching. In tandem with Alexander's course, Miller also taught third year students his course on the composition and delivery of sermons.

In the 1837-8 academic year, a course in "Sacred Rhetoric" was added to the curriculum and did not replace either Alexander's or Miller's courses. In the 1841-2 academic year, a note was added to the seminary catalogue to the effect that, "The students of the seminary are required to deliver orations, and to exhibit compositions, as often as it is judged expedient by the professors."⁵⁵ In other words, the faculty in that year added regular oral performance for students in all classes to the official pattern of assessment of student learning.⁵⁶

In addition to ecclesiastical history and church government, J.W. Alexander taught sermon preparation and sacred rhetoric. Extant student notes from his lectures on rhetoric make clear that he approached this subject in an interdisciplinary manner. He urged students to write every day and to pay attention to matters of style; there should be "no day without a line" of text written by the one who would develop his skills in sacred rhetoric. The Greco-Roman classics should be studied regularly and in their original languages. Dwelling with the masterpieces of classical literature would aid the development of rhetorical excellence. In particular, he urged that the works of Cicero, Quintilian, and other classical orators should be studied carefully.⁵⁷

In lecturing on sacred rhetoric, J.W. Alexander drew heavily on his experience as both an accomplished preacher and a professor of rhetoric at the College of New Jersey. He also carried on the tradition of teaching about both preaching and the dynamics of effective oral communication established by his father and Samuel Miller in their respective third year courses. The archival evidence makes quite clear that from day one of the seminary's existence, teaching future pastors how to preach and how to speak was a central priority in the curriculum.

In the course catalogue for the 1855-6 academic year, following the listing of courses, a note explaining the oral performance requirement made students aware of "exercises in composition and delivery throughout the course [of studies]."⁵⁸ The PTS catalogue for 1862-3 includes a course for all first year students on "extemporaneous speaking" as well as a note that all students should expect regular exercises in "composition, reading, and delivery without notes."⁵⁹ This points to an emerging emphasis on the development of excellence in oral communication without being tied to notes or text. A few years later, in the 1865-6 catalogue, the new course in extemporaneous speaking for first year students was complemented by a course for first year students entitled "Homiletics" and a course for second

---

[55] *Catalogue 1841-1842* (Princeton, NJ: Robert E. Hornor, 1841), 11.
[56] The catalogue likely only made explicit here what had actually been a longstanding curricular practice.
[57] James Waddell Alexander Manuscript Collection, Special Collections, Princeton Theological Seminary Library, box 3, file 2.
[58] *Catalogue 1855-1856* (Philadelphia: C. Sherman and Son, 1855 [sic]), 15.
[59] *Catalogue 1862-1863* (Trenton, NJ: Murphy, Betchtel, 1862), 17.

year students on "Homiletical Criticism."[60] The emphasis on speech and preaching was extracted from the traditional third year courses in pastoral theology and the preparation and delivery of sermons developed by Alexander and Miller. A further opportunity to develop oral communication skills was added to the list of course offerings: "Special instructions and exercises in the art of Elocution, without charge to the students, by the very best qualified teachers in the country."[61] During this same academic year, the faculty petitioned the General Assembly to add a fourth year to the curriculum, part of which would be spent in a course on preaching. In this revised curricular scheme, elements of ministerial theory and practice functioned not so much as a capstone (as was the case in the period of the patriarchs), but as an emphasis that permeated the curriculum.

Curricular developments in speech and preaching were further elaborated in the 1869-70 catalogue. The description for the pastoral theology course included, among other things, a focus on preaching. A new section of the catalogue devoted to "Rhetorical Exercises and Sermonizing" provides important details about this dimension of the curriculum:

> Dr. C.W. Hodge presides at the weekly speaking of the Junior and Middler Classes, each member of which is, in turn, expected to deliver original discourses, *memoriter*.
>
> The weekly preaching of the Senior Class, which is likewise *memoriter*, is under the direction of Dr. McGill, who also has exercises with all the classes…in *extempore* speaking, in writing sermons, and in preparing written criticism upon the sermons of others….
>
> Special instruction is given in the art of elocution, with appropriate vocal exercises by Prof. S.G. Peabody, who is in constant attendance at the seminary, and by professors Mark Bailey of New Haven, and Robert Kidd of Indiana, by whom the institution is successively visited at different periods in

---

[60] *Catalogue 1865-1866* (Princeton, NJ: Blanchard, 1866), 17.
[61] Ibid., 19.

> each session. This is without cost to the students, the expense being borne [sic] by generous friends of the Seminary.
>
> Every student is required, prior to graduation, to exhibit to the Professor of Homiletic Instruction two lectures and four popular sermons, which shall be approved by him.[62]

Similar announcements were published in PTS catalogues throughout the remainder of the nineteenth century. Changes to the standard notice had mainly to do with the faculty members who staffed this aspect of the curriculum. The designated practical theologian on the faculty—McGill, followed by William Miller Paxton—always assessed the weekly sermons presented by seniors and had to give approval for the "two lectures and four popular sermons" requirement for graduation. The various PTS faculty members who staffed the "weekly speaking" of the Junior and Middler classes from 1874 to 1904 included variously professors C.W. Hodge, Patton, Armstrong, Warfield, Davis, Purves, Green, and DeWitte. The elocutionary exercises were covered by the team of Peabody and Bailey—with the addition of Theodore E. Perkins in 1874—through the 1877-1878 academic year.[63] Beginning the following year, instruction in elocution was handled by Henry W. Smith. Smith taught elocution at the seminary for the rest of McGill's and the entirety of Paxton's tenure on the faculty, spanning more than a quarter of a century.

The curricular pattern for the latter years of McGill's tenure included first year courses in homiletics and "extemporary speaking," a second year course on "homiletical criticism," no explicit course of preaching or oral communication during the third year, and, for those who opted to avail themselves of the supplemental fourth year, an advanced course on preaching.[64] A note in the catalogue indicated that McGill used Swiss Reformed theologian Alexandre Vinet's book *Homiletics or the Theory of Preaching* along with lectures and "writing skeletons [outlines]" as the basis for the first year course in preaching.[65] During the last year of

---

[62] *Catalogue 1869-1870*, (Philadelphia: Caxton Press of Sherman and Co, 1869) 15-6.
[63] *Catalogue 1874-1875* (Philadelphia: Caxton Press of Sherman and Co., 1874), 16.
[64] Ibid., 12.
[65] Ibid., 15. In his book *Homiletics*, Karl Barth made this assessment of Vinet's approach to preaching: "The Swiss Vinet (professor at Lausanne) was a faithful disciple of Schleiermacher who is still influential even today. His starting point was the possibility of viewing homiletics as a special form of rhetoric. He was not trying to paganize homiletics, for, as we recall from Schleiermacher, natural life at its deepest level is

McGill's regular service on the faculty, the overall curricular pattern with respect to preaching and speech changed rather significantly. For academic year 1882-3, a more robust schema emerged: first year students took courses in homiletics, extemporary speaking, and elocution; second year students took courses in homiletical criticism and in elocution; third year students took a course in elocution; and students who remained for the optional fourth year took an advanced course in preaching.[66] From this point forward, the curriculum required that students take a course in elocution for each of the three years of the main academic program.

When William Paxton arrived as McGill's replacement, the pattern of required courses in preaching and speech became even more demanding. For the first half of Paxton's tenure on the faculty, students in the regular three year program took eight courses in preaching and speech: first years took courses in "homiletical exercises" and elocution; second years took courses in homiletics, "Criticism of Sermons," and elocution; third years took courses in "Homiletics: Analysis of Texts," "Homiletical Criticism," and elocution. The optional fourth year included the usual advanced course in preaching.[67] This pattern shifted slightly in the 1892-3 academic year with the amalgamation of the second year courses in homiletics and criticism of sermons.[68] Explicit references to Vinet's *Homiletics* disappeared from the *Catalogues* with the arrival of Paxton.[69] Instead, the following description typified Paxton's approach to

---

already Christian and therefore true rhetoric is to be regarded fundamentally as homiletics. Rhetoric and the art of rhetoric consist of putting oneself into others' shoes and identifying oneself with their innermost being so as to be able to speak for them. This innermost being in us is not evil but an advocate for the good, and it is the duty of Christian preaching to bring it to expression, so that during a sermon we are constantly reminded of our true selves. In this way, rhetoric is filled with spiritual content, so that when the ideal of speech between people is achieved, i.e., when the innermost being of the one converses with the innermost being of the other, Christian discourse ensues. It is typical of Vinet that a biblical text does not have to be the basis of such discourse. Should it be asked whether a preacher is addressing believers or unbelievers, Schleiermacher would answer in favor of believers, but Vinet, with a much more comprehensive dialectic, replies that preaching must always be for both. It must lead those who do not yet know it to the truth of Christianity, and it must explain this truth further for those who already have a closer knowledge of it." Karl Barth, *Homiletics* (Louisville, KY: Westminster John Knox, 1991), 25-6.

[66] *Catalogue 1882-1883* (Philadelphia: Caxton Press of Sherman and Co., 1882), 13.
[67] *Catalogue 1883-1884* (Philadelphia: Caxton Press of Sherman and Co., 1883), 13.
[68] *Catalogue 1892-1893* (Princeton, NJ: Princeton Press, 1892), 20.
[69] *Catalogue 1883-1884*, 15.

teaching preaching under the "Ecclesiastical, Homiletical, and Pastoral Theology" department heading:

> The study of Homiletics begins in the Junior year. The method of instruction is by Lectures. The course includes: The proper idea and essential elements of a Sermon; the Classification of Sermons; the choice of Texts; Origination of Thought; Invention; Assimilation; the drawing of the Theme; Analysis of Texts and the different classes of Divisions; Practical exercise in the making of Divisions, with criticisms of Sermons delivered in the presence of a Professor.
>
> The course of Lectures in Homiletics is continued in the Middle year, including Lectures on Introductions; methods of treating the different heads of a discourse; Illustrations in preaching, together with practical exercises in preaching and criticisms by a Professor.[70]

In a funeral address in honor of Paxton, his colleague B.B. Warfield quoted one of Paxton's former students: "He was eminently a pastor in the pastoral chair. The teaching was concrete....He taught not so much the philosophy as the art...but with devotional spirituality, on a high level and with just balance."[71] Warfield further noted that Paxton "had no literary ambitions. His chosen method of expression was oral...he seemed to have a positive dislike for print."[72] Paxton's one—very short—book *Homiletics: Classifications of Divisions*, was a detailed and utterly practical taxonomy of the two possible types of sermons: topical and textual. Paxton insisted that preaching be done without notes and in a highly organized and lucidly logical manner. Though he wrote little, students and faculty colleagues alike deeply appreciated Paxton's facility in the pulpit and his ability to develop effective preachers.

While the teaching of speech communication for ministry and the dynamics of effective preaching had been taught from the seminary's very first days, this crucial dimension of the PTS experience reached its most elaborate curricular form in the final decades of the nineteenth century. It

---

[70] *Catalogue 1891-1892* (Princeton, NJ: Princeton Press, 1891), 21.
[71] Benjamin Breckinridge Warfield, "Memorial Discourse," 42.
[72] Ibid., 45.

is not by accident that PTS came to be known widely as "the school of the prophets" and as the school that produced princes of the pulpit.

Ecclesiastical Theology: Church Government and Discipline

All of the professors who taught practical theology at PTS during the nineteenth century provided meaningful and, in many ways, determinative leadership at the national level for the Presbyterian Church. Alexander (1807), Miller (1806), McGill (1848), and Paxton (1880) had all served as Moderators of the General Assembly, as had their faculty colleagues Charles Hodge (1846) and William Henry Green (1891).[73] Though they did not serve as moderators, John Breckinridge and J.W. Alexander ministered in high-profile leadership positions at the national level of the church. Moreover, every one of the practical theologians on the PTS faculty in the nineteenth century had served for several years as pastor of a Presbyterian congregation. While possessing various honorary academic degrees and often being widely published, the members of the PTS faculty who taught in the area that would today be called practical theology were called to join the faculty right out of their pulpits. No one who taught practical theology at PTS during the first half of its life was an ecclesiastically disengaged scholar; each one provided robust and sustained leadership at the congregational, presbytery, and General Assembly levels and continued to do so during his tenure as a member of the PTS faculty.

Leadership experience in the church came in handy when teaching about the nature and forms of the church as well as about leadership for the church. Church government and pastoral leadership played an important role—if secondary to preaching—in the various configurations of practical theology at PTS in the nineteenth century. Samuel Miller provided the baseline scholarship and teaching about church government in the seminary's patriarchal era. The importance of church government and discipline was developed further and given particular prominence in the middle decades of the nineteenth century under the professorial hand of Alexander McGill.

Beyond some sermons and occasional pieces, McGill published little until the end of his life, at which time he prepared three books for publication. Only his substantive tome on the principles of Presbyterian

---

[73] In addition to serving as GA moderators, they also served variously in positions of leadership on national committees of the church.

church government made it into print.[74] The book was essentially a compilation of forty years of polity lectures or as he described them, "…principles in the granite foundation of my own convictions, laid by the Bible as interpreted by the Westminster literature of the seventeenth century, and the reproduction thereof, with lucid and masterly exposition, by Drs John M. Mason and Samuel Miller, in the first half of this century."[75] In this work, for which McGill claimed originality only in the arrangement of topics, he held that he was explicating the principles of polity that are embedded in Scripture.[76] This rather dry if exhaustively informative expression of McGill's life work stands as a testimony to the maturity of his thought in practical ecclesiology. The work covered the nature of the church and its membership, provided an extended consideration of various aspects of the pastoral office, treated the offices of elder and deacon, and concluded with an examination of ecclesial judicatories and the nature of corporate worship.[77] According to McGill, the teaching of polity as practical ecclesiology matters a great deal because, "abstractions will never define and mysticism will never unite the Church. Her nature is concrete. The gospel is a religion of facts, and the revelation which contains it is history more than philosophy promulgated for the redemption of man."[78] Further, and affirming the insights of Charles Hodge, McGill held that the church is a theocracy guided by Scripture through the faithful and appropriately articulated leadership of pastors, elders, and deacons.[79]

Courses in church government and discipline in the last quarter of the nineteenth century began midway through a student's time at PTS. Middler students had to take a course on the constitution of the church. Senior students took a course in church government and discipline. For those students opting for a fourth year of study, an advanced course in "Ecclesiastical Law and Discipline" was required.[80] The standard catalogue description for the teaching of church government captures well McGill's approach to the subject:

---

[74] Alexander Taggart McGill, *Church Government. A Treatise Compiled from his Lectures in Theological Seminaries* (Philadelphia: Presbyterian Board of Publication and Sabbath Work, 1888).
[75] McGill, *Church Government*, 3.
[76] Ibid., 4.
[77] Ibid., 5-6.
[78] Ibid., 9.
[79] Ibid., 10.
[80] See, for example, *Catalogue 1874-1875*, 12.

Church Government is made a study of the second year, mostly by lectures. These embrace the nature of the Church, and the different schemes of Church polity; membership in the Church; the baptized; the full communicants; officers of the Church; commission, succession, and parity of Ministers; ruling Elders, in the warrant, qualifications, duties, and tenure of the office; Deacons, in the origin, importance, distinct and perpetual use of the office; Church Courts, in their warrant, gradation, and power.[81]

Doubtless, McGill illustrated the principles and rules with ample and engaging cases drawn from his considerable leadership experience and voluminous correspondence on matters of polity. This basic pattern remained intact through the final year of McGill's service on the faculty.

Though William Paxton's driving passion was preaching and the teaching of preaching, he also taught church government. During his first year on the faculty, Paxton made some key changes to what he inherited from McGill. Most significantly, he subsumed the teaching of church government under the rubric of "Ecclesiastical Theology."[82] With this move Paxton signaled that polity should be seen as a form of practical theology of and for the church. It should be part of theological reflection and not merely ecclesiastical technique.

The study of this subject commenced with first year students in the study of several topics in ecclesial history and ecclesiology: "the true idea of the Church; the organization of the Church; the Head of the Church; the claim of Papal Supremacy; Officers of the Church; Apostolic Succession; Office of Ministry; Ruling Elders, etc."[83] In order to make room for more coursework in homiletics, Paxton also combined McGill's classes for middlers and seniors on the subject into one course for middlers. For the first half of Paxton's tenure, no course in church government was offered to seniors; in its place, he taught an additional course in homiletics.[84]

Beginning in academic year 1893-1894, the pattern for teaching ecclesiastical theology changed yet again. From this point forward until the end of Paxton's career, ecclesiastical theology began in the middler

---

[81] Ibid., 15.
[82] *Catalogue 1883-1884*, 16.
[83] Ibid.
[84] Ibid.

year with a course entitled "Government and Discipline of the Church" followed by a course in "Church Government and Discipline" for seniors.[85] These courses might as easily have been called Practical Ecclesiology I and Practical Ecclesiology II.

Though they clearly gave priority to homiletics and speech, McGill and Paxton provided a thorough education in church government and discipline that deftly integrated church history, ecclesiology, and wise practice. In subsequent eras, faculty in the area of practical theology would never again give such pride of place to the subject of polity and leadership. Rather than functioning as one of the primary learning goals, this subject matter would in coming decades be moved increasingly to the margins of the curriculum.

Pastoral Theology, Missions, and "Christian Social Science"

Preaching and polity did not exhaust the subject of practical theology at PTS in the latter half of the nineteenth century. The curriculum during this period also intermittently included such subjects as pastoral theology, worship, missions, and "Christian social science." While courses for seniors in pastoral care and in the "Ordinances of Worship" were offered consistently during this period, some fluidity in the configuration of the curriculum related to practical theology seems perpetually to have been the norm. For example, when John Breckinridge joined the faculty in 1836, teaching about missions was added. When he resigned from the faculty, a course devoted to missions did not appear again in the curriculum until academic year 1895-6.[86]

In academic year 1888-9, an existing course for seniors in Christian ethics was elaborated in terms of "Christian Social Science."[87] As spelled out in the catalogue for 1894-5, the notion of Christian social science addressed, "…the teachings of Christianity as to the family, the nation, and the school; and the argument for Christianity from the superiority of its social system."[88] As was characteristic of the entirety of practical theology at PTS in the nineteenth century, this subject matter began with principles derived from Scripture and applied them to existing social realities and institutions. Christian sociology in this very early form was essentially a one way movement from text to context.

---

[85] *Catalogue 1893-1894* (Princeton, NJ: Princeton Press, 1893), 20.
[86] *Catalogue 1895-1896* (Princeton, NJ: Princeton Press, 1895), 24.
[87] *Catalogue 1882-1883*, 13.
[88] *Catalogue 1894-1895* (Princeton, NJ: Princeton Press, 1894), 26.

Perhaps the most significant curricular development related to practical theology in the latter years of the nineteenth century occurred in relation to the reintroduction of the study of mission. The study of mission—with heavy emphasis on foreign mission work—included an explicit focus on practical theology.[89] The catalogue description for the 1895-6 academic year indicates that the subject of missions was to be studied in an interdisciplinary fashion:

> The course in Missions treats of the philosophy, Biblical basis, history and Scriptural norms of missions, and affords instruction in the methods of awakening, developing and directing the Church's interest in foreign missions. It comprehends the study of the place of foreign missions in comparative religion; the universalistic element in Biblical theology, the history of missions from the close of the Apostolic period to the evangelical revival of the eighteenth century; the history, methods and results of Protestant missions; *practical theology in relation to foreign missions.*[90]

The description reads as if a certain conceptualization of the theological encyclopedia were brought to bear on the special subject of foreign missions. The operative conception of practical theology would likely have focused on the role and work of the missionary pastor. From the following year—when the course in mission moved to a biennial pattern—and into the first decade of the twentieth century, the course description included the practical theology component to the study of foreign missions.

Beginning in academic year 1882-3, the topic of "Theological Encyclopædia" began to be included explicitly in the courses offered to first year students.[91] This subject, which originated in German speaking lands in the early part of the nineteenth century, examined the parts and the whole of theological education. In these attempts at comprehensive schemas for understanding theology, practical theology usually functioned as the application of other areas of the curriculum to the life of the

---

[89] That there were no courses explicitly devoted to mission in other years does not mean that the topic was ignored. It was covered as part of other courses.
[90] *Catalogue 1895-1896*, 28. Emphasis added.
[91] *Catalogue 1882-1883*, 13. While the topic of theological encyclopedia may have been addressed in courses prior to 1882 in the seminary curriculum, this is the first year in which it appeared as part of the explicit, advertised curriculum.

church.[92] The theological encyclopedia provided incoming students with an intellectual roadmap for the study of theology and for the place of practical theology in the ecology of seminary education.

Practices of Formation in Practical Theology

Practical theology at PTS was never simply a matter of lectures and book learning. It also entailed engagement by students and faculty alike in a demanding pattern of religious practices. Such involvement came in several forms: daily prayer; Sunday morning corporate worship; Sunday afternoon conferences; a student led meeting on missions; a monthly gathering for intensive corporate prayer; involvement in local churches; and various forms of mission related activity.

Daily prayer took place twice a day throughout the week on the seminary campus. Seniors led these times of worship in the mornings and professors led them in the evenings. Attendance by every student and every faculty member at every service was expected.[93] The PTS learning community convened almost as many times per week for common prayer as it did for class.[94]

Every Sunday morning, the community gathered for common worship in Miller Chapel. Each of the professors would preach and lead worship on a rotating schedule. This pattern of Sunday morning corporate worship for the entire PTS community took place throughout the nineteenth century and continued on into the early decades of the twentieth century.

On Sunday afternoons, students and faculty came together again for a different kind of religious exercise. In the Oratory—the central classroom space on campus—the members of the PTS learning community would gather for Sunday afternoon conferences. The faculty members took turns reflecting and conversing more informally with students about various subjects related to the life of the church, the work of pastoral ministry, the shape of the Christian life, and the glories of foreign and domestic mission.[95] Students provided the "devotional exercises" that created the context for the faculty discourses.

---

[92] For an historical treatment of the enterprise of theological encyclopedia and the various conceptions and models developed, see Farley, *Theologia*, 49-124.
[93] For example, see *Catalogue 1874-1875*, 17.
[94] According to catalogue information about the frequency of "Lectures and Recitations," students attended class fourteen to sixteen sessions per week. For example, see *Catalogue 1890-1891* (Princeton, NJ: Princeton Press, 1890), 19.
[95] For example, see ibid., 24.

Remarkably, these Sunday afternoon conferences, which had been instituted by Archibald Alexander and Samuel Miller in the seminary's early years, remained a key feature of weekly life at the seminary for the entirety of the nineteenth century and into the early part of the twentieth.

Sunday evenings involved yet another community religious gathering. For at least the latter quarter of the nineteenth century, students met for "Missionary meetings."[96] These meeting were eventually shifted to Wednesday evenings. Beginning in the catalogue for the 1902-3 academic year, the list of the previous year's speakers at the missionary meetings were included.[97] Presumably, such a list functioned as an enticement to prospective students who were mission minded.

Twice daily prayer during the week and three gatherings on Sundays did not exhaust the seminary's pattern of religious practices. Faculty and students also gathered on the first Monday of the month for a "concert of prayer" led by the faculty.[98] Several seminary catalogues note that "various other meetings for devotion or mutual exhortation are maintained either by the students as a body, or by each class separately, by the graduates of the several colleges, etc."[99] Many other forms of group spiritual endeavor, small groups, and cooperative mission activities were undertaken at the initiative of students.

Students were encouraged to participate in the life and work of area congregations. Though there was no formalized system for coordinating field education opportunities in the nineteenth century, the catalogue noted that, "Opportunities for active usefulness and observation of pastoral life are afforded in the Churches of Princeton and its vicinity…within some ten miles of the Seminary."[100] Students were encouraged to get experience in leading religious meetings of various kinds and teaching in church school settings.

Taken as a whole, the pattern of course work in subjects of a practical theological character, regular assessment of performance in preaching and elocution, engagement in frequent corporate worship and devotional activities within the seminary community, and ad hoc observation and involvement in local congregations provided powerful and comprehensive formation in practical theology. Theory and practice

---

[96] *Catalogue 1874-1875*, 17.
[97] *Catalogue 1902-1903* (n.p. : C.S. Robinson, 1902), 50-1.
[98] Ibid.
[99] Ibid.
[100] Ibid.

reinforced each other in the curriculum and in the daily life of the PTS learning community.

Practical Theology in Relation to Race and the Civil War

The discussion of race and practical theology begun in the previous chapter needs to be revisited here before concluding a treatment of practical theology at PTS in the latter half of the nineteenth century. Reflections on race and the Civil War provide something of a critical index to the character of the theory and practice of practical theology during this period.

J.W. Alexander, McGill, and Paxton had rather different patterns of involvement in matters of race in American society. As noted above, while he was a member of the faculty of the College of New Jersey, J.W. Alexander served for many years as the pastor of the First Presbyterian Church of Color—now known as the Witherspoon Street Presbyterian Church—in Princeton. He often reminisced about the congregation with great fondness, as when he wrote from Princeton in 1835 that, "…I believe my happiest hours are spent on Sunday afternoons in labouring [sic] among my little charge [the congregation of colored persons]."[101] His pastoral leadership for the black congregation met occasional resistance and jeering from whites in town.[102]

Despite his evident affection for the Witherspoon Street Presbyterian Church, J.W. Alexander also tended to view blacks in paternalistic terms. He believed that slaves in the South were better off than free blacks in the North and that the best way to achieve emancipation was through Christian conversion of the slaves. During a visit to his native Virginia in 1842, Alexander reflected:

> Nothing so much engages my thoughts as the spiritual case of the negroes. I seize every chance to preach to them. Of no people, I think, is a larger portion regenerate. They [the slaves in the South] are unspeakably superior to our Northern free blacks, retaining a thousand African traits of kindliness and hilarity, from being together in masses….
>
> My mind has been, and is, filled with the negroes. What I say on this point I say with, I do believe, as much love for the

---

[101] James W. Alexander, *Familiar Letters*, 1:227. Brackets in original.
[102] Ibid., 1:263.

race as any man feels; and with an extent of observation perhaps as large as I can pretend to on any subject, having seen the worst as well as the best of their condition. And the result of all, increasingly, is, what you I am sure would agree to if you were on the spot, that the *average physical evils* of their case are not greater than of sailors, soldiers, shoeblacks, or low operatives; while their *moral evils* are unspeakably great. My point is this, then: The soul of the negro is precious and must be saved. Aim at this, at the first, at this directly, at this independently of their bondage, and the other desirable ends will be promoted even more surely than if the latter were made the great object. A gradual emancipation is that to which the interior economy of the North-Southern States was tending, is tending, and will reach; it is desirable; in my view it is inevitable; it is craved by thousands here [in the South]; but an emancipation even gradual may arrive in such sort as to leave a host of blacks to be damned, who, by the other means, may be Christianized, while their eventual freedom is not less certain. It is the salvation of the slave, which is infinitely the most important, which moreover Southern Christians *can* be led to seek, and of which the very seeking directly tends to emancipation. I say this, on the obvious principle, that when the owner by seeking the salvation of his slave, gets (as he must) to love him, he will not rest (I speak of the mass) without trying to make him a freeman. I cannot describe the pleasure I have had in preaching and talking to the slaves: if I have ever done any good, this is the way.[103]

Alexander viewed slavery as a "transition-state" for the nation that should "be terminated as soon as possible."[104] For this reason, he did not support the annexation of Texas because he believed it would only spread and prolong the plague of slavery.[105] In his view, emancipation should be gradual so as not to do terrible harm to freed slaves.[106] According to one of Alexander's reflections from December of 1855, increasingly heated public controversy over slavery should have a proper focus so as not to divide the country and to do further damage to blacks:

---

[103] Ibid., 1:353-4. Emphasis in original.
[104] Ibid., 2:52.
[105] Ibid., 1:385 and 2:18.
[106] Ibid., 2:65.

> I am fully persuaded, that if all parties would be patient, would drop the naked question of slavery, and would bend all powers towards abating the *abuses* of slavery, it would result in the speedy emancipation of all who should be fit to enjoy freedom. In this way history shows us that slavery has heretofore ceased and determined. Hush the angry quarrels, and appease the pride of slave-holders, and thousands among them would go even for legislative reform, in the matters of marriage, property, separation of households, reading the Bible, and so forth. This, I think, will take place anyhow; but in a less favourable [sic] way, so long as Northern violence retards the measures.[107]

In addition to his evangelical gradualism and his disdain for Northern abolitionists and Southern abuses alike, he also agreed with his father, Archibald Alexander, in support for the colonization movement.[108]

Alexander McGill had a complicated history on matters of race and had a great deal to say about the subject. He had many friends among southern Presbyterians and even joined the faculty of Columbia Theological Seminary for a brief period immediately prior to his appointment at PTS. He consistently spoke against the evils associated with the theory and practice of slavery. In order to preserve the unity of the church, he sought to steer a middle way between Northern and Southern extremes in the decades leading up to the Civil War. One of his sons served as a surgeon for the Army of the Potomac during the war. In the last year of the war, he compiled a digest of General Assembly statements supporting emancipation and the equal treatment of blacks. As late as 1877, he delivered an address to the American Colonization Society in which he argued that all blacks should be encouraged to return on a voluntary basis to Africa in order both to solve the race problems associated with Reconstruction and to hasten the Christian conversion of the entire African continent.

In an address to the Pennsylvania Colonization Society in 1862, McGill held that "the light of reason, the voice of revelation, and the finger of Providence, combine as they never combined before" to support

---

[107] Ibid., 2:218. Emphasis in original.
[108] Ibid., 1:297. In this entry, he noted that his father had colonization "more at his heart than any thing [sic] in the world."

the unity of the human race (based, in part, on a reading of Acts 27.26), a belief in particular providence with respect to the times and places of particular ethnic groups, and the call of God to evangelize the whole world.[109] McGill believed that divine providence would work in the unfolding American history so as to bring about the elimination of slavery and the return of freed slaves—now Christian and educated—to Africa in order to transform a continent for Christ. Moreover, America's continued viability as a nation depended upon resolution of the race question.[110] In short, that meant freeing, educating, and sending back to Africa freed slaves because, to put it baldly, "The black man cannot stay here."[111] McGill believed that tensions with former slave masters and with hostile whites in the North would make it impossible for former slaves to live equal and fully flourishing lives. Instead, God was at work to bring about "another exodus" in which former slaves would be the instrument of divine action bringing knowledge of God to a heathen continent.[112] In the midst of the greatest national crisis since the Revolution, McGill argued that, "colonization, under God, in this dark hour, is the only hope of America."[113]

In the final year of the Civil War—three years after his address to the Pennsylvania Colonization Society—the Presbyterian Board of Publication put out a book by McGill entitled *American Slavery, as Viewed and Acted on by the Presbyterian Church in the United States of America*.[114] This little book provided a digest—with sparse comment—of key General Assembly actions on slavery and race issues from 1774 to 1864. McGill argued, "…From the beginning, [the church's] utterances on the subject have been mature, comprehensive, and consistent. There is not one deliverance, to be found on record, which we would suppress or conceal."[115] He maintained that the General Assembly had always been in favor of "the ultimate emancipation of the slave, and the overthrow of the whole system as an evil thing."[116] Further, he argued that the church had

---

[109] Alexander T. McGill, *The Hand of God with the Black Race: A Discourse Delivered Before the Pennsylvania Colonization Society* (Philadelphia: William F. Gedded, 1862), 3.
[110] Ibid., 5.
[111] Ibid., 15.
[112] Ibid., 16-7.
[113] Ibid., 18.
[114] Alexander Taggart McGill, *American Slavery as Viewed and Acted on by the Presbyterian Church in the United States of America* (Philadelphia: Presbyterian Board of Publications, 1865).
[115] McGill, *American Slavery*, 3.
[116] Ibid., 4.

always worked toward the "amelioration of the system," had urged religious education of slaves and their children, and the use of freed slaves for the evangelization of the African continent (through the colonization movement focused on Liberia).[117] The dual themes of gradualism and moderation between the extremes of slavery supporters and abolitionists that had marked the approach of Alexander and Miller on these same topics are in evidence in McGill's interpretation of General Assembly actions. McGill himself had served on the 1845 special committee that sought to develop a moderate position between "extremes of radical abolitionism on the one hand, and pro-slavery fanaticism on the other."[118] Because Scripture did not expressly forbid slavery, this special committee could not bring itself to recommend to the General Assembly an outright condemnation of slavery. Instead, they averred that there is much evil connected with the institution of slavery and that slave owners should treat their slaves as fellow human beings, not as mere property.[119] McGill tended to see the effects of the various efforts toward gradual change, education of slaves, and the colonization of Liberia in positive terms:

> Thus, it may well be claimed, at every point of view, that if there be one thing on which, more than anything else, the whole energies of our church were converged for twenty years before this war [i.e. the Civil War] began, it was the welfare of slaves in the territory of these United States; in that very way which has proved most effectual in preparing them for the great result God is working out, at present—and which this church aimed at from the beginning—freedom, with qualifications to use and enjoy it.
>
> The harvest is now on hand. The mighty providence of God is breaking off the fetters of the slave.[120]

While McGill's extract from the northern General Assembly minutes of 1864 similarly spoke of the emancipation of slaves through the federal Emancipation Proclamation of 1863 as an act of divine providence, this book has all the feel of a rear guard action.[121] Statements of slavery and

---

[117] Ibid.
[118] Ibid., 25.
[119] Ibid., 27.
[120] Ibid., 43.
[121] Ibid., 70.

race made by General Assemblies over the course of three quarters of a century apparently did not do much to change actual behavior and attitudes of Presbyterians in the North or in the South. Mark Noll's assessment of the crisis over biblical interpretations of slavery in the antebellum churches hits the mark more accurately:

> With debate over the Bible and slavery at such a pass, and especially with the success of proslavery biblical arguments manifestly (if also uncomfortably) convincing to most Southerners and many in the North, difficulties abounded. The country had a problem because its most trusted religious authority, the Bible, was sounding an uncertain note. The evangelical Protestant churches had a problem because the mere fact of trusting implicitly in the Bible was not solving disagreements about what the Bible taught concerning slavery. The country and the churches were both in trouble because the remedy that finally solved the question of how to interpret the Bible was recourse to arms. The supreme crisis over the Bible was that there existed no apparent biblical resolution to the crisis....It was left to those consummate theologians, the Reverend Doctors Ulysses S. Grant and William Tecumseh Sherman, to decide what in fact the Bible actually meant.[122]

McGill's little book on the Presbyterian Church and slavery was more an exercise in ecclesial self justification and self deception than a vindication of the views of a beleaguered and righteous church. Perhaps the most positive aspect of McGill's volume is that he saw in the emancipation of slaves the providential hand of God at work.

McGill continued strongly to support the colonization movement long after the end of the Civil War. In 1877—the last year of Reconstruction and amid the "long depression" of 1873-9—he continued his unmitigated advocacy for the voluntary removal of blacks to Liberia.[123] In "*Patriotism, Philanthropy, and Religion: An Address before the American Colonization Society*," McGill affirmed and celebrated emancipation while renewing the

---

[122] Mark A. Noll, *The Civil War as a Theological Crisis* (Chapel Hill, NC: University of North Carolina, 2006), 50.

[123] For a description of Reconstruction, see entry of same in *The Oxford Companion to United States History*, edited by Paul S. Boyer (New York: Oxford, 2001), 653-5. For a treatment of the "Long Depression" (the longest in American history), see "Depressions, Economic," in ibid., 183.

call for support of the colonization cause as a way to solve the ongoing American race problem and to Christianize the African continent.[124] Though he affirmed a commitment to the "advancement anywhere...both at home and abroad" of blacks, only colonization, he argued, would relieve the suffering and "social degradation" of freed blacks during Reconstruction and the depression then taking place.[125] Moreover, black missionaries—with ancestral roots in African climates—would be more likely to survive the physical difficulties presented by work in Africa than white missionaries.[126]

By contrast with his immediate predecessor, William Paxton wrote little if anything about race in American society. One looks in vain for comments or insights on race matters among Paxton's published sermons, addresses, memorial discourses, or lecture outlines. Race seems not to have been his focal concern.

The three practical theologians at PTS in the latter half of the nineteenth century exhibited widely varying behaviors with regard to race in America. J.W. Alexander served for several years as founding pastor for a black Presbyterian Church in Princeton and expressed both affection and paternalism toward blacks. Alexander McGill both celebrated emancipation as an act of divine providence and maintained support for the African colonization movement to the end of his life. William Paxton left no record of having ever addressed race in either his pastoral or professorial roles. The primacy of place accorded scriptural revelation, the high esteem given to the Westminster documents, and the relatively broad engagement with secular literature made possible only a modest, moderate, and, at key points, misguided engagement by the PTS practical theologians of the latter half of the nineteenth century with one of the most important issues facing the church and the larger society.

Summary and Concluding Reflections

The PTS faculty members who taught in the area of practical theology between 1850 and 1902 sought to honor and carry forward the original vision of the patriarchs. J.W. Alexander, Alexander McGill, and William Paxton affirmed the primacy of evangelical piety in the dual foci of piety and learning across the curriculum. The broad Christian humanism of Alexander and Miller, while assumed, was not further developed. Instead,

---

[124] Alexander T. McGill, *Patriotism, Philanthropy, and Religion: An Address before the American Colonization Society, January 16, 1877* (Washington, D.C.: n.p., 1877), 3-4.
[125] Ibid., 3 and 5.
[126] Ibid., 8-9.

their successors elaborated upon the basic framework for practical theology in technical directions, particularly in relation to sacred rhetoric or homiletics and in relation to church government and discipline.

The terminology used for practical theological subject matter was somewhat fluid during the latter half of the nineteenth century at PTS. When McGill was inaugurated in 1854, his inaugural address was entitled "Practical Theology."[127] For one academic year, his title was changed in such a way as to incorporate the term "practical theology."[128] It is not entirely clear why the title was dropped the following year. When at various points McGill used the term "practical theology," he deployed it as a comprehensive rubric for a range of ministerial disciplines and practices. The term "pastoral theology" used by Alexander and Miller became for McGill a subcategory under the larger rubric. William Paxton seems to have favored the term "Ecclesiastical Theology" for the subjects covered today under the rubric of practical theology. Toward the end of the nineteenth century, the term "practical theology" was extended to cover a form of theological reflection upon the theory and practice of foreign mission work.

J.W. Alexander, McGill, and Paxton engaged in various forms of interdisciplinary work. Each of them turned to secular sources for insights that would enrich and develop treatment of subject matter related to ministerial practice. Such interdisciplinarity tended to use non-theological materials as resources for technical enhancement of content derived from revelation, theological tradition, and church practice. The subject of "Christian Social Science" at PTS—taught by a member of the theology department—essentially meant techniques and tips for applying Christian principles to the institutions of family, school, and society. During this period of the seminary's history, there was little if any dialogical engagement between practical theology and such emerging disciplines as psychology and sociology. Any interaction with these fields took place on an apologetic and unidirectional basis.

The approaches to practical theology articulated and practiced by J.W. Alexander, McGill, and Paxton were subject to the very same limitations as the patriarchs' approaches. These limitations come most clearly into view when considering the ways in which the PTS practical

---

[127] McGill, "Practical Theology: An Inaugural Discourse," 35-60.
[128] A note in the minutes of the PTS board of directors from 1860 reads, "Dr McGill's chair divided into a chair of Church History and a Chair of Practical Theology." William O. Harris, *Digest of the Minutes of the Board of Directors, 1812-1929* (unpublished manuscript, 1992), 32.

theologians dealt with the most pressing contextual issues of the nineteenth century: slavery and race. While opposing the abuses of slavery and consistently urging both a gradualist approach to the end of the institution and an effort to resolve racial difficulties in America through the colonization movement, none of the PTS practical theologians could or would condemn slavery outright. The main reason for their inability to condemn slavery directly lay in their interpretation of Scripture and in their conviction that reliable truth only flows from biblical text to contemporary context. By century's end, considerations of and concern for race in the US dropped entirely off the map of practical theology at PTS. The overriding concerns at the turn of the century remained what it had been since the beginning: evangelical conversion of individual souls and edification of the church.

Chapter 3
Practical Theology and the Reorganization of the Seminary

When the First Presbyterian Church of Princeton invited J. Gresham Machen to fill its pulpit as stated supply in 1923, its members already knew him well. A member of Princeton Theological Seminary's New Testament faculty, Machen had taught a Sunday school class at First Church for many years and had even been elected by the teachers to serve as superintendent of the Sunday School in 1913.[1] Machen was a leading voice in the conservative wing of the denomination, and he was not shy about using the pulpit of First Church to attack liberals in the denomination and to defend the orthodox standards of the church. His final sermon in 1923, "The Present Issue of the Church," would set off a firestorm. Sounding themes treated extensively in his writings, Machen accused Protestant liberals of dishonesty. As he put it, "The plain fact is, disguised though it may be by the use of traditional language, that two mutually exclusive religions are contending for the control of the church today."[2] The only reasonable course of action, he went on to argue, was for liberals to leave the denomination.

Not all in the congregation appreciated Machen's preaching. Henry van Dyke, former pastor of the Brick Presbyterian Church in New York, ambassador to the Netherlands and Luxembourg under Woodrow

---

[1] *The First Presbyterian Church of Princeton: Two Centuries of History*, ed., Arthur Link (Princeton: Princeton University Press, 1967), 94-6.
[2] Quoted in Darryl Hart, *Defending the Faith: J. Gresham Machen and the Crisis of American Protestantism in Modern America* (Baltimore: John Hopkins University Press, 1994), 60.

Wilson, and current professor of English literature at Princeton University, resigned his pew after Machen's sermon. He sent the following letter to the leaders of the congregation and made copies available to newspapers in Philadelphia and New York City.[3]

> Dear Sir,
>
> Having had another Sabbath spoiled by the bitter, schismatic and unscriptural preaching of the stated supply of the First Presbyterian Church of Princeton...I desire to give up my pew in the church.
>
> The few Sabbaths that I am free from evangelical work to spend with my family are too precious to waste in listening to such a dismal, bilious travesty of the gospel. We want to hear about Christ, the Son of God and the Son of man, not about the Fundamentalists and Modernists, the only subject on which your stated supply seems to have anything to say, and what he says is untrue and malicious. Until he is done, count me out and give up my pew in the church. We want to worship Christ our Saviour.

Six months later, Machen stepped down as stated supply of First Church. The Session asked Dr Charles R. Erdman to take his place. Erdman had served two Presbyterian congregations in Pennsylvania prior to coming to PTS as Professor of Practical Theology in 1906. The match was a good one. Erdman served as pastor of First Church for nearly ten years, while continuing his responsibilities as professor at the seminary.

Van Dyke returned to his pew shortly after Erdman's arrival, a fact noted by the conservative periodical, *The Presbyterian*: "Does the return of such a pronounced and avowed modernist as Dr. van Dyke to the old church, under the new pastor, mean that he is anticipating more liberal preaching under the new regime?...Does this action of Dr. van Dyke signify that two parties are developing in the faculty of Princeton Seminary?"[4] Erdman sent a response to *The Presbyterian* and *The Presbyterian Advance* in which he defended his orthodoxy and stated

---

[3] The letter appear in the *Philadelphia Public Ledger*, Jan. 5, 1924; the *Newark Evening news*, January 5, 1924; the *New York Times*, January 4, 1924 and the *Trenton Evening Times*, January 4, 1924, as well as church journals like *The Presbyterian*.

[4] *The Presbyterian*, January 15, 1925, 4.

that any division that might be present in the seminary faculty was not theological but a matter of "spirit, methods or policies." He continued: "This division would be of no consequence were it not for the unkindness, suspicion, bitterness and intolerance of those members of the faculty, who are also editors of *The Presbyterian*."[5]

As the only faculty member on the editorial board, Machen was outraged. In a letter to *The Presbyterian*, he accused Erdman of "doctrinal indifferentism," a willingness to tolerate Presbyterian pastors and professors who did not hold a strict interpretation of the Westminster confessional standards. His disagreement with Erdman was not a matter "of this doctrine or that, but of the importance which is to be attributed to doctrine as such."[6] The Presbyterian Church's doctrinal standards, he argued, are a system of revealed truth based on Scripture. They bind its congregations together. They are essential to its identity and mission, for they give expression to the gospel. To tolerate pastors and professors who depart from these standards—regardless of one's own orthodoxy—reveals "indifferentism" toward the importance of doctrine in the church's life.

Erdman *was* more open than Machen to theological differences in the Presbyterian Church, though he was by no means a liberal.[7] He represented an inclusive evangelicalism, a perspective aptly described by Bradley Longfield as "conservative in theology, tolerant in spirit, and evangelistic in purpose."[8] Like many evangelicals of the period, Erdman

---

[5] *The Presbyterian Advance*, January 22, 1925, 24.
[6] *The Presbyterian*, 20.
[7] In *A Presbyterian Power Struggle: A Critical History of Communication Strategies Employed in the Struggle for Control of the Presbyterian Church, U.S.A., 1922-1926* (Ph.D. dissertation, Northwestern University, 1974), Delwain Nykamp identifies three distinct positions within the Presbyterian Church at this time. *Modifier inclusivists* were theological liberals who believed that the church needed to adapt to modern life, revise outmoded doctrines and practices and become more responsive to twentieth-century realities. *Traditional exclusivists* upheld Reformed orthodoxy and strove to ensure that only clergy with that theology were ordained. *Traditional inclusivists* were theologically traditional but open to other theological perspectives among the clergy. They believed that a united church stood the best chance of carrying out its mission in a changing social context and resisted the polarization of the liberals and orthodox. There were *no* modifier inclusivists, or liberals, on the PTS faculty at this time. The faculty majority were traditional exclusivists, who advocated Reformed orthodoxy (also known as strict, conservative, or militant Calvinism). A minority of faculty, like Erdman, were traditional inclusivists. It is noteworthy that all members of this minority had ties to practical theology, including Frederick Loetscher who initially taught homiletics before moving to the area of church history. The members of this minority, other than Loetscher, had extensive pastoral experience, in contrast to the faculty majority.
[8] Bradley J. Longfield, *The Presbyterian Controversy: Fundamentalists, Modernists, & Moderates* (New York: Oxford University Press, 1991), 132.

did not believe that doctrinal and denominational controversies should stand in the way of Christian unity in service, evangelism, and mission. Mutual cooperation across denominational lines had been very important during World War I. Erdman was wary of returning to a narrow denominationalism that eviscerated this ecumenical spirit between church bodies and within the Presbyterian Church.

The "van Dyke" incident, as these events came to be called, reflected the deep conflicts and polarization of the 1920s. In many ways, this period is not unlike the present. Modernists and fundamentalists were at war within denominations and in highly charged national events and crusades. It was during this period, for example, that the entire nation was riveted to the courtroom proceedings of the Scopes Trial (1925), in which a public school teacher was put on trial for teaching evolution. By the 1920s, religious pluralism was a reality in American life, especially in urban areas where many immigrants were concentrated.[9] Between 1870 and 1910, 20 million immigrants arrived in the US, swelling the ranks of Roman Catholics to 14.2 million by 1906. Between 1881 and 1920, 2 million Jews immigrated to the US, mostly from eastern Europe, expanding their membership to 3.4 million.[10] The perceived threat to Anglo-Saxon Protestantism elicited strong responses. The Ku Klux Klan, for example, experienced tremendous growth during the 1920s. By some estimates, it had between 4 and 5 million members, including 20,000 in Detroit alone.[11]

The 1920s was a time in which the cultural differences between urban and rural life also came to the fore. Between the end of the Civil War and 1900, the percentage of Americans living in cities had risen from 20% to 40%. By 1920 this number was over 50%.[12] The cultural innovations of the "Roaring Twenties" were deeply rooted in urban culture:

> "Newly franchised women competed for jobs and the title of Miss America. Freud became a household name; sex came to dominate headlines, movies, and conversations; and the divorce rate soared. The waltz gave way to the Charleston;

---

[9] Robert Handy refers to this as the "second disestablishment" of American religion. See, *A Christian America: Protestant Hopes and Historical Realities* (New York: Oxford University Press, 1971).
[10] Robert Wuthnow, *The Restructuring of American Religion: Society and Faith Since World War II* (Princeton: Princeton University Press, 1988), 23-4.
[11] Longfield, *Presbyterian Controversy,* 26.
[12] Ibid.

jazz moved north from New Orleans; and Sabbath worship succumbed to Sunday golf."[13]

These cultural changes evoked shock and outrage in many Protestant quarters, which remained largely rural. While over 50% of the American population now lived in urban areas, more than 65% of Protestant clergy still served rural congregations.[14] At least in part, the Fundamentalist and Modernist controversy of the 1920s was rooted in the very different cultural patterns of urban and rural America, though some of the larger and more prominent fundamentalist congregations were located in urban areas.

It is no accident, thus, that the van Dyke incident would quickly embroil Machen and Erdman in such heated and public controversy. The country as a whole was experiencing a great deal of conflict. For quite some time, moreover, the Presbyterian Church had been caught up in this polarization. During this period, it held more heresy trials that any other denomination in the United States. The PTS faculty played an important role in these conflicts, throwing light on tensions within the seminary itself.

Denominational Conflict

One of the earliest flare-ups in the denomination ignited over modern biblical criticism. Scholars like Charles Briggs at Union Seminary in New York City (a Presbyterian institution at that time) began teaching higher biblical criticism as early as the 1880s. Briggs raised questions about traditional beliefs like Moses' authorship of the Pentateuch and the scientific accuracy of the creation story. He was put on trial at the 1893 General Assembly and was stripped of his ordination for teachings "contrary to the doctrine of Holy Scripture and the standards of the church and in violation of his ordination vows."[15] Union chose to break ties with the denomination after the Briggs trial. Henry Smith, at Lane Seminary, lost his ministerial credentials for defending Briggs's view of Scripture.

Throughout this debate, the PTS faculty, led by B.B. Warfield, championed the conservative point of view and were challenged, in turn, by theological liberals.[16] Reviewing a centennial volume by PTS faculty, scholars at the University of Chicago Divinity School charged the PTS

---

[13] Ibid., 26-7.
[14] E. Brooks Holifield, *A History of Pastoral Care in America: From Salvation to Self-Realization* (Nashville: Abingdon Press, 1983), 149.
[15] Quoted in Longfield, *Presbyterian Controversy*, 23.
[16] See Hart's discussion of Warfield's contribution to the debate in *Defending the Faith*, 38.

authors with portraying the Bible as a "revealed system of truth" and with ignoring the impact of historical circumstances on its development.[17]

A second battle was waged over the Westminster standards, the sole confessional standards of the Presbyterian Church since its founding in the United States. In 1903, the presbyteries approved modification of these standards, emphasizing God's love for all of humanity and the salvation of all who die in infancy. Conservatives worried that these changes represented a liberal drift in the denomination, compromising the doctrines of reprobation and limited atonement. To counter this drift among ministerial candidates from liberal seminaries, they championed a five-point declaration of "essential and necessary" doctrines. This was approved by the 1910 General Assembly and reaffirmed in 1916 and 1923, with Machen's vocal support. The declaration required all candidates for ordination to affirm the inerrancy of Scripture, the virgin birth, substitutionary atonement, the bodily resurrection of Christ, and the miracle-working power of Christ. Liberals perceived the five point declaration as an expression of intolerance by theological conservatives toward those with whom they disagreed. In response to the 1923 reaffirmation, a group of liberals wrote a document commonly known as the Auburn Affirmation, which challenged the General Assembly's right to impose these five doctrinal standards without the approval of a majority of presbyteries. It was signed by 1,274 clergy and theologians.[18]

A third battle was launched over ecumenical initiatives.[19] In this conflict, the majority of the PTS faculty sided against the seminary's president. Building on the extensive cooperation of various denominations during World War I, thirty-five presbyteries sent overtures to the GA urging the denomination to seek union with other "evangelical churches" in America. The 1920 General Assembly passed a proposal to enter into the "United Churches of Christ in America," which was sent to presbyteries for approval. Charles Erdman and the seminary's president, Ross Stevenson, were ardent supporters of the proposal. Gresham Machen actively campaigned against it, claiming it omitted "not some, but practically all, of the great essentials of the Christian faith."[20] The proposal did not receive enough presbytery support to pass.

---

[17] Gerald Birney Smith, Shirley Jackson Case, and D. D. Luckenbill, "Theological Scholarship at Princeton," *American Journal of Theology*, 17 (1913), 94-102.
[18] The Auburn Affirmation is available at http://en.wikipedia.org/wiki/Auburn_Affirmation. For discussion, see Longfield, *Presbyterian Controversy*, 77-9.
[19] Ibid., 49
[20] Quoted in ibid.

Public involvement of PTS faculty in denominational conflicts continued when Erdman ran for moderator of the 1924 GA against Clarence Macartney, a member of the seminary's Board of Directors. Macartney was the conservatives' candidate and won with 464 votes to Erdman's 446. When Erdman was elected to this position the following year, he was publicly opposed by Machen. Machen characterized Erdman as the candidate of the "modernist and indifferentist party in the church," whose willingness to compromise with liberalism would eventually open the doors of the church to modernism.[21]

Conflict at Princeton Theological Seminary

Charles Hodge once quipped, "I am not afraid to say that a new idea never originated in this seminary." His comment was echoed by the seminary's first president, Francis Landey Patton, who declared with pride at PTS's centennial celebration that "the theological position of Princeton Seminary has remained unchanged" during the first one-hundred years of its existence.[22] While this reflects PTS's strong commitment to strict Calvinism until its reorganization in 1929, it also indicates the relatively small and inbred nature of the faculty during this period. Much of the conflict at PTS during the first three decades of the twentieth century revolved around how much the seminary should adapt to a changing social context.

One change that seemed minor at the time, but later had great significance, was the creation of the office of the president by the Board of Directors in 1902. Previously, the senior member of the faculty played the role of chief administrative officer and led faculty meetings.[23] Creation of the office of president seemed inconsequential because president Patton saw his role as maintaining the seminary's theological and educational traditions. When Patton retired in 1913, the Board of Directors appointed B.B. Warfield to serve as acting president and the following year considered only two candidates: Warfield and Ross Stevenson. Warfield's brother was the chair of the board, and Stevenson was a board member. After two lengthy and heated meetings, the board decided on Stevenson.

---

[21] J. Gresham Machen, "The Present Situation in the Presbyterian Church," *Presbyterian*, May 14, 1925, 8.
[22] Francis Landey Patton, "Princeton Seminary and the Faith," in *The Centennial Celebration of the Theological Seminary of the Presbyterian Church in the United States of America* (unpublished), 354.
[23] William K. Selden, *Princeton Theological Seminary: A Narrative History, 1812-1992* (Princeton: Princeton University Press, 1992), 82.

Stevenson was not educated at PTS and, thus, had not been enculturated into the PTS ethos. Moreover, he believed that a key task of his presidency was to reform the faculty and curriculum. He was proactive in this regard because he believed the seminary needed to change. As he put it in personal correspondence to Harris Kirk:

> "Princeton Seminary has still a great influence in the Northern Church. This influence, however, has been on the wane for several years past, largely because the Professors have gotten out of touch with the church and look upon the Seminary more as a conservator of the past than a servant of the present."[24]

Stevenson believed the seminary should serve "the whole church," not one party within the denomination.

In Stevenson's efforts to change the seminary, he was opposed by the majority of the faculty: B. B. Warfield, Robert Wilson, Geerhardus Vos, William Green, William Armstrong, Caspar Hodge, and Oswald Allis. He was supported by a minority of three: Charles Erdman, Frederick Loetscher, and Richie Smith. All three were members of the department of practical theology and had served churches prior to joining the PTS faculty.[25] Among the traditionalists, William Green alone had significant pastoral experience and that had been many years prior.

The faculty majority was determined to keep "Old Princeton," leading to conflict over two issues: governance of the seminary and the curriculum. Since 1826, PTS had been governed by both a Board of Directors and a Board of Trustees. The former was older and composed primarily of pastors, all of whom were PTS graduates and former students of Hodge and Warfield. Like the faculty majority, it saw its task as the preservation of the seminary's nineteenth century legacy. In 1929, a special commission of the GA recommended that the two boards be consolidated into one and clarified the responsibilities of the president, faculty, and new board. These changes were strongly opposed by the faculty majority and the Board of Directors. When the modifications were approved by the General Assembly, Gresham Machen, Oswald Allis, Robert Wilson, Cornelius van Til (an instructor in theology) and a number of students withdrew from the seminary and founded Westminster Theological Seminary to carry on the legacy of "Old Princeton."

---

[24] Quoted in ibid., 89.
[25] Frederick Loetscher later moved to the Department of Church History.

In the years leading up to the seminary's reorganization, conflict over the curriculum emerged as a second flashpoint. Here, the difference between the understandings of the purpose of seminary education held by the faculty majority, on the one side, and president Stevenson and the faculty minority, on the other becomes very clear. It was no accident that the faculty who supported changing the curriculum were located in the area of practical theology. As men with pastoral experience, they were committed to helping the seminary move away from its scholastic approach to theological education and toward giving more attention to preparation for ministry. They believed that the integration of theory and practice should be an important goal of the curriculum.

Two studies of theological education during this period help us see how static the PTS curriculum had become, especially in comparison to other schools of theology: the Kelly Study (1924) and the Brown and May Study (1934). Examining the curricula of 161 theological schools in the United States and Canada, Robert Kelly discovered that the curriculum at PTS was similar to those of most other schools in 1872 but quite different by 1895.[26] In many curricula, less emphasis was now placed on exegetical theology and more on historical and practical theology. Moreover, new courses had been added in sociology, ethics, the psychology of religion, religious education, English Bible, and world religions. By the 1920s, many schools allowed students to pursue specialized tracks, preparing for future ministries in mission, social service, and religious education, as well as in congregations. As early as 1912, the University of Chicago Divinity School accommodated eighteen ministerial vocations in its curriculum.

While new courses were introduced into the PTS curriculum during this period, they clearly occupied a secondary status in a curriculum that continued to emphasize the "classical" disciplines and original languages. The curriculum's unifying vision was provided by Charles Hodge's system of theology. Opposition to changes in this pattern is evident in the faculty's response to the introduction of English Bible into the curriculum. This initiative was a response to a student petition and a request of the Board of Directors. Warfield expressed the objections of the faculty majority: "Our theological seminaries can never make 'the English Bible' the basis of their instruction or a thorough knowledge of it

---

[26] Robert Kelly, *Theological Education in America: A Study of One Hundred Sixty-One Theological Schools in the United States and Canada* (New York: George H. Doran Company, 1924).

the main object of their efforts."[27] He introduced a resolution in the faculty to ensure that courses in English Bible would not receive credit in "minors" and, as such, would have the status of a secondary elective. The same was true of new courses in sociology and the psychology of religion, which were taught by adjunct faculty. As George Haines comments, "Princeton looked with disdain upon this shift from the dogmatic to the practical" across theological education.[28]

A second study of theological education during this period offers further insight into the curricular conflict at PTS. In 1934, William Adams Brown and Mark May published a multi-volume research report sponsored by The Institute of Social Religious Research.[29] Brown and May discovered four major changes in the curricula of Protestant theological schools during the twentieth century's first three decades: (1) enlargement of the subject matter covered; (2) widespread adoption of an elective system; (3) more diversified courses and training for different ministerial vocations; (4) changes in educational theory and practice that placed greater emphasis on giving students the opportunity to learn through field education and reflection on practice.[30] Once again, the majority of the PTS faculty resisted reform of the curriculum along these lines.

An example of this resistance is found in the faculty majority's attempt to block the introduction of an elective system. Shortly after Stevenson became president, a joint committee of faculty and the Board of Directors proposed a reduction in the number of required courses in order to make more room for electives. Warfield spoke against this proposal, arguing that students would opt for easier courses over more essential ones.[31] Machen, likewise, feared that an elective system might surreptitiously introduce elements of modernism into the seminary. The proposal passed, but only in response to Board pressure and the belief of some members of the faculty majority that a worse proposal might follow if it were defeated.

---

[27] Quoted in Ronald T. Clutter, "The Reorganization of Princeton Theological Seminary Reconsidered," *Grace Theological Journal,* 7:2 (1986), 183.

[28] George L. Haines, "The Princeton Theological Seminary, 1925-1960," (Ph.D. Dissertation, School of Education, New York University, 1966), 45.

[29] William Adams Brown and Mark May, *The Education of American Ministers* (New York: Institute of Social and Religious Research, 1934) 4 Volumes.

[30] Mark May, *The Education of American Ministers, Volume 2, The Institutions That Train Ministers* (New York: Institute of Social and Religious Research, 1934), Chapter 4.

[31] Benjamin B. Warfield, *Notes on Certain Proposed Readjustments of the Curriculum* (Princeton, New Jersey: Privately printed, 1914), 7. See Clutter's discussion, "Reorganization," 186-8.

These two studies point to a major shift in theological education during the first three decades of the twentieth century, which was largely driven by innovations in university-based divinity schools. Conrad Cherry characterizes this as the emergence of a *professional model* of theological education, explored more fully below.[32] The PTS faculty majority strongly opposed any movement in this direction; the faculty minority resisted it as well. This is an important point in our story. The practical theologians who fought for the reform of the seminary were committed to a view of practical theology and seminary education that did not flow from liberal theology or Reformed orthodoxy. They developed an alternative trajectory of practical theology grounded in a Reformed evangelical perspective. Later in this chapter, we will examine this trajectory as represented in the writings of Charles Erdman. In order to grasp the distinctiveness of this perspective, we must first trace the contours of the professional model of theological education and the understanding of practical theology that accompanied it.

Professional Education and the Religious Education Movement

The development of a professional model of theological education in university-based divinity schools was an attempt to move beyond problems created by the *encyclopedic pattern of theological education*. This is a pattern of theological education emerging in Germany during the first part of the nineteenth century and gradually migrating to the United States under the influence of American scholars who had studied in Germany.[33] Theology was divided into four specialized fields of research, which served as the organizing principle of theological education: biblical studies, church history, systematic theology, and practical theology.[34] One of the strengths of this fourfold pattern was the production of specialized knowledge. This was also its weakness. As theological disciplines became more specialized, their relationship to one another grew less obvious. Moreover, their relationship to the church and public life grew more tenuous. Cherry makes the very important point that beneath the fourfold pattern of the theological encyclopedia was a deeper and more powerful *twofold* schema: the distinction between

---

[32] Conrad Cherry, *Hurrying Toward Zion, Universities, Divinity Schools, and American Protestantism* (Bloomington, IN: University of Indiana Press, 1996), Introduction, Chapter 4.
[33] For an overview, see Robert Wood Lynn, "Notes Toward a History: Theological Encyclopedia and the Evolution of Protestant Seminary Curriculum, 1808-68, *Theological Education* (Spring 1981), 118-44.
[34] See Farley, *Theologia*.

theory and practice.[35] The specialized, "scientific" knowledge of biblical studies, church history, and dogmatic theology lay on the side of theory; the "application" fields of practical theology lay on the side of practice. It was unclear how theory and practice informed one another, not only at the level of research, but also, in the curriculums of theological education. The rise of a professional model of the theological education was an innovative attempt to overcome this dichotomy.

The University of Chicago Divinity School led the development of this new model, under the guidance of William Rainey Harper (president of the university) and Shailler Matthews (dean of the divinity school). Chicago strove to develop a form of professional education with the same high standards as schools of law, medicine, engineering, and teaching. It tried to overcome the dichotomy between theory and practice by portraying modern professionals as needing both. Professionals in all fields must acquire a specialized body of knowledge based on scientific research and then bring this knowledge to bear on particular areas of practice. Like doctors and lawyers, clergy were seen as needing both a strong graduate education in the theological disciplines and supervised practice, comparable to the case study approach in law schools and internships in medical schools. Theoretical knowledge and practical competence stand at the heart of a professional model of clergy education.[36]

This model both informed and was informed by developments in practical theology. Particularly important was the emergence of the Religious Education Movement in 1903, which attempted to professionalize the leadership of the teaching ministry. Strong programs in religious education were established at Chicago and Union (New York), which offered specialized tracks in the seminary curriculum and masters programs in Religious Education. Later, doctoral programs were added. Drawing on liberal and social gospel theology, these new

---

[35] Cherry, *Hurrying toward Zion*, 151.

[36] Ibid., 139-41. Cherry characterizes the theory/practice relationship at Chicago as functionalism. Functionalism is a biological metaphor based on active organisms' adaptation to a changing environment. Organisms must develop different biological functions that allow them to cope with different challenges in their context, like procuring food, reproducing, and fleeing danger. This framework became especially prominent under the influence of Darwin's theory of evolution, which portrayed various species as engaged in an ongoing process of selective adaptation. The most important form of functionalism to influence professional theological education and practical theology during this period was the philosophical and educational pragmatism of John Dewey. Dewey portrayed human beings as engaged in an ongoing process of adaptation to changing contexts and as having unique capacities for reflection and imagination that enable them to cope with the problems these contexts pose.

programs emphasized the immanence of God in the unfolding, evolutionary processes of history, which often was conceptualized in terms of personalism (i.e. God acts to evoke the "personalizing" dimensions of culture, society, and personality found in modern democratic forms of life). The influence of John Dewey's theory of education was also great. The goal of religious education was no longer to hand on the religious traditions of the past, but to help people reshape these traditions to make sense of the challenges of modern life. Professional religious educators were to be fully grounded in the specialized knowledge of modern education and social science. They were to use this knowledge to reshape educational practice in the church, which, in turn, would allow the church to both adapt to and shape modern life. In a professional model of theological education, theory and practice were mutually influential.

PTS did not participate in the emergence of a professional model of theological education and had no faculty who were active participants in the Religious Education Movement during the early decades of the twentieth century. In large part, this was due to the faculty majority's fierce resistance to any innovations in curriculum or theology that might open the doors of the seminary to liberalism and modernism. In hindsight, this was a mixed blessing. On the one hand, it allowed PTS to retain links with theological perspectives other than liberalism and protected it against the severe critique of the professional model of theological education during the 1930s. On the other hand, PTS remained caught in the death grip of Reformed orthodoxy and was not able to generate curricular innovations that might have contributed to theological education.

The one exception was in the area of practical theology. Charles Erdman represents the beginning of a trajectory of practical theology that would continue to develop at PTS over the course of the twentieth century. It placed emphasis on theology as central to the identity of so-called "practical fields," not social science, psychology, or educational philosophy. Moreover, it attempted to develop a theology that was a clear alternative to Reformed orthodoxy, on the one hand, and theological liberalism, on the other. Without question, the most important figure in this development was Charles Erdman. Erdman was forced to clarify his position in the face of the intellectual and political attacks of Gresham Machen. Before this chapter turns to Erdman's alternative perspective, therefore, the next section details Machen's fierce commitment to maintaining Reformed orthodoxy at PTS.

Gresham Machen

Gresham Machen is often portrayed as a leading voice of fundamentalism in the Fundamentalist/Modernist conflict of the 1920s. While Machen was a leading spokesman for Reformed orthodoxy, he cannot be easily pigeon-holed into a catch-all category like fundamentalism. He was not a typical fundamentalist. While he was deeply concerned about the changes taking place in American society, he was an ardent, even radical libertarian, who opposed the church's involvement in politics and moral crusades and the intrusion of the government in the affairs of individuals and voluntary associations. Likewise, he was against prohibition, a decidedly minority position among both liberal and conservative Presbyterians during the 1920s. A conservative New Testament scholar who argued for biblical inerrancy, Machen refused to participate in the conflict over evolution, even when asked by his friend, William Jennings Bryan, to give expert testimony at the Scopes trial. He opposed women's suffrage but was a life long member of the Democratic Party and one of the few Presbyterians to vote for the first Roman Catholic to run for president, Al Smith.[37]

Machen is thus far more complex than the one-dimensional caricature often drawn of him. This is also true of his desire to preserve the theology and educational patterns of the seminary's past. Machen developed his theology and his understanding of theological education in a social context far different than that of his PTS predecessors. Throughout the nineteenth century, Scottish Common Sense Realism and Baconian inductivism were virtually the norm in American higher education.[38] When Charles Hodge portrayed theology as a science along these lines, he could argue on the basis of a philosophy and model of science that was widely accepted. Likewise, evangelical Protestantism remained a dominant force throughout the nineteenth century—in higher education, public discourse, and Christian denominations. While Hodge and his colleagues might argue over denominational distinctives with their Protestant brethren, they shared many theological assumptions with other Protestants.

---

[37] Longfield, *Presbyterian Controversy*, Chapter 2.

[38] Sydney E. Ahlstrom, "The Scottish Philosophy and American Theology," *Church History* 24:3 (Sep., 1955), 257-72. Mark Noll explains: "For most of the nineteenth century, then, the Princeton theologians merely shared widespread cultural values in their convictions about the Bible, Scottish Common Sense Philosophy, and scientific empiricism. The distinctive Princeton achievement was to absorb these cultural assumptions into their Calvinism without losing that Calvinism." "The Princeton Theology" in *Reformed Theology in America: A History of Its Modern Development*, ed., David Wells (Grand Rapids: Eerdmans, 1985), 27.

In contrast, Machen faced a context in which these intellectual and religious perspectives could no longer be taken for granted. Historicism in the humanities and positivism in science were serious alternatives to the older Common Sense Realism. Liberalism was making inroads in mainline Protestant denominations and higher education. The culture as a whole was rapidly becoming more pluralistic and secular. In this charged and rapidly changing context, Machen viewed himself as fighting to preserve a valued religious and theological heritage in the face of threats from without and within. This helps us understand why he drew such sharp boundaries between his own position and that of others. In the face of competing theological and secular paradigms, Machen believed that it was essential for the Presbyterian Church to take a clear and unequivocal stand.

Biography

Machen's biography throws light on his response to changes taking place in American culture and religion during the early decades of the 1900s. Especially important are Machen's deep Southern roots. He was born on July 28, 1881 in Baltimore, where he lived until graduating from John Hopkins. Baltimore was the "capital" of the South after the Civil War. Situated strategically between the North and South, it was a thriving commercial center and a place where many of the southern aristocracy relocated to escape the devastating poverty of the post war South. Machen's father, Arthur, did not fight for the Confederacy but had a brother who did. He was asked to become the District Attorney of Maryland but refused, because it "might have required him to prosecute those who adhered openly to the Southern cause."[39]

Arthur Machen wed Mary Gresham, a southern belle twenty-two years his junior, who was raised in a prominent family in Macon, Georgia. Under her influence, J. Gresham Machen was raised in the southern version of Old School Presbyterianism, studying the Westminster Shorter Catechism as a child. He attended the Franklin Street Presbyterian Church, whose pastor, J. J. Bullock, was a strong supporter of the Confederacy and led his congregation out of the Northern branch of the Presbyterian Church to join the Southern branch in 1866. Knowledge of Machen's southern roots is integral to understanding his actions. His libertarianism and belief that the church should concentrate on spiritual matters, not politics, reflect the thinking of the leading southern Presbyterian theologian of the Civil War era, James Henley Thornwell.

---

[39] Longfield, *Presbyterian Controversy*, 31.

Mary Gresham Machen was an active member of The United Daughters of the Confederacy throughout her adult life. Under her influence, her son was exposed to a cultural ethos described by historians as "the legacy of the lost cause."[40] In the face of defeat in war and economic devastation at home, many Southerners began to glorify the agrarian and spiritual values of the Old South. As Bradley Longfield puts it: "In prose, poetry, and oratory the UDC glorified the South's love of liberty, gallant men, gentle women, noble institutions, and proud people. Having been overcome by the materialistic Yankees, postwar Southern women cultivated the memory of a better time and a superior civilization."[41] A life long bachelor, Machen maintained a very close relationship with his mother until her death, exchanging letters two or three times a week and vacationing together. It is thus no accident that Machen viewed the changing values and secularization of American culture as the triumph of materialistic utilitarianism and mercantilism. Nor is it an accident that he viewed secession as an honorable course of action, an option he exercised after the General Assembly reorganized the seminary in 1929 and destroyed, in his mind, Old Princeton.

One further biographical note on Machen's early life is worth mentioning. Following his graduation from John Hopkins, where he majored in classics, Machen was unclear about the career he should pursue. After dabbling in law and banking, he decided on a trial year at PTS. He ended up earning the Bachelor of Divinity degree and even won the New Testament prize his senior year. Upon graduation, however, his vocational plans remained unclear, so he studid for a year in Germany at Marburg and Göttingen. His exposure to the Marburg theologian, Wilhelm Herrmann, a leading proponent of liberal theology, evoked a crisis of faith.

Herrmann challenged the very heart of Machen's Southern Presbyterianism. He argued that modern historical scholarship relativized the Bible and church doctrine. Religious experience alone could serve as the foundation of faith. Even after Machen accepted the invitation to join the PTS faculty for a one year appointment in New Testament, he remained in crisis. Only gradually, under the influence of PTS faculty members William Armstrong and Benjamin Warfield, did he find answers to the questions that Herrmann had raised. Henceforth, he was to become a staunch defender of Princeton's understanding of Reformed orthodoxy.

---

[40] Ibid., 36-8.
[41] Ibid., 37.

Machen's Defense of Reformed Orthodoxy and His Understanding of Practical Theology

Like his predecessors on the PTS faculty, Machen viewed theology as a science. He once wrote: "Theology, we think, is just as scientific as chemistry."[42] He had in mind a Baconian view of science located within the philosophical framework of Common Sense Realism. Truth is obtained inductively through an open minded examination of facts, their classification, and the formulation of careful hypotheses that provide the best explanation. Theological science, however, is not confined to the framework of naturalism. It expands the range of facts to include the influence of supernatural forces on human history, especially the history narrated in Scripture. Indeed, Machen argued that Scripture not only contains the facts of the history of redemption, but also their doctrinal interpretation. He frequently illustrated this point with the example: "'Christ died'—that is history; 'Christ died for our sins'—that is doctrine."[43] Scripture offers both, and each of the theological disciplines contributes to the organization of these facts and interpretations into a coherent system.

This model of theology-as-science is closely related to Machen's understanding of faith, which placed great emphasis on knowledge. Faith as trust requires knowledge about the object of faith. As Machen put it, "A Man can believe only what he holds to be true. We are Christians because we hold Christianity to be true."[44] He placed great emphasis on the cognitive dimension of faith, which engenders trust in God.

Machen's portrait of science, theology, and faith stands in continuity with the traditions that dominated Princeton Theology throughout the nineteenth century. Yet there also are elements of discontinuity, primarily in matters of emphasis. In the face of competing theological and secular paradigms, he tended to exaggerate certain parts of the older tradition and lose sight of the tensive relationship between theological polarities that was a part of Old Princeton.[45] This is the case in three areas.

First, Machen resolved the relationship between knowledge and piety in the direction of cognitive beliefs. In the writings of Charles Hodge, knowledge and piety had remained in a dynamic, if unresolved, tension,

---

[42] Grescham Machen, "The Relation of Religion to Science and Philosophy: A Review," *The Princeton Theological Review*, 24:1 (1926), 51.
[43] Machen, *Christianity & Liberalism* (Grand Rapids, Eerdmans, 2009), 27.
[44] Gresham Machen, "Christianity and Culture," *Princeton Theological Review*, 11:1 (1913),5.
[45] For a sympathetic but critical examination of Machen, see George Marsden, "Understanding J. Gresham Machen," *The Princeton Seminary Bulletin* 11:1 (1990), 46-60 and "J. Gresham Machen, History, and Truth, *Westminster Theological Journal*, 42:1 (1979), 157-75.

though movement in a more cognitive direction had already begun to take place in the writings of B.B. Warfield and Francis Landey Patton.[46] Perhaps Machen exaggerated the importance of knowledge because of his opposition to liberalism's emphasis on religious and historical experience as a source of knowledge of God. Whatever the case may be, he had little positive to say about the role of personal piety in the formation of knowledge of God or in seminary education. He portrayed the conviction of sin, conversion, and communion with God as "one of the grounds for our belief…that we cannot share."[47] At most, such experiences confirm the knowledge found in Scripture and systematized in the Westminster standards.

At times, Machen even appears to have worried that piety may be a threat to knowledge of God. In a 1912 convocation address, for example, he told PTS students that the "scientific spirit" they will encounter in their studies may create a sense of "infinite loss."[48] At the seminary, they will not approach the Bible "with the desire of moral and spiritual improvement" but with the "desire to know." This "scientific spirit" may seem "incompatible with the old spirit of simple faith."[49] Machen said nothing about the ways the seminary might form the piety of its students or the sort of knowledge students might gain through worship, study, prayer, or Christian friendship. To put it in more contemporary terms, cultivating intellectual knowledge is granted priority over spiritual formation in seminary education. The danger of this sort of seminary education is that it will graduate students chock full of "head knowledge" but with little capacity to lead their congregations as spiritual communities. This will prove to be a crucial difference between Machen and Erdman, with important implications for their views of practical theology.

Second, Machen exaggerated the importance of intellectual apologetics to the exclusion of the "living apologetic" of congregational witness. Like his PTS predecessors, Machen portrayed apologetics as the

---

[46] As Mark Noll points out, the relationship between piety and knowledge are both acknowledged by Hodge and the Princeton Theologians generally but "no entirely satisfactory integration occurred." "The Princeton Theology," 23. See also, his introduction to Charles Hodge, *The Way of Life* (Carlisle, PA.: Banner of Truth, 1978) and "Charles Hodge as an Expositor of the Spiritual Life," *Charles Hodge Revisited: A Critical Appraisal of His Life and Work*, eds. John Stewart and James Moorhead (Grand Rapids: Eerdmans, 2002), 181-216. For a fuller discussion of the understanding of piety in "Old Princeton," see Andrew Hoffecker, *Piety and the Princetonians: Archibald Alexander, Charles Hodge, and Benjamin Warfield* (Phillipsburg, NJ: Presbyterian and Reformed Publishing Co., 1981).
[47] Machen, "Christianity and Culture," 5-6.
[48] The quotations in this paragraph are found in ibid., 3.
[49] Ibid.

task of defending the faith against intellectual adversaries and of explaining its meaning in a particular socio-cultural context. He also argued that theological apologetics must engage the contemporary arts and sciences and "consecrate" them for Christian purposes, opposing them when they contradict the gospel but using them to the glory of God when they do not.[50] Here, Machen followed a line of thinking that can be traced through the Old Princeton Theology all the way back to John Calvin.

Missing in his writings, however, is any real appreciation of the "living apologetic" of a church's way of life. Here again, Machen so exaggerated one pole of apologetics—a reasoned defense—that he failed to value and develop the other pole—a living apologetic in which the gospel is embodied in the life of a congregation in a particular time and place. Perhaps he was concerned about the historicism of theological liberalism, which he believed would relativize the faith. Machen's unwillingness to engage the interaction of context and witness at the level of congregational life was a serious omission. It represented another point of contrast between him and Erdman, who affirms a role for contextual analysis in the service of congregational witness and mission. This had implications for their understanding of practical theology.

Third, Machen was so concerned with protecting "Presbyterian particularism" that he eliminated any room for theological variation within the Reformed tradition.[51] It is important to recall that Machen faced a social context in which religious and cultural pluralism were increasingly a part of American public life. His response was complex. He took his bearings less from his PTS predecessors than from the Southern Presbyterian theologian, James Thornwell, noted in passing above. Thornwell was well known for the doctrine of the "spirituality of the church," which portrayed the church and state as having distinct spheres of jurisdiction and no right to meddle in one another's affairs. The sphere of the church is the spiritual life, not politics or moral crusades. Following Thornwell's lead, Machen acknowledged a pluralistic cultural sphere in which a wide range of voluntary organizations and cultural options exist. As a libertarian, he believed that the state should stay out of this sphere.

But Machen's view of the Presbyterian Church was quite different. While the Presbyterian Church might only be one actor among others in a pluralistic social context, there was no room for theological pluralism *within* this particular religious community. As we have seen, Machen

---

[50] Ibid., 5.
[51] "Presbyterian particularism" is Darryl Hart's phrase, see *Defending the Faith*, cited above.

was a forceful proponent of the five point declaration of "essential and necessary" doctrines that must be affirmed by Presbyterian clergy.

In effect, Machen argued that the Westminster standards were not one perspective among others. They are the Presbyterian Church's *only* viable perspective because they express the facts and doctrines of Scripture in a revealed system of Christian truth. This ruled out any place for theological liberals in the church. It even called into question the tolerant spirit of Reformed evangelicals like Charles Erdman, whom Machen portrayed as "indifferent" to doctrine. In *Christianity and Liberalism*, Machen even argued that theological liberalism "is not Christianity at all," but "so entirely different from Christianity as to belong to a different category."[52]

In his desire to eradicate theological pluralism in the Presbyterian Church, Machen placed sharper boundaries around the denomination than his PTS predecessors. Charles Hodge, for example, defended Reformed orthodoxy but was clear that the earthly church does not have the spiritual insight or authority to separate "the wheat from the tares."[53] As the Presbyterian Church struggled with theological pluralism over the course of the twentieth century, it would clarify its understanding of what it means to confess the faith and the status of confessional standards.[54]

What sort of impact did Machen's theological position have on his understanding of seminary education and the contribution of practical theology within the theological enterprise as a whole? The clearest picture of what Machen had in mind can be discovered in the first convocation address he gave at Westminster Theological Seminary, the school he founded after leading a group of faculty colleagues and students out of PTS. On September 25, 1929, he gave the following speech: "Westminster Theological Seminary: Its Purpose and Plan."[55]

Machen began by describing the Bible as the center of Westminster Seminary, for it is the record of God's self revelation and the "once and for all" redemption of humanity in Jesus Christ.[56] Accordingly, the study

---

[52] J. Gresham Machen, *Christianity and Liberalism* (Grand Rapids: Eerdmans, 1923), 6-7.
[53] See Clutter's helpful overview of the differences between Hodge and Machen concerning the purity of the church in "Reorganization of Princeton Seminary," 191.
[54] See, for example, Edward Dowey, *A Commentary on the Confession of 1967 and an Introduction to The Book of Confessions* (Philadelphia: Westminster, 1968).
[55] J. Gresham Machen, "Westminster Theological Seminary: Its Purpose and Plan" in *Selected Shorter Writings*, ed. D.G. Hart (Phillipsburg, NJ: P&R Publishing, 2004), 187-94.
[56] Machen also includes philosophical apologetics in the curriculum, which establishes the plausibility of theism in the face of intellectual alternatives. While he mentions the importance of common sense in this address, he does not explicitly argue for the perspective of Common Sense Realism as the basis of philosophical apologetics at Westminster.

of original languages and exegetical Theology are the starting point of theological education. This is followed by biblical Theology, which traces the history of revelation in the Bible. But it is systematic Theology that is the "center" of Westminster's curriculum: "[S]tanding on the foundation of biblical theology, it seeks to set forth, no longer in the order of the time when it was revealed, but in the order of logical relationships, the grand sum of what God has told us in his Word," "a system of theology, a great logically consistent body of truth." Machen went on to state that at Westminster this system will be Calvinist, as this is "set forth so gloriously in the Confession and catechisms of the Presbyterian Church," a clear reference to the Westminster standards.

Machen concluded by briefly describing two additional disciplines in Westminster's curriculum. Church history allows the church to understand the ways past generations have responded to God's word in thought and deed. Machen then described practical theology, which received the least attention in his address. Westminster graduates will be people with a "message" and the department of homiletics and practical theology is tasked with helping them to deliver this message "as to reach the hearts and minds of men." But this department "cannot itself teach a man how to preach; that he must learn, if at all, by the long experience of subsequent years." It can, however, help new preachers avoid errors and start rightly.

Machen's portrait of practical theology made perfect sense in light of his theological commitments. The weight of the theological curriculum was on biblical studies and systematic theology, which work together to help students grasp the revealed system of truth found in the facts and doctrines of Scripture. Missing, however, are key elements of practical theology that were an important part of Charles Erdman's understanding of this field and would subsequently become an important part of the Princeton tradition of practical theology in the twentieth century. To gain a better sense of what these are, we turn now to Charles Erdman.

Charles Erdman
Biography

Charles Erdman was born in Fayetteville, New York in 1866. His father, William, was raised in the Dutch Reformed Church, but after attending Union Theological Seminary in New York was ordained in the New School Presbyterian Church in 1860. New School and Old School Presbyterians had split in 1837. The latter emphasized doctrinal orthodoxy and church order; the former downplayed denominational differences in the service of the church's evangelistic mission. William Erdman, a close friend and colleague of the evangelist, Dwight L. Moody, served on the staff of Moody's Chicago Avenue Church for three years and helped found the Moody Bible Institute. Moody also downplayed denominational differences in the service of his evangelistic ministry. He exposed William and his son to the Keswick Holiness movement, which emerged in Great Britain in the 1870s. This movement emphasized the continuing power of sin and the need for repeated "fillings" by the Holy Spirit to live a life of sanctity and service.[57]

When Erdman enrolled at PTS, he was forced to negotiate the relationship between his religious upbringing and the strong dose of Old School, Reformed orthodoxy he received from the PTS faculty. There is at least one indication of restiveness with his PTS education. He took a year off to gain a more comprehensive understanding of the Bible under his father's tutelage. When Erdman later reflected on this year, he wrote:

> "Seminary authorities in those days felt that extensive Bible study was unnecessary. They took the position that all who enrolled to study for the ministry were thoroughly schooled already in the Bible. This was fallacious. I, for one, wasn't, at least not to the extent necessary, even though my father was a clergyman. The emphasis back in my seminary days was given to Latin, Greek, and Hebrew."[58]

After he graduated from PTS in 1891, Erdman started a new congregation in Overbrook, Pennsylvania, where he stayed for six years. He then was called to the First Presbyterian Church of Germantown, Pennsylvania. During this period, he was offered a faculty position in homiletics at PTS but choose to remain at Germantown. In 1906, he accepted an invitation to join the PTS faculty in a new chair in Practical Theology. The Board of Directors created this position to "give emphasis to the practical side of seminary teaching" and bring greater balance to a curriculum heavily weighted toward specialized, academic studies.[59] Erdman's responsibilities included all fields in practical theology other

---

[57] B. B. Warfield wrote a scathing critique of the theology of the holiness movement in *Perfectionism*, which included explicit discussion of Keswick theology. See Benjamin Breckinridge Warfield, *Perfectionism* (New York: Oxford University Press, 1931).

[58] Quoted in Longfield, *Presbyterian Controversy*, 137.

[59] Elmer Homrighausen, Charles T. Fritsch, Bruce M. Metzger, "In Memoriam: Charles Rosenbury Erdman, July 20 1866-May 10, 1960," *The Princeton Seminary Bulletin,* 54 (November, 1960), 36.

than preaching and liturgics. He was also asked to guide students "in their practical Christian work in nearby cities" and to teach English Bible.[60]

The addition of English Bible was controversial. Some on the faculty viewed it as "watering down" the curriculum.[61] In his inaugural lecture, Erdman argued that the "practical aim" of his approach to English Bible would fit well in practical theology and might be called the "Literary and Homiletic Study of the Bible." In addition to providing a "comprehensive view of the Bible," it aimed "at such a special, practical, spiritual and evangelistic interpretation of the Bible as will directly equip the preacher for his pulpit and the pastor for his personal work."[62] During his twenty years at PTS, Erdman wrote thirty-five books, most of which were commentaries on books of the Bible written along these lines. He also served as an editorial consultant to the *Scofield Reference Bible* in 1908.

Erdman differed from his colleagues at PTS in yet another way.[63] He did not live the somewhat cloistered academic life of many faculty members. We have already mentioned his ten years of service as the pastor of First Church, Princeton while on the faculty. He also regularly preached and lectured at conferences. He served on the Board of Trustees of the Westminster Choir College and founded the Princeton chapter of the YMCA. He served as president of numerous organizations, including the YMCA Board of Directors, the Columbus Boy-Choir School, and the Princeton Symphony Orchestra Association. He was a long time member and then president of the denomination's Board of Foreign Missions. He knew four presidents of the United States: Woodrow Wilson, Grover Cleveland, Theodore Roosevelt, and Calvin Coolidge. In short, Erdman had a broad view of the church and American society. It is little wonder that he worked easily with people of diverse theological persuasions and was willing to lead a minority of faculty in opening up the seminary to perspectives other than Reformed orthodoxy.

Erdman's Understanding of Practical Theology

In light of Erdman's background and his education at PTS, he is best characterized as a *Reformed evangelical*. Erdman was quite traditional theologically. He was committed to the Westminster standards, as he

---

[60] Ibid.
[61] See Clutter, "Reorganization," 181-3.
[62] Charles Erdman, "Modern Practical Theology, " *The New York Observer*, January 3, 1907, 18. This lecture also is available at http://digital.library.ptsem.edu/default.xqy?terms=Charles+Erdman Accessed June, 2008.
[63] The information in this paragraph is found in Homrighausen et al, "Memoriam," 37.

frequently noted in his exchanges with Machen. He was not a modernist or a liberal; he was Reformed theologically and even orthodox. Yet he was shaped by nineteenth century evangelicalism, which led him to be tolerant of theological perspectives besides Reformed orthodoxy. This inclusivity is grounded in two theological trajectories found in Erdman's writings.

First, Erdman emphasized the evangelical mission of the church, which led him to stress ecumenism in the service of this mission at home and abroad. In *The Work of the Pastor*, he wrote that "missionary churches are live churches" and "nonmissionary churches are dying or dead."[64] He pointed to implications for seminary education:

> Unless the minister is interested in the world outside his parish, unless he longs for the evangelization of the world, unless he has the "mind of Christ" towards the world for which Christ died, he cannot lead his people to have the mind "which was also in Christ Jesus"…Much of the trouble regarding missions can be traced back to the days of preparation for the ministry. Many candidates for ordination, more or less versed in Hebrew, Greek, Church history and theology, are woefully ignorant regarding the world work of their own denomination, and are without any training for the missionary leadership of the churches which they have been called to serve.[65]

Through his father's close association with D.L. Moody and his own involvement in the missionary movement, Erdman was strongly inclined to press for unity across denominational and theological lines in the service of the church's mission. At the 1910 Edinburgh World Missionary Conference, he experienced first hand a gathering of missionary leaders from around the world who were committed to the "evangelization of the world in this generation," to recall the central conference theme taken from one of John Mott's books.[66] In his emphasis on ecumenism in mission, not defense of denominational doctrines, Erdman was an inclusive, Reformed evangelical.

Second, Erdman placed great theological emphasis on the role of the Holy Spirit in the Christian life—in bringing persons to Christ, edifying the Body of Christ, and equipping the church to carry out its mission. His

---

[64] Charles Erdman, *The Work of the Pastor* (Philadelphia: Westminster Press, 1924), 245.
[65] Ibid., 245-6.
[66] David Bosch, *Transforming Mission: Paradigm Shifts in Theology of Mission*, (Maryknoll, NY: Orbis Books, 1991), 336-7.

most extensive treatment of this topic is found in *The Spirit of Christ*. He developed a trinitarian perspective in which the Spirit of God is described as actively involved in the world from the very beginning of creation but as playing a new role with the coming of Christ: "Christ had been revealing the nature and redeeming love of the Father; henceforth, in turn, the Spirit will reveal the glory of the Son."[67] He drew out the implications of this understanding of the Spirit for the Christian life:

> He (the Spirit) began to work with a new instrument, namely, the truth concerning our crucified, risen and ascended Lord. He began to develop the life of believers in a new and more intimate relation to God, namely, that of "sons" in fellowship with a loving Father. This was possible only when redemption had been accomplished and when the Father had been revealed by the Son.[68]

Erdman's understanding of the Holy Spirit showed clear signs of the influence of the Keswick movement. He described Christian ministers and congregations as in need of a "new enduement of the Spirit," which was not a one time event but must occur repeatedly in the life of the church.[69] Yet his portrait of life in the Spirit showed contact with broader traditions of Christian spirituality. He was remarkably ecumenical for a Reformed theologian teaching at PTS during this era. He cited positively Jeremy Taylor and Brother Lawrence's understanding of the "practice of the presence of God" and described one of the key tasks of pastoral leadership as "nurture of the spiritual life" of the congregation.[70] These are themes he developed extensively in *The Work of the Pastor*, where he argued that a chair in "experimental" theology would be an advance on Protestant faculties.[71] Spiritual formation of the congregation, Erdman claimed, equips the church to carry out its mission as a witness to Christ.[72] The centrality Erdman gave to the Spirit leads him to portray the

---

[67] Charles Erdman, *The Spirit of Christ: Devotional Studies in the Doctrine of the Holy Spirit* (New York: George H. Doran Company, 1926), 30.
[68] Ibid., 68.
[69] Ibid., 31-2, 39, 41.
[70] Ibid., 21, 91.
[71] Erdman, *Work of the Pastor*, 6. See also, 4-6, 37-40, and Chapter 4. By "experimental," Erdman is pointing to what we might call today "spiritual theology."
[72] Erdman, *Spirit of Christ*, 100.

Christian life in stark contrast to Machen's doctrinal emphasis. In terms that could almost be directed against his seminary colleague, he wrote:[73]

> A man may recite an orthodox creed and belief, and yet be self-deceived as to his relation to Christ; he may be a defender of the faith...and yet be a Pharisee.
>
> We "grieve the Spirit"...in theological controversy. Frank, fair, and kindly discussion of divergent views is stimulating and helpful, but bitterness, dogmatism and temper are destructive of spiritual power.
>
> Many modern Bible teachers and self-constituted "Defenders of the Faith" need to be reminded that there are limits to their own omniscience.
>
> It is also a mistake to suppose that church unity must consist in unanimity of belief. This never has existed among the followers of Christ, and is hardly to be looked for today.

In short, Charles Erdman is best described as a Reformed evangelical. While subscribing to orthodox, Reformed doctrine, he was evangelical in his emphasis on ecumenism in the church's mission and on the spiritual life, which take precedence over confessional distinctives. How did this theological perspective shape Erdman's understanding of practical theology?

Erdman drew on a tradition of practical theology stretching back to Friedrich Schleiermacher, the father of modern liberal theology. Schleiermacher authored the first modern theological encyclopedia in which practical theology is described as a distinct branch of theology.[74] As a Reformed evangelical, however, Erdman warranted his theological proposals in ways that did not follow the patterns of liberal theology. Rather, he appealed to an understanding of the church's mission that is grounded in Scripture and the present work of the Holy Spirit. To grasp the significance of these theological patterns, further explanation is necessary.

---

[73] Ibid.,11, 48-9, 84, 93.
[74] Friedrich Schleiermacher, *Brief Outline of Theology as a Field of Study: Revised Translation of the 1811 and 1830 Editions*, trans. Terrence N. Tice, 3rd ed. (Louisville, KY: Westminster John Knox Press, 2011).

Erdman offered his most extensive discussion of practical theology in two places: his inaugural lecture, "Modern Practical Theology," and *The Work of the Pastor*.[75] In both writings, he acknowledged the tradition of "modern" practical theology and pointed to prominent members of this field in the nineteenth and twentieth century, like Johannes J. van Oosterzee, Alexandre Vinet, Patrick Fairbairn, W.G. Sheed, James Hoppin, Washington Gladden, and R.A. Torry.[76] But he argued that the subject matter and tasks of practical theology are much older than their relatively recent depiction in the context of modernity. Indeed, they are as ancient as the letters of Paul and the Acts of the Apostles. Erdman also noted writings in the Christian tradition that deal with the subject matter and tasks of this field, including writings by John Chrysostom, Gregory the Great, Bernard of Clairvaux, and the Reformers of the sixteenth century century—Martin Luther, Ulrich Zwingli, and John Calvin.[77] While practical theology as a specific field may be relatively recent in the history of theology, its subject matter and tasks are as old as the church itself. Drawing on this broad understanding of practical theology, Erdman identified three key characteristics of this field.

First, practical theology deals with the "application of truth to life" and "the methods whereby revealed truth is brought to bear upon the life of the individual, upon the church and the community, and is given wider acceptance in the world."[78] It is clear from Erdman's debates with Machen and throughout his writings that he did not have in mind here the straightforward application of doctrine. He repeatedly described practical theology as an "art and science." As a science, it develops principles that guide practice, based on scripture, tradition, knowledge of human nature, empirical research, and the social sciences.[79] As an art, it is learned by observation and practical experience in particular situations, which are best cultivated in classroom settings by the use of case study material.[80]

Second, practical theology is organized into distinct branches, which focus on the tasks of pastors as leaders of congregations. Here, Erdman followed the standard literature of practical theology. These branches include homiletics (preaching), liturgics (worship), ecclesiastics (church/denominational governance), poimenics (the cure of souls,

---

[75] Cited above.
[76] Erdman, *Work of the Pastor*, xiv-xv.
[77] Ibid., xii-xiii.
[78] Ibid., ix.
[79] Ibid., 67.
[80] Ibid.

including pastoral care and spiritual nurture), catechetics (Christian education), archagics (leadership of organizations), and alieutics (evangelism and overseas missions).[81] Within practical theology, pastoral theology deals with all but the first three of these fields.[82] Erdman emphasized repeatedly that theological education cannot prepare students for ministry by focusing exclusively on academic scholarship and preaching: "The Church is realizing that a man may be an erudite scholar, but still a very wretched preacher; and further, that he may be a profound theologian and an eloquent orator, but a pitifully poor pastor—a great hero in the toga, but a sorry figure as soon as he grasps the shepherd's staff."[83]

Third, practical theology reflects on the work of clergy and the mission of congregations in a changing social context. Erdman argued that the contemporary church faces new challenges in modern society, including more complex forms of congregational organization, new forms of social service in an industrializing and urbanizing society, and the relationship of congregations to denominational boards, para-church movements, ecumenical bodies, and missionary organizations.[84] While Erdman encouraged pastors to learn from social survey material and modern psychology and drew on such material in his writings, he never carried out empirical research himself or engaged in an extensive dialogue with the social sciences.[85] His primary focus as a practical theologian was elsewhere. This is due to the weight he gave, as a Reformed evangelical, to Scripture and the Holy Spirit in the Christian life. This set him apart from theological liberalism, on the one hand, and Reformed orthodoxy, on the other. The importance he gave to Scripture and the present activity of the Holy Spirit are clearly seen in the way Erdman justified his theological proposals.

Two examples of Erdman's warranting procedures illustrate patterns found throughout his writing. Both come from *The Work of the Pastor,* in which Erdman developed a pastoral theology of clergy leadership. The first example is the way Erdman justified his understanding of the pastoral office and the sort of theological education that prepares persons for this office. He began by noting its "divine origin." Jesus appointed apostles to "found and organize his Church, and, under the guidance of

---

[81] Ibid., ix-x. "Modern Practical Theology," 17-8.
[82] Here, "pastoral theology," refers to theological reflection on the work of the pastor. It will be used in a narrower and more specific way later in the twentieth century. See Chapter 5.
[83] Erdman, *Work of the Pastor*, x.
[84] "Modern Practical Theology," 17.
[85] For a reference to social surveys, see, Erdman, *The Work of the Pastor*, 43.

his Spirit...officers were ordained."[86] He then traced the development of this office in the New Testament, arguing that the biblical image of the shepherd captures best the work of the pastor. While this image includes preaching, it also captures a broad range of activities by which the pastor engages in the spiritual edification of the people.

Erdman then drew out the implications of this perspective for practical theology in the context of theological education. He argued that preparation for the pastorate involves several key elements: knowledge of the modern context, "technical training" in the art (skills and methods) and science (principles and theories) of practical theology, and the "spiritual preparation" of pastors, who must learn how to rely on the Holy Spirit in leading congregations. Erdman described the latter as the cultivation of habits of prayer, meditation, and the devotional reading of Scripture and spiritual classics.[87] In short, Erdman warranted his description of the pastoral office and the role of practical theology in educating persons for this office by (1) appealing to the authority of the New Testament as it reflects Jesus's calling and training of apostles, (2) drawing on the New Testament's depiction of the leaders of congregations to depict the pastoral office as engaged in spiritual edification, which includes but extends beyond preaching, and (3) describing the challenges facing pastors and congregations in the modern context, derived from his own experience as a pastor and from social scientific research.

A second example is Erdman's description of catechetics, or Christian education. Here, he began by distinguishing his own position from the newly emerging Religious Education Movement, which he believed describes religion and education generically and works within a "naturalistic" framework that excludes divine revelation and regeneration by the Spirit.[88] In contrast to the Religious Education Movement, he argued that Christian education must take its bearings from God's redemption of the world in Jesus Christ as narrated in Scripture. The mission of the church is to make disciples of all people, which is the "broadest and noblest meaning" of teaching in Christianity.[89] He then employed social survey data to underscore the importance of Christian education of children and youth. In an increasingly secular context, he argued, the educational ministry now falls almost exclusively on congregations, families, and para-church organizations due to the

---

[86] Ibid., 1.
[87] Ibid., 4-6.
[88] Ibid., 120.
[89] Ibid., 121.

secularization of public education.[90] Erdman's warranting procedures here are similar to those summarized above. He granted unique authority to Scripture's witness to God's revelation in Christ, which determines the distinctive nature of teaching in the Christian community. He also drew on pastoral experience and social scientific research to describe the challenges facing the teaching ministry in the modern context.

Summary and Concluding Reflections

This chapter examined PTS during a time of major social change in American society that led to turmoil in the Presbyterian Church and the seminary. In the various attempts to reform the PTS curriculum during this period, practical theology was a lightening rod. The faculty majority resisted the introduction not only of more electives and English Bible, but also of courses teaching the knowledge and skills of practical theology. Our examination of Gresham Machen has disclosed some of the reasons for this resistance, especially his commitment to defending Reformed orthodoxy in the face of competing theological and secular paradigms.

In sharp contrast, our examination of Charles Erdman has uncovered a trajectory that will prove to be somewhat rare in the American practical theological field during the twentieth century. Unlike liberal theology, which would dominate this field in future decades, Erdman's Reformed evangelical theology emphasized the authority of Scripture, ecumenism in the church's mission, and life in the Spirit. These provided the framework in which he located contextual analysis, dialogue with the social sciences, and the interaction of theory and practice. It is not too much to say that Erdman set in motion a trajectory at PTS that emphasized the *theological* identity of practical theology. This will be a hallmark of PTS practical theology across the twentieth century.

---

[90] Ibid., 122-4, 127-46.

Chapter 4
Reformed and Ecumenical:
Practical Theology and New Currents of Theology

This chapter follows the story of practical theology at Princeton Theological Seminary during John Mackay's presidency (1936-59). It compares changes to the PTS curriculum, especially programmatic developments in practical theology, to those of other seminaries and divinity schools. To gain a more concrete picture of practical theology under Mackay, this chapter highlights the life of Elmer Homrighausen.[1]

Homrighausen was a key figure in PTS practical theology during the Mackay years. Appointed as the Thomas Synnott Professor of Christian Education in 1938, he was installed as the first Charles R. Erdman Professor of Pastoral Theology in 1954, a position he held until retiring in 1970. In addition to teaching courses on Christian education, preaching, evangelism, pastoral counseling and church leadership, he moonlighted in the departments of Bible and History.[2] He was chair of the practical theology department from 1953-60 and served as dean of the faculty from 1955-65.

---

[1] The best resources on Homrighausen are Arnold B. Lovell, "Communicating the Christian Faith: A Study of the Relationship between Education and Evangelism in the Work of Elmer G. Homrighausen" (Dissertation, Presbyterian School of Christian Education, May 1995) and Dana Wright, *Elmer Homrighausen*, Talbot School of Theology: Christian Educators, at http://www.talbot.edu/ce20/educators/view.cfm?n=elmer_homrighausen. See also, "Elmer George Homrighausen," *The Princeton Seminary Bulletin* 4:1 (1983), 45-9.

[2] Homrighausen began teaching "An Introduction to the English Bible," previously taught by Erdman, in 1940-1. In 1945, he taught "The Renaissance, the Reformation, and the Counter-Reformation (1450-1688)."

While this chapter covers Homrighausen's work more fully below, it introduces two vignettes here in order to build a bridge to the previous chapter. In 1923-4, Homrighausen enrolled at PTS in a one year Bachelor of Theology program. This was the year that the controversy at PTS entered a more serious and public phase: Machen published *Christianity and Liberalism*, the General Assembly reaffirmed the five point doctrinal standards for the third time, the "van Dyke" incident occurred, and Erdman ran for moderator of the Presbyterian Church against Clarence Macartney.

That year, as Homrighausen later recalled, students heatedly discussed the issues polarizing the faculty.[3] He recollected that some students took "delight in asking questions in classes taught by Dr. Machen which would provoke him to become polemical."[4] Homrighausen took six courses from faculty aligned with Machen and nine, most of which were in practical theology, from faculty aligned with Stevenson and adjuncts.[5] A course taught by adjunct faculty George Johnson would have the deepest influence on Homrighausen, introducing him to two competing theological perspectives that would preoccupy him for the next ten years.

Johnson's course was entitled "The Psychology of Religion" and focused on the "study of the psychological aspects of religion with particular reference to the phenomena of conversion, revivals, worship, prayer and mysticism."[6] It provided Homrighausen with his first exposure to human science perspectives on the religious life. In his graduate work at the University of Dubuque, which included course work at the University of Chicago Divinity School, Homrighausen would enter into a deeply sympathetic conversation with the socio-evolutionary and psychological perspectives of the Religious Education Movement and theological liberalism. As he later reflected, during this "liberal" period, he learned that "God was no longer remote; religion was no longer merely a matter of correct ideas. It became a life. God was part of life and history."[7] He never abandoned this insight, even after he broke with theological liberalism.

---

[3] Homrighausen reflected on this year at two points. Campbell Wyckoff invited him to share his thoughts on the history of Christian Education in a two hour, tape recorded interview on March 18, 1976. He also wrote down his thoughts in "Princeton Seminary and Biblical Studies: Personal Reflections, 1938-1959," found in papers held by John Homrighausen, Homrighausen Collection, Special Collections, Princeton Theological Seminary Library. Both sources are discussed in Lovell, "Communicating the Christian Faith," cited above.
[4] Ibid., 52.
[5] Ibid., 57-9.
[6] *The Princeton Seminary Bulletin,* 17:3, 47.
[7] Elmer Horighausen, "Calm After Storm," twelfth article in the series "How My Mind Has Changed in This Decade," *Christian Century,* 56:1 (April 12, 1939), 477.

Ironically, it was in this same course that he first encountered Karl Barth's critique of theological liberalism in European Christianity.[8] Homrighausen would later become one of the earliest translators and interpreters of Barth for an American audience. He developed a personal friendship with Barth and his close colleague, Eduard Thurneysen. In his comprehensive examination of the rise of neo-orthodoxy in the United States, Dennis Voskuil describes Homrighausen as one of the most significant contributors to this movement's Barthian trajectory.[9]

Knowledge of Homrighausen's introduction to these competing theological impulses not only provides a starting point for charting his intellectual development, but also throws light on curricular reforms during the Mackay years. A central goal of the president and faculty was to forge a new Reformed identity beyond the "Old Princeton Theology." At the institutional level, this did not involve a break with theological liberalism, as was the case at institutions like the University of Chicago Divinity School and Union Theological Seminary (NY), where liberalism had flourished. PTS never entered a "liberal" period. Yet, many individual members of the PTS faculty *had* gone through a liberal period in their intellectual development. Homrighausen is a case in point. He understood theological liberalism from the inside and was appreciative of its analysis of the human dimension of religion from the perspectives of psychology, social history, sociology, and evolutionary thinking. This made him wary of jettisoning altogether the perspectives of the human sciences on the contemporary world. This was also true of other PTS faculty members. A number of new courses added to the PTS curriculum during this period drew on psychology, sociology, history, and anthropology.

A second part of Homrighausen's story illuminates the seminary's disengagement with Reformed orthodoxy and Christian fundamentalism throughout the Mackay years, even as it welcomed European dialectical theology, American Christian realism, and Reformed evangelicalism. Mackay invited Homrighausen to join the PTS faculty in 1937 while both were attending the World Conference on Church, State, and Society in Oxford. Homrighausen accepted and was approved by the Board of Trustees, pending ratification by the General Assembly.

As soon as Homrighausen's nomination went public, Samuel Craig attacked him in the pages of *Christianity Today*. Craig, a former member

---

[8] Wykoff interview. Quoted in Lovell, "Communicating the Faith," 59-60.
[9] Dennis Vokuil, *From Liberalism to Neo-orthodoxy: The History of a Theological Transition, 1925-1935* (Cambridge: Cambridge University Press, 1974).

of the PTS Board of Directors, had broken ties with the seminary after its reorganization in 1929 and helped establish Westminster Theological Seminary. One of Homrighausen's classmates from 1923-4, Cornelius Van Til, joined the assault in *The Presbyterian Guardian*. A Machen disciple, Van Til left PTS to join Westminster's faculty after one year as instructor in theology. Craig lambasted Homrighausen's view of scripture, and Van Til, his sympathies with Barth. Van Til wrote that "by embracing and propagating this sort of theology Princeton Seminary is now undermining and attacking—and in fifth column fashion—all that for which the Hodges, Warfield, and Machen stood."[10] When Homrighausen's name was brought before the General Assembly committee in charge of such matters, Craig and Clarence Macartney spoke against his ratification. Mackay was forced to withdraw the nomination. The General Assembly approved his nomination in 1938, but only after strategic maneuvering by Mackay.

Almost ten years after the seminary's reorganization, Homrighausen endured the same political and theological attacks that had wracked PTS in the twentieth century's first decades. It is little wonder that there was virtually no nostalgia for Old Princeton during the Mackay years, except among a few faculty like Andrew Blackwood, professor of homiletics.[11] As Hugh Kerr aptly wrote, "It is no secret that many contemporary professors at the Seminary feel completely out of touch theologically with their predecessors of a generation or more ago on such issues as Biblical criticism, apologetics, the sacraments, and the interpretation of the Westminster Confession of Faith."[12]

Homrighausen's story tells us much about PTS under Mackay's guidance. While theological liberalism held little appeal, neither did Reformed orthodoxy. The seminary was committed to forging a more inclusive Reformed identity, which avoided subscribing to a single theological position and participated in the worldwide ecumenical and missionary movements. Its new president, John Mackay, led the way.

---

[10] Cornelius Van Til, "A Substitute for Christianity," *The Presbyterian Guardian,* 12:10 (Feb. 10, 1943), 35. Samuel G. Craig, "Developments at Princeton Seminary," *Christianity Today,* 8:7 (November, 1937), 127. Further attacks by Craig in this journal appeared in July, 1939 and January and April, 1938.

[11] For an overview of Blackwood's relationship to "Old Princeton," see Jay E. Adams, *The Homiletical Innovations of Andrew W. Blackwood* (Grand Rapids: Baker Books, 1975).

[12] Hugh T. Kerr, ed., *Sons of the Prophets* (Princeton: Princeton University Press, 1963), xii-xiii.

John Mackay

A native of Inverness, Scotland, John Mackay was educated at Aberdeen University and PTS, graduating from the latter in 1915. After a year of study in Spain, Mackay and his new wife became missionaries in South America, where he was principal of the Anglo-Peruvian College of Lima and earned a doctorate at San Marcos University in Lima, Peru. After eight years, he joined the faculty of the National University of Lima as professor of philosophy. In 1932, Robert Speer invited him to join the staff of the Presbyterian Board of Foreign Missions, with oversight of the church's missionary activities in South America and Africa. Speer subsequently played a role in inducing Mackay to accept the presidency of PTS in 1936. Throughout his years at PTS, Mackay remained deeply involved in the worldwide missionary and ecumenical movements.

When Mackay arrived, he found a school in need of healing and a new guiding vision of its mission. He began to outline his vision for the seminary in his inaugural lecture as president, "The Restoration of Theology."[13] He underscored the need for Christian theology to engage the implicit "theologies" of the surrounding culture. This was a task, he argued, that theology could accomplish only if it lived in the tension between high standards of scholarship and passionate commitment to the "Universal Christian Church." He also encouraged PTS to open its doors to the "renaissance of evangelical learning which has flushed the horizon of European thought" in order to dispel "false conceptions" regarding the Reformed faith. He charged the seminary to make "adequate provision for the progress of its students in learning and piety," students who were preparing to become pastors, scholars, missionaries, Christian educators, and ecumenical leaders.[14] Mackay's emphasis on both piety and learning is a commitment that had been present from the very beginning of PTS, as has been noted in earlier chapters. In Mackay's view, however, the formation and interaction of piety and learning needed to become more explicitly missional and ecumenical at PTS. During his presidency, this belief took on flesh and bones in three ways: faculty appointments, establishment of a doctoral program, and reform of the curriculum.

Among the twenty professors appointed to the faculty during Mackay's presidency, nine hailed from countries other than the US. This not only brought persons to the faculty who had not been embroiled in the

---

[13] John Mackay, "The Restoration of Theology," *The Princeton Seminary Bulletin*, 31:1 (1937), 7-18.
[14] John Mackay, "The Role of Princeton Seminary," in *The Princeton Seminary Bulletin*, 38:4 (March, 1945), 1.

Presbyterian controversies of the 1920s, but also accomplished Mackay's goal of bringing new currents of theology to PTS. By the end of the Mackay era, the faculty had grown to sixty-four professors of all ranks, including full time, part time, visiting and guest lecturers. In part, this was due to steady growth in the student body. When Mackay arrived, the student body consisted of 209 students; when he retired, it had 485.

In 1940, Mackay received the Board of Trustees approval to establish a doctoral program for students preparing to become professors in academic institutions, initially offering a ThD. Within four years, eighteen students had enrolled in the program. In a statement by the faculty, one of the reasons offered for starting this program was the great difficulty Presbyterian seminaries were having "finding suitable candidates" for faculty positions.[15] In the ensuing decades, the presence of a robust PhD program was to have a formative impact on PTS. While it remained strongly committed to the church and congregational life, it attracted faculty and students capable of working at the doctoral level from various denominations and countries. "We have one foot in the academy and the other in congregations and the world-wide church," as one PTS faculty member put it. By any measure, this doctoral program has proved remarkably successful. In 2001, only Chicago Divinity School had more graduates under the age of 53 in academic positions in the member schools of the Association of Theological Schools.[16]

Reform of the curriculum began in earnest in 1939-40. Seven areas of study—Old Testament, New Testament, Church History, Apologetics, Systematic Theology, Practical Theology, and Ecumenics—were consolidated into four departments: Biblical Literature, History, Systematic Theology, and Practical Theology. These departments now provided the basic structure of the curriculum. In addition, greater attention was given to field education, which gained its first full-time director in 1941 and became an academic requirement in 1945.[17] In 1955, an interdepartmental committee established a required practicum for juniors and middlers designed to integrate field and course work. Field placements gradually became more diversified, including placements in congregations,

---

[15] *The Princeton Seminary Bulletin*, 34:1 (July 1940), 26.

[16] Barbara G. Wheeler, Sharon L. Miller, and Katarina Schuth, "Signs of the Times: Present and Future Theological Faculty," http://www.auburnseminary.org/sites/default/files/Signs%20of%20the%20Times.pdf, 14. Accessed on February 25, 2011.

[17] George Haines, *The Princeton Theological Seminary 1925-1960*, (dissertation, School of Education, New York University, 1966), 112-3.

college campuses, prisons, hospitals, and Clinical Pastoral Education programs. By 1959, twenty-two students participated in full time CPE placements, the largest number of students of any seminary in the East.[18]

During this period, Christian education became an important part of the curriculum. In 1941, the General Assembly urged all Presbyterian schools of Christian education to affiliate with seminaries for financial reasons. PTS assimilated the Tennent College of Christian Education in 1944, previously located in Philadelphia. The Masters in Christian Education was initially a three-year course of study that included all courses required for the Bachelor of Divinity, except biblical languages and preaching.

One way of discerning changes in the curriculum during the Mackay years is to examine course requirements and offerings. The chart on the following pages compares the curricula of 1925, before the seminary's reorganization, and 1960, the year after Mackay retired.[19] What trends are evident when these course offerings are placed side by side? How do they compare with curricular reforms taking place in other schools of theology? These questions are answered, in part, through a major study of theological education during this period conducted by H. Richard Niebuhr, James Gustafson, and Daniel Day Williams (referred to below as the Niebuhr study).[20] In a summary of their findings, they identified five trends:[21]

1. A reemphasis upon the importance of the traditional disciplines of theological study in the biblical, church-historical, and systematic fields;
2. An introduction of non-theological disciplines into the curriculum such as psychology, history of philosophy, and sociology;
3. An introduction of new courses in practical theology, including worship, administration, Christian education, and ecumenics;
4. A vast increase in field experience as seminaries became more involved in the work of their respective churches;
5. A tendency for the accelerated number of prescribed courses to limit independent and advanced study.

---

[18] Ibid, 117.
[19] Ibid., 120-2.
[20] H. Richard Niebuhr, Daniel D. Williams, and James Gustafson, *The Purpose of the Church and Its Ministry* (New York: Harper and Brothers, 1956) and *The Advancement of Theological Education* (New York: Harper and Brothers, 1957).
[21] Niebuhr, Williams, and Gustafson, *Advancement*, 21-2.

Course of Study, 1925[22]	Course of Study, 1960
Junior year	
Hebrew	Hebrew
Old Testament History	Old Testament History
Old Testament Introduction	Old Testament Book Studies
New Testament Greek	New Testament Greek
New Testament Introduction & Exegesis	New Testament Book Studies
	New Testament History
English Bible (taught by Erdman)	
Church History	Church History
Apologetics and Theism	Introduction to Christian Philosophy
Systematic Theology	Revelation, Authority, & Christian Doctrine of Man
	Ecclesiastical Theology
Homiletics	Homiletics
Public Speaking	Fundamentals of Expression
	Preaching
	Field Work Practicum
Middler year	
Introduction to the Pentateuch	Old Testament Introduction
Introduction to the Poetical Books	Prophetic Books with Exegesis
Biblical Theology of the Old Testament	
Gospel History	Introduction to the New Testament
	New Testament Exegesis
Church History	Church History
	History of American Christianity
Evidences of Christianity	History of Christian Doctrine
Systematic Theology	Jesus Christ & the Christian Doctrine of Redemption
English Bible (taught by Erdman)	
Principles and Methods of Missions	
	Christian Education
	Church Music
	Worship
	Field Education Practicum
	Preaching

---

[22] Courses in the same subject areas are in parallel columns. Blank lines in a column indicate omitted or new courses, though occasionally courses have been shifted from one year to another.

Course of Study, 1925[23]	Course of Study, 1960
Senior year	
Exegesis of the Prophetical Books	
Introduction to the Prophetical Books	
Apostolic History	
Biblical Theology of the New Testament	
Church History	
Christian Sociology	Christianity and Society
Systematic Theology	Doctrine of the Church & the Christian Life
Pastoral Theology	Pastoral Ministry of the Church
Homiletics	Homiletics
	Preaching
	Church Administration
	Church Polity
	Ecumenics
	Christian Ethics
	Theological Colloquium

All of these trends are evident in changes in the PTS curriculum during the Mackay years, with slight variations. With regard to the first trend, a reemphasis on the "traditional" disciplines, PTS had never deemphasized these disciplines. What *did* change during the Mackay years was the way these disciplines were approached. Gone were the older courses on apologetics and the "evidences" of Christianity, which had been such an important part of Old Princeton. Dogmatic theology, moreover, was no longer organized around a single system of Reformed theology—namely Hodge's. The loci of church doctrine still provided the structure of required courses but these were taught with a view to the variety of ways doctrines are treated in the Reformed tradition and contemporary theology. This was an important part of the seminary's shift to a more inclusive and ecumenical understanding of Reformed identity.

A number of required and elective courses included psychology, sociology, and philosophy, the second trend of the Niebuhr study. In the 1960 PTS catalogue, for example, psychology was described as a component of twenty-four courses, sociology of eight, and philosophy of

---

[23] Courses in the same subject areas are in parallel columns. Blank lines in a column indicate omitted or new courses, though occasionally courses have been shifted from one year to another.

seven.[24] The above chart clearly reveals the addition of new courses in practical theology, the third trend. These included expanded course work in preaching, as well new courses in Christian Education, church music, worship, church administration, and pastoral ministry. We have already noted above a greater emphasis on field education, the fourth trend.

The fifth trend of the Niebuhr study is the expansion of required courses, which made it harder for students to do advanced work in a particular subject area. On the surface, this would appear to be true of the PTS curriculum. In 1925, students needed ninety-six credit hours to graduate. By 1960, this had become 135, plus four hours of field work. This reflects required courses in new subject areas like Christian ethics, history of American Christianity, and Christian education. This shift must be interpreted carefully. In 1925, a curricular requirement typically could only be met by taking one particular course. In 1960, introductory courses were required, but beyond this, students could fill an area requirement by choosing from a number of courses. Overall, elective courses tripled during the Mackay era, affording students far more choices than in 1925. It is true, however, that requiring courses in more subjects areas did limit a student's freedom to pursue advanced study in a particular field, a major point of the Niebuhr study.

This brief examination of the PTS curriculum through the lens of the Niebuhr study makes it clear that during the Mackay years PTS's curriculum grew to be more in sync with mainline theological education than it had been between 1885[25] and 1929, when it had championed militant orthodoxy. In his study of university-based divinity schools, Conrad Cherry describes these trends as marking a transition from a professional model of theological education to a model that attempted to cultivate a *general theological perspective* among students.[26] This descriptor aptly characterizes the approach to theological education at PTS during this period. This is fairly remarkable, for the distance between PTS and divinity schools like Chicago and Union had been enormous during the first part of the twentieth century. Yet Reinhold Niebuhr joined Union's faculty in 1928 and was followed by Paul Tillich in 1933. Emil Brunner gave lectures at PTS in 1928, and the faculty soon included many members sympathetic to neo-orthodoxy and Christian realism, like Elmer Homrighausen, Otto Piper, Hugh Kerr, Paul Lehmann, and George

---

[24] Haines, *Princeton Theological Seminary*, 125.
[25] 1885, as mentioned in chapter three, was the first time PTS showed a curricular profile different from other theological schools in the Kelly study.
[26] Cherry, *Hurrying Toward Zion*, 141-3.

Hendry. Why did this convergence across theological education occur, and what does Cherry mean by the cultivation of a general theological perspective?

This paradigm shift in theological education at institutions as different as PTS and Union was prompted in part by the radically different social context created by two world wars and a major economic depression. This called into question the optimism and evolutionary moral progressivism of theological liberalism, which had provided the assumptions for the professional model of theological education at many divinity schools. It also called into question the commonsense realism and Westminster confessionalism of Reformed orthodoxy, which had provided the assumptions for the PTS curriculum from its founding until its reorganization in 1929. Across Protestant theological education, many theologians returned to the biblical roots of Reformation theology. They emphasized the reality of human sin and evil, the transcendence of God, and the sheer grace of God's reconciliation of the world in Jesus Christ. Educating professional clergy who were capable of helping the church adapt to the modern world was viewed as a totally inadequate goal for theological education. Equally inadequate was the goal of internalizing and defending denominational distinctives. The crises of modernity were too great, and the need for ecumenicity in mission too obvious.

Across theological education, thus, the widely shared goal was to cultivate among students a general theological perspective. By this, Charry means a broad and deep understanding of Christian Scripture, tradition, and contemporary theology, all of which raise questions about modernity's quest for autonomy. Cultivating this perspective was thought to provide students with a framework that could both guide their future ministries and enable them to interpret the contemporary world in light of the gospel.

Practical Theology: The Contribution of Clinical Pastoral Education

Practical theology both shaped and was shaped by these developments in theological education. The most innovative approach to practical theology during this period emerged out of Clinical Training programs, later called the Clinical Pastoral Education Movement. The story of this movement has been well told elsewhere.[27] Suffice it to say that CPE began in small training programs in hospital settings under the leadership of Richard Cabot, Russell Dicks, and Anton Boisen. Students were directly involved in ministry of some sort—commonly as chaplain interns—and invited to

---

[27] See, for example, Allison Stokes, *Ministry after Freud* (New York: Pilgrim Press, 1985).

reflect on their experiences through case studies, verbatims, personal supervision, and group discussions with fellow interns. In Anton Boisen's famous phrase, students were to learn about theology, their pastoral identities, and ministry by reflecting on "living human documents." Boisen believed that theological reflection on human beings in particular situations was every bit as important as reflection on the written texts studied in biblical studies, church history, and dogmatic theology.[28]

From these small beginnings, the CPE movement grew dramatically during the 1940s and 1950s. By the end of the 1950s, CPE programs were established in 117 centers with relationships to over forty schools of theology.[29] This had an important impact on Protestant theological education. As late as 1939, few schools of theology offered courses in pastoral counseling. By the 1950s, almost all did. By the mid-fifties, moreover, seven universities offered advanced graduate programs in theology and personality, pastoral psychology, pastoral counseling, or pastoral theology.

There is no question that the enormous success of the CPE movement was due in part to cultural trends. Following World War I, psychology exploded into popular consciousness and entered the vocabulary of everyday American life. Americans were interested in what psychology had to say about raising children, improving marriages, helping children do well at school, and succeeding at work. They also began entering therapy, sparking a rise in the mental health professions. Between 1940 and 1957, the American Psychological Association grew from 3,000 to 16,000 members, including more than 9,000 psychiatrists.[30] As the American economy shifted from small businesses to large corporations—the percentage of people in white-collar jobs doubled between 1940 and 1956—many businesses began using personality tests to screen prospective managers. Working with people and symbols had become more important than working with things.

---

[28] See the excellent overview of Boisen's life and works at http://www.acpe.edu/networks/boisen_bio.htm. Accessed June, 2010. Boisen used the term "living human documents" in a variety of places. See, for example, *The Exploration of the Inner World: A Study of Mental Disorder and Religious Experience* (Philadelphia: University of Pennsylvania Press, 1936), 185. Cf., articles found in *Register of the Chicago Theological Seminary*, 35:1 (January, 1945); *Religious Education: Journal of the Religious Education Association*, 25:3 (1930); and the *Journal of Pastoral Care*, 9:1. Special thanks to Robert Leas for this information.
[29] The statistics in the paragraph come from Holifield, *History of Pastoral Care*, 271.
[30] Ibid., 263.

Philip Reiff describes these trends as the "triumph of the therapeutic" in American culture.[31] Undoubtedly, the explosion of popular interest in psychology and the growth of the mental health professions helped fuel the success of the CPE movement. Yet it would be too simple to interpret CPE as merely a reflection of the triumph of the therapeutic in American life. CPE was critical of these trends, even as it was shaped by them. While this movement was diverse, some of its leading members contributed to a new understanding of practical and pastoral theology along three lines.

First, key figures in the CPE movement emphasized the development of a theological perspective beyond liberalism and orthodoxy. This, of course, was not true of all in the CPE movement. Some simply carried over the theological assumptions of liberalism and were more interested in what psychology had to teach theology than vice versa. They remained close to the position of the Religious Education Movement, which continued to dominate academic guilds in Christian education during this period. Yet there were many in the CPE movement who attended closely to the theological critique of modern life found in the writings of Paul Tillich, Reinhold Niebuhr, and others. This led people like Seward Hiltner, David Roberts, and Wayne Oats to develop a theological perspective on pastoral care and counseling as a ministry of the church.

Second, leading representatives of CPE brought theology into conversation with other fields, especially psychology. They were strongly committed to *interdisciplinary thinking*. The correlational method of Tillich exerted particular influence. It portrayed theology as listening to the questions of the present era in order to forge meaningful theological answers. In Tillich's view, the deepest questions with which people were struggling at that time did not focus on how they might adapt to modern life. Rather, they grew out of a questioning of modernity, fully cognizant of the anxiety, despair, and demonic forces it had unleashed. Like Tillich, many leading figures in the CPE movement found these questions brought to expression in the psychoanalytic perspectives of Freud and the neo-Freudians, which differed greatly from John Dewey's perspective, which was central to the Religious Education movement. Human beings were not merely problem solvers; rather, the human psyche was deeply conflicted, riddled with anxiety and struggling to find meaning in a mass society. Psychoanalysis provided the CPE movement with what we would call today

---

[31] Philip Rieff, *The Triumph of the Therapeutic: Uses of Faith after Freud* (New York: Harper Torchbooks, 1966).

a hermeneutic of suspicion, a critical perspective on popular culture's appropriation of psychology for personal improvement and the ego's adaptive competence. It portrayed human consciousness as caught in a web of potent even mechanistic forces in the unconscious, which render human reflection and volition ambiguous. The task of pastoral counseling was not merely to help people "adjust" to society. Rather, it was to evoke "insight," an awareness of forces within and without that shape human consciousness. These forces must be integrated emotionally and reflectively if people are to grow in their capacities for freedom and self-realization.[32]

Third, proponents of the CPE movement emphasized the importance of *theological reflection on clinical and ministerial practice*. This served as a context in which students gained theological knowledge and learned interdisciplinary thinking learned. It allowed persons to develop the judgment and wisdom needed to make good decisions in particular circumstances. It also afforded them the opportunity to reflect on their pastoral identities. In the following chapter, we will examine Seward Hiltner, who articulates the contribution of the CPE movement in a particularly powerful way.

What sort of influence did the CPE movement have on theological education in general and PTS in particular? For the most part, it was compartmentalized or, perhaps better, departmentalized.[33] It influenced particular areas like field education and the "practical field" but had relatively little impact on "traditional" theological disciplines or on theological curriculums as a whole. This certainly was the case at PTS. There is no question that the CPE movement had real influence. It was during this period that field education was linked to a new, "integrative" practicum, which supported theological reflection on practice. During the 1940s, Elmer Homrighausen and Sam Blizzard team-taught courses, like "Church and Family," which were interdisciplinary in nature and made use of case study material and student "task groups" that studied particular problems in congregations. Yet it is also true that Homrighausen and other members of the practical theology department continued to rely heavily on the lecture method of teaching, linked with precepts that allowed students to ask questions related to course material and their field education experiences. The impact of CPE on the "traditional" disciplines and the

---

[32] For an extended discussion of the shift in pastoral theology from the language of adjustment to insight and self-realization, see Holifield, *History of Pastoral Care*, Chapter 6.

[33] See Cherry's comments in this regard in *Hurrying toward Zion*, 145. He argues that the CPE movement provided important models for the sort of contextual education that began to emerge in the 1960s.

curriculum as a whole was minimal. In this regard, PTS was no different than many schools of theology during this period. As Cherry notes, the research of specialized theological disciplines continued to set the terms of theological education. The legacy of the theological encyclopedia and its twofold theory-practice scheme lived on, even as the subject matter of the "traditional" fields changed.

The remainder of this chapter examines the thinking of one member of the department of practical theology during the Mackay years, Elmer Homrighausen. The stories and contributions of other members of the department during this period are also important, including those of Donald Wheeler, Andrew Blackwood, Harold Donnelly, Edward Roberts, Wilbert Beeners, Donald Macleod, and Campbell Wyckoff. Each brought something important and unique to the development of practical theology at PTS. We focus on Homrighausen for several reasons. As noted at the beginning of the chapter, Homrighausen played a unique role in practical theology and in the seminary community as professor of Christian education and pastoral theology, chair of the department, and dean of the faculty. At the time of his death, the president of the seminary, James McCord, described Homrighausen as "the most beloved Princetonian of his generation."[34] Homrighausen is also an important figure historically. As noted above, he was one of the first American translators of Karl Barth and developed an American strand of Barthian practical theology, which he described as "neo-orthodox evangelicalism of the Reformed tradition."[35] Finally, Homrighausen's writings in the area of practical theology well represent Mackay's hope that PTS would begin to embody a Reformed identity that was more ecumenical and missional than in the past.

Elmer Homrighausen
Biography

Elmer G. Homrighausen was born in 1900, in Wheatland, Iowa, a small farm town of 600 residents. The community had a strong German ethnic identity. Homrighausen grew up speaking German, and his family belonged to the Reformed Church in the United States, commonly known as the German Reformed Church. There, he studied the Heidelberg Catechism in a three-year confirmation class. While

---

[34] James McCord, "Tribute to Elmer G. Homrighausen," Memorial Service, Jan. 9, 1982, Miller Chapel, Princeton Theological Seminary, Tape Recording. Quoted in Lovell, "Communicating the Christian Faith," 29.
[35] Homrighausen, "Calm after Storm," 477.

Homrighausen appreciated the tradition in which he was raised, he remembers it as strongly moralistic:

> My boyhood religion was a matter of dread at the thought of God's judgement. Religion was related to things solemn—to death, to heaven and hell. The moral law hung like a sword of Damocles over my defenseless head. God as an all-seeing judge, his church the place to which I *had* to come, and his minister the spy and vicar of God.[36]

Somewhat ironically, Homrighausen would later be characterized by his colleagues and students as an extremely warm, affable, and even joyful person who was "universally liked" in the Princeton community. He was a friend of the intellectual giants of Princeton, like Albert Einstein, yet retained the capacity to show respect and kindness in fielding "off the wall" questions from even the most aggressive students.[37] When asked by a student why he always seemed to be so ebullient and full of life, he responded, "My parents were told when I was two years old that I could not live. I learned this later on, and I determined to thank God every day the sun rose, and to live that day to the fullest."[38]

Homrighausen attended Mission House College in Plymouth, Wisconsin, founded by ministers educated by the most prominent contributors to Mercersburg theology, Philip Schaff and John Nevin. His time there included two years in the Mission House seminary, after which he spent his formative year at PTS. He was subsequently ordained in the Reformed Church of the United States and became the pastor of a congregation in Freeport, Illinois. Before his arrival at PTS, he served the Carrollton Avenue United Church in Indianapolis from 1917-38.

While serving these churches, Homrighausen began work on a masters and, then, doctorate at Dubuque University as a limited-time resident. This

---

[36] Ibid.

[37] One of Homrighausen's former students shared an account in which a student confronted Homrighausen angrily in class about the very idea of teaching the Bible, which he believed was impossibly outdated. Homrighausen responded by summarizing the student's position in a manner that was better than the student himself. He continued by saying, "Here is how I see it" and went on to share his own perspective. "What struck me most of all," the former student said, "was the way he treated this student and others with such dignity and respect. That has stayed with me in my own teaching." Personal interview, September, 2010.

[38] This incident was reported in the tribute by McCord, noted above. It is quoted in Lovell, "Communicating the Christian Faith," 30.

allowed him to take courses at the University of Chicago from such notables as Shirley Jackson Case, Shailer Matthews, and George Albert Coe (at Northwestern). He was thoroughly exposed to the historical and functional understanding of religion regnant at Chicago during this period, as well as the tenets of theological liberalism. This influenced his dissertation entitled "The Significance of Justin Martyr in the History of Early Christianity, or the Significance of Justin Martyr as a Witness to the State of Christianity in the Middle of the Second Century." In 1937 John Mackay approached Homrighausen about joining the PTS faculty as the Thomas Synnott Professor of Christian Education. As noted at the beginning of this chapter, his appointment was delayed for a year due to criticism by alumni sympathetic to Old Princeton. Homrighausen actually began his teaching responsibilities at PTS in 1938.

Toward a Neo-orthodox Evangelical Practical Theology in the Reformed Tradition

In 1939 Homrighausen contributed to *The Christian Century* series, "How My Mind Has Changed in This Decade," which centered on his encounter with dialectical theology, especially the writings of Karl Barth.[39] He describes his thinking as passing through five stages:

1. Curious awareness of Barth's writings during his graduate school years.
2. Active rebellion against dialectical theology from the perspective of theological liberalism.
3. Ardent discipleship of Barth's perspective. This period was prompted by reading the second edition of Barth's *Commentary on Romans* shortly after arriving at the Freeport pastorate. During this period, he translated two volumes of Barth's sermons and one volume of his addresses.[40] He travelled to Bonn to meet Barth and, subsequently, began corresponding with both Barth and

---

[39] Homrighausen, "Calm after Storm." Homrighausen mentions Emil Brunner, Karl Heim, Herman Kutter and Edward Thurneysen as dialectical theologians who also influenced his thinking. These figures, moreover, led him to a new encounter with Paul and Luther.

[40] Karl Barth and Eduard Thurneysen, *Come Holy Spirit*, transl., George Richards, Elmer Homrighausen, and Karl Ernst (New York: Round Table Press, 1934). Karl Barth, *God's Search for Man*, transl., George Richards, Elmer Homrighausen, and Karl Ernst (New York: Round Table Press, 1935). Karl Barth, *God in Action*, transl. Emer Homrighausen and Karl Ernst (New York: Round Table Press, 1936).

Thurneysen. He also wrote a protest article against the liberal intelligentsia and several articles on Barth's potential contribution to American Christianity.[41]

4. Construction of a new theological perspective beyond liberalism. This stage commenced with the publication of Homrighausen's first book, *Christianity in America: A Crisis*.[42]

5. Development of a more critical perspective on Barth in which he articulated his own theological position. He described this as a dialectical theology that has "indigenous interpretation and application" for an American context.[43]

Since this article was written in 1939 and Homrighausen did not retire until 1970, this narrative self-description is most helpful in understanding his movement away from liberalism and encounter with Barth's theology. By the fifth stage described above, moreover, many of the themes of his later work had begun to emerge. What, then, are the most important features of Homrighausen's mature perspective?

At the heart of Homrighausen's project is the recovery of the *theological grounds* of Christian ministry—the ministry of clergy, laity, and the congregation as a whole. This is central to Homrighausen's sense of vocation. When asked why he entered the field of Christian education in the department of practical theology, he responded: "It is primarily because I regard the practical field as in desperate need of being undergirded by sound theological structure."[44] Later, reflecting on his time at PTS, he put it this way: "I felt that all Practical Theology needed to become centered more fully in a theology of the Word. Practical Theology needed to become *theological*."[45] Homrighausen's emphasis on theology continues a central feature of the trajectory of practical theology established by Charles Erdman. This will continue to be the case in future decades at PTS, even when people like Seward

---

[41] Elmer Homrighausen, "A Young Minister's Counter-Revolt," *Christian Century*, 48:1 (February 18, 1931), 236-8; "Barthianism and the Kingdom," *Christian Century*, 48:2 (July 15, 1931), 922-5; "Barth and the American Theological Scene," *Union Seminary Review* 46 (July, 1935), 283-301.

[42] Elmer Homrighausen, *Christianity in America: A Crisis* (New York: Abingdon Press, 1936).

[43] Homrighausen, "Calm after Storm," 479.

[44] Elmer Homrighausen, "The Minister and Religious Education," *Christian Education*, 21:4 (April, 1938), 236, n5.

[45] "Personal Reflections," cited above in note 3.

Hiltner, James Loder, and Charles Bartow give more explicit attention to the interdisciplinary nature of practical theology.

In a series of articles published in 1938-40, Homrighausen developed his theological perspective in direct contrast to the Religious Education Movement.[46] This prompted critical responses from George Albert Coe and Harrison Elliott, leading lights of this movement.[47] The Religious Education Movement, Homrighausen argued, is Exhibit A in why practical theology needs to develop a new and more solid theological foundation. It has lost its "critical detachment" from modern intellectual trends and "thereby capitulated to a naturalistic and positivistic idea of religion," becoming little more than an "annex to a type of humanistic religion."[48] In terms that appear to take direct aim at Coe's *A Social Theory of Religious Education*, Homrighausen outlined this movement's assumptions:

> To be sure, God may be mentioned, but God is conceived as immanent in the social process, as a part of nature, capable of being experienced in man's high devotion to "ideal social ends." In short, the social "religious attitude" is substituted for definite personal relations to a personal God and definite ends. "The beyond" element is swallowed up in present experience.[49]

As a result of these theological assumptions, Homrighausen argued, the Religious Education Movement offers little more than the cultivation of a "vague religious attitude" and various forms of social idealism.[50]

---

[46] These include "The Minister and Religious Education," cited above; "The Real Problem of Religious Education," *Religious Education,* 34:1 (January-March 1939), 10-7; "The Salvation of Christian Education," *International Journal of Religious Education,* 15:9 (May, 1939), 12-3, 40; "Religious Education vs. the Church," *Christian Century,* 56:2 (November 29, 1939), 1465-6; "The Task of Christian Education in a Theological Seminary," *The Princeton Seminary Bulletin*, 34:1 (1940), 3-21. He continues this critique in "The New Emphasis in Christian Education," *Christendum,* 7:1 (Winter 1942), 81-9; and "Christian Education After Ten Years of Ecumenical Thinking," *International Journal of Religious Education* 15:9 (May 1950), 176-85.

[47] George Albert Coe, "Religious Education Is in Peril," *International Journal of Religious Education,* 15:5 (January 1939), 9-10. Harrison Elliott, *Can Religious Education Be Christian?* (New York: The Macmillan Company, 1940). In this book, Elliott was not responding to Homrighausen but to the broader critique of the Religious Education movement by proponents of the "new theology."

[48] Elmer Homrighausen, "The Real Problem of Religious Education," 16.

[49] Ibid., 14.

[50] Elmer Homrighausen, "Minister and Religious Education," 242-3.

From Homrighausen's perspective, the larger issue at stake is the question of authority. The Religious Education Movement accepted uncritically "the modern outlook which has made man autonomous."[51] This shaped its perspective at every level—from the uncritical authority it grants the natural and social sciences and secular philosophies of education, like John Dewey's, to its depiction of the goal of religious education as the enhancement of human autonomy by cultivating the capacity to reflect on contemporary problems in light of religious values. This impulse, he argued, permeates much more than the Religious Education Movement. From the Renaissance forward,

> The authority of life in modern times has gradually shifted from that contained within the Christian tradition, particularly the Word of God, to that which is contained within the context of this world. The supreme good was interpreted in terms of human wellbeing autonomously determined, individual and corporate. The transcendent was swallowed up in the immanent, or the transcendent was interpreted in terms of data in personality and the social order.[52]

He continues:

> From the time of Kant on, the Christian religion has been regarded not as a revelation from God made manifest in history and immanent through faith and the power of the Holy Spirit in the church, but as a datum of human experience. Objective revelatory authority was displaced by the religious consciousness.[53]

Following Barth's lead, Homrighausen offered a prophetic critique of the "autonomous modern man," who has unleashed the horrors of the twentieth century. The church will have something to offer modernity only if it recovers its own message and mission. This is the fundamental goal of his theological project.

---

[51] Homrighausen, "Barth and the American Theological Scene," 298. The theme of autonomy is also found in "The Real Problem of Religious Education," 15; "The Task of Christian Education," 13; and "Christian Theology and Christian Education," 354.
[52] Homrighausen, "Christian Theology and Christian Education," 354.
[53] Ibid.

Homrighausen believed that the unique message of the church for the modern world is the gospel. He followed Barth's reversal of the logic of theological liberalism and modernity's quest for autonomy. The gospel is not the answer human beings discover in their autonomous search for meaning, value and power. It is the good news of God's search for humanity, to recall the title of one of Barth's sermon collections translated by Homrighausen.[54] The gospel is the message of God's incarnation and reconciliation of the world in Jesus Christ. The movement is from God to humanity, an act of sheer grace in which God offers salvation to a world caught in sin and death. When the Religious Education Movement uncritically adopted modernity's quest for autonomy, it brought into the church, like a Trojan horse, certain assumptions that violate the very logic of the gospel.

Homrighausen proposed an alternative foundation for the teaching ministry. He consistently described this foundation as a theology of revelation, based on the "objectivity" of God's Word in Jesus Christ. By "objectivity," he did not mean that theology can capture in static, propositional statements of doctrine the meaning of God's revelation, along the lines of Protestant orthodoxy. Rather, he meant that theology "follows after" God's Word. It orients itself to God's self revelation in Jesus Christ, the coming of the transcendent God to humanity, and to the present activity of the Holy Spirit, who enables this Word to be heard and given response in varied cultural and historical contexts. The "objective" foundation of theology is the otherness of the Word, which breaks into human experience and is appropriated through the Holy Spirit. It is not merely a natural outgrowth of human experience. Homrighausen also granted special authority to Scripture as it gives witness to the Word, to the historic experience of the church brought to expression in creeds and practices, and to "Christian experience" in the context of a community of faith seeking to give faithful witness to God's Word.

Constructing a Theology of the Church

Over the course of his writings, Homrighausen touched on many theological themes derived from his interpretation of the gospel as God's self revelation and reconciliation of the world in Jesus Christ. Without question, the theme he treated most extensively was the church, called into being and given its mission by the gospel. All of his books dealt

---

[54] Homrighausen, *God's Search for Man*, cited above, n38.

with the church, as did most of his articles.[55] Homrighausen's theology of the church provided the foundation of his theory of Christian ministry, developed most extensively in the areas of Christian nurture, evangelism, and pastoral care.

Homrighausen never completely abandoned the historical and functional understanding of Christianity he learned at Chicago during his graduate years. The church *does* take different forms and carry out different social functions in various historical contexts. But this is not the first thing that must be said about the nature and purpose of the church from a theological perspective. Rather, theology must begin with a clear affirmation that "the church is not fundamentally a human institution. It has a divine origin and function."[56] As Homrighausen insisted:

> [The church] is a living movement, the incarnation of the Spirit of Christ in human flesh and blood. And the Church is definitely brought into being not by a vague humanly-constructed "philosophy of religion," or "social philosophy," or "personality building technique," but by definite historic events witnessed to in the Bible.[57]

As such, the church derives its mission from its divine origin in Christ. While Homrighausen describes this mission in a variety of ways, the most important concept he uses is *witness*. "I have come to see that witness is the church's and the Christian's major task."[58] Elsewhere, he notes: "The Church exists because Christ lived, and it is…the continuing incarnation of the living Christ. As such, the Church must witness to God in Christ."[59]

The theme of witness goes all the way back to Homrighausen's dissertation on Justin Martyr.[60] As his thinking matured, he identified four

---

[55] Elmer Homrighausen, *Choose Ye This Day: A Study of Decision and Commitment in Christian Personality* (Philadelphia: Westminster Press, 1943); *Christianity in America*, cited above, n40; *I Believe in the Church* (Nashville: Abingdon Press, 1959); *Let the Church Be the Church* (New York: Abingdon-Clkesbury Press, 1940).
[56] Homrighausen, *Christianity in America*, 164.
[57] Homrighausen, "The Salvation of Christian Education," 13.
[58] Homrighausen, "Christian Education After Ten Years of Ecumenical Thinking," 185.
[59] Homrighausen, "The Minister and Religious Education," 239.
[60] Elmer Homrighausen, "The Significance of Justin Martyr in the History of Early Christianity, or the Significance of Justin Martyer as a Witness to the State of Christianity in the Middle of the Second Century." (S.T.D. dissertation, University of Dubuque Graduate School of Theology, 1930).

key dimensions of the church's mission as witness. First, witness is the mission of bearing the message of the gospel. A witness is not the Redeemer. A witness is a person or community that points beyond itself to the good news of God's salvation of the world in Jesus Christ. As early as *Christianity in America: A Crisis*, Homrighausen criticized the American church for defining its mission in other ways, as serving "progress, or democracy, or bourgeois capitalistic culture."[61] In so doing, it has lost its capacity to confront American society "with a common witness to the Word of God entrusted to, and *only* to, the Church."[62]

Second, the church as witness has the mission of embodying in its own life some measure of the salvation God offers to all people in Christ. Through its fellowship, worship, and service it testifies to the grace it has received. In Homrighausen's development of this dimension of witness, he remained solidly Reformed, in contrast to the Anabaptist ecclesiologies that have become prominent in the twenty-first century. He wrote:

> It should be said that when the Church is properly conceived it does not become a peculiar community, although it will always seem peculiar in a world "under sin"; rather, it becomes humanity under God, in Jesus Christ, through the Spirit…As such the Church is the vanguard of true human community.[63]

This is an important point. Even as Homrighausen strongly advocated a renewed emphasis in practical theology on the church as a distinct community with its own message and mission, he portrayed this as a form of participation in God's mission to the world. The divine election that brings the church into being does not set it apart as a community of special privilege but as a fellowship that gives witness to the possibilities of humanity restored to a right relationship with God. It is the "vanguard" of the true humanity revealed in Christ Jesus.

Third, the church's mission as witness has an apologetic dimension. This is an understanding of theology that Homrighausen gleaned from his dissertation on Justin Martyr, a great patristic apologist. Homrighausen appreciated the way Justin used philosophy and ethics to communicate the Christian faith and repeatedly commented in his dissertation on the "need

---

[61] Homrighausen, *Christianity in America*, 159.
[62] Ibid.,142.
[63] Homrighausen, "Christian Theology and Christian Education," 360.

for a new apology today."[64] This is one of the points where Homrighausen departed from Barth. He never relinquishes the apologetic task of Christian witness, the task of rendering the gospel in forms of thought and life that are both fitting and intelligible in a particular socio-historical context.[65] Yet the deeper logic of this task remains thoroughly Barthian. Revelation sets the terms of the witness rendered. In his inaugural lecture at PTS, Homrighausen described the apologetic dimension of witness:

> It is one thing to recover the Bible and the body of truth in the Christian tradition. It is quite another to translate (not adapt!) the meaning of that truth into terms of the contemporary age...This service, however, must be done in every age...It is a type of incarnation, in which the Word must again become flesh.[66]

Finally, the church's mission as witness is a form of participation in the self-giving love of Christ, which in extreme circumstances can lead to suffering and death. Here again, we find a theme that entered Homrighausen's thought in his dissertation on Justin Martyr. Justin was martyred during a period when the church faced persecution, and he viewed martyrdom as the ultimate form of witness. Homrighausen later drew on this image to understand Karl Barth. During one of his meetings with Barth in Bonn, Barth shared with him the proofs of *Theologische Existenz heute!* As Homrighausen read the proofs, he was struck by Barth's courage amid the crisis of the German church, commenting later that he "knew he was in the presence of what the New Testament calls a *witness*, or a *martyr*."[67] The church should not seek this sort of suffering; it simply attempts to embody Christ's sacrificial love out of loyalty to God. But when it faces radical evil and must choose between loyalty to God and the servants of evil, it must be prepared to make the ultimate witness.

A Theology of Christian Nurture

Homrighausen drew on this theology of the church as witness to develop his understanding of evangelism, Christian education, and

---

[64] See Lovell's extremely helpful discussion of this point in "Communicating the Christian Faith," 80-91.
[65] For examples of Homrighuasen's apologetic orientation, see "The Real Problem with Religious Education," 11, "Christian Theology and Christian Education," 356, and "Theology and Christian Education," 420.
[66] Homrighausen, "The Task of Christian Education in a Theological Seminary," 19.
[67] Quoted in Lovell, "Communicating the Christian Faith," 132.

pastoral care.[68] By far, he gave the greatest attention to a theory of Christian nurture, which he sometimes refered to as Christian *paideia*. Here, he articulated his understanding of Christian education. Homrighausen's theory of Christian nurture, thus, illustrates the way his theology of the church shapes his various theories of Christian practice.

Homrighausen was clear that the recovery of Christian nurture in the contemporary church is not simply a matter of reforming curriculum, teaching methods, or structures of Christian education. Rather, it must begin "at the deeper level of evangelical Christianity itself. The need is for a theology which will undergird the Church's task of Christian nurture with a sound unified approach."[69] This entails becoming clear about the primary goal of Christian nurture. Two examples of Homrighausen's articulation of this goal reveal the way he consistently grounded Christian nurture in his theology of the church:

> The primary business of Christian education is to make living members of the Christian community of which Jesus Christ is the center, sustainer, and hope. This can be done only by grafting life, through commitment, into the living Christ, by enlightening the minds of those so ingrafted with the historic theological thought of the church, and by bringing those so committed and ingrafted into an intelligent, creative and missionary membership in the historic and existing community.[70]

---

[68] Homrighausen's various writings on Christian Education and Christian nurture are cited throughout this chapter, as are those articles on evangelism that are directly related to Christian nurture. A sampling of his thinking on evangelism includes: "Axioms of Evangelism," *The Pastor,* 17:4 (December, 1953), 3-6; "Evangelism in Such a Time," in *The Ecumenical Era in Church and Society: A Symposium in Honor of John A. MacKay* (New York: The Macmillan Company, 1959); "Communicating the Christian Faith," *Theology Today,* 1:4 (January, 1945), 487-504; "Evangelism and the Presbyterian Reformed Churches," *Presbyterian World*, 19:2 (June, 1949), 71-6; "Evangelistic Calling," *Pastoral Psychology,* 7:69 (December, 1956), 55-7; "The Holy Spirit and the Renewal of Witness," *Theology and Life,* 7:1 (Spring 1964), 46-57; and "What is the Witness of Presbyterianism?" *The Presbyterian World* 22:4 (December, 1953), 152-8. One of Homrighausen's few writings on pastoral care is his inaugural lecture upon the occasion of his shifting to the Erdman chair in pastoral theology, "Toward a Pastoral Church," *Princeton Seminary Bulletin*, 48:4 (May, 1955), 10-9.

[69] Elmer Homrighausen, "Wanted: The Recovery of the Christian Paideia," *Religion In Life,* 15:1, 126.

[70] Homrighausen, "The New Emphasis in Christian Education," 86-7.

> Is Christian education mere evolutionary development of the natural man into a harmoniously social creature, or is it the deliberate guidance of a person through divine truths and personal agencies (for the true meaning of the Church is a personal tradition and fellowship) into an experience with God which He proposes through a self-initiated act of revelation in Jesus Christ?[71]

Christian nurture is based on God's self revelation in Christ and takes shape within the church, called into being by this revelation. It occurs through the fellowship and practices of the church as a living community of faith, as well as the specific points of teaching and learning in this community. It grafts individuals into this community and, thereby, into Christ.

One of the most innovative dimensions of Homrighausen's depiction of Christian nurture was the way he accentuated the *dynamic quality of nurture*. It is not merely a matter of being socialized into a particular community of faith. Rather, it is a matter of confronting the living Word of God again and again across the Christian life. Quite literally, the members of the Christian community must bear witness to the gospel in their relationships with one another. Homrighausen wrote:

> Nurture must be accompanied with and supported by the message of Christianity centering in Jesus Christ. The major question is: Can there be any Christian nurture without faith which is a continuous response to the divine initiative and which is never a possession of man?...A comprehensive Christian nurture involves both an emphasis upon continuity and discontinuity, nurture and evangelism.[72]

Homrighausen explored the dynamic quality of Christian nurture most extensively in his discussion of its relationship to evangelism.[73] At one point, he declared: "It is our contention that all Christian education must be evangelistic, and that all Christian evangelism must be

---

[71] Homrighausen, "The Salvation of Christian Education," 13.
[72] Homrighausen, "Christian Theology and Christian Education," 362.
[73] In addition to the articles cited in this paragraph, see also, "Christian Education after Ten Years of Ecumenical Thinking," 180, "Religious Education vs. the Church," 1466, "The New Emphasis in Christian Education," 82, "Christian Theology and Christian Education," 361-2.

educational."[74] This is due to the nature of the message to which the church gives witness:

> The Gospel of God demands that we tell the good news with the idea of enlisting others in its cause. It is an offer which demands acceptance on man's part. It does not come up out of man's life; it comes to man's life. It is a personal call and demands a response."[75]

Elsewhere, he argued that if the gospel addresses human beings whose "sinfulness has resulted in a radical breach of relationship between God and man, then man has to be confronted with God's truth and love in such a way that he may make a choice for or against it."[76] Evangelism, thus, is not directed exclusively toward those outside the church, as it is commonly portrayed. Rather, it is an essential part of Christian nurture of people *within* the community of faith:

> There will be a continuous evangelization for those who have grown up in the Christian *paideia*, with a view to bringing children and youth to an ever-growing voluntary acceptance in faith of the heritage in which they live and move and have their beings, the center of which is Jesus Christ. The child will grow up as a member of the Christian *paideia*, but will also be led to know that *he* has *become* a believer by personal decisions, one or several of which have been crucial. In fact, the Christian *paideia* deliberately creates tensions within the life of growing children so that they may know that even though they belong to the Christian community they do not thereby become *naturally* or *automatically* Christian.[77]

Elsewhere, Homrighausen made it clear that he had adults in mind as much as children and youth. There will be "constant conversions" in the process of "evangelistic Christian education" as individuals hear God's Word anew in different circumstances and stages of their lives.[78]

---

[74] Elmer Homrighausen, "Evangelism and Christian Nurture," *The Christian Review*, 8:4 (October, 1939), 274.
[75] Ibid., 276.
[76] Homrighausen, "Christian Theology and Christian Education," 361.
[77] Homrighausen, "Wanted: The Recovery of the Christian Paideia," 136.
[78] Homrighausen, "Evangelism and Christian Nurture," 276.

What are some of the practical implications that flow from this understanding of an evangelistic Christian nurture? Four are lifted up in Homrighausen's writing. First, as is already evident in the above discussion, Christian nurture is broader than the specific programs and practices of Christian education designed to foster teaching and learning. It depends on the quality of fellowship and service found in the congregation and Christian home. If these communities fail to embody the message and mission of the church, then no amount of education will be capable of filling the void.

Second, the educational ministry must recover its historic emphasis on "divine content," giving pride of place to Scripture and Christian tradition.[79] In a number of places, Homrighausen went so far as to argue for a positive understanding of the term indoctrination. He believed that it does not refer to rote memorization or handing on a closed system of church doctrines along the lines of Reformed orthodoxy. Rather, indoctrination is the process of communicating the beliefs of the church, based upon divine reality, in a manner that transforms the mind and life of learners.[80] It is personal, not merely intellectual, "a communication from personality to personality of the divine activity of God for man's redemption."[81] The gospel claims the whole of a person—mind, emotions, and will—but "how will a man *know* unless he can *understand* the Gospel's claims?"[82]

Third, while teaching methods are important, they are secondary to the teacher's role as a witness to the gospel. Homrighausen argues that there are real limits to what can be accomplished through teaching and education, for "only God can make anyone a Christian."[83] He continues: "It is impossible for any person to communicate his faith to another. Always the teacher is engaged as a witness to the thing itself," leaving room for the free response of the student.[84] Learning and growing in the life of discipleship is not a matter of mastering facts but of "coming into possession of divine wisdom…which has come through a deep, personal, faith-produced

---

[79] Homrighausen, "The Real Problem of Religious Education," 16; "Christian Education after Ten Years of Ecumenical Thinking," 177; "The Task of Christian Education," 13; "Religious Education vs. the Church," 1466.
[80] Homrighausen, "The Task of Christian Education," 14.
[81] Ibid. For other positive references to indoctrination, see "Salvation of Christian Education," 13, "Christian Theology and Christian Education," 357.
[82] Homrighausen, "Salvation of Christian Education," 13.
[83] Homrighausen, "Christian Theology and Christian Education," 356.
[84] Ibid.

understanding and appropriation of revealed truth."[85] Teaching methods are not to be despised, but they are only "prepatory ways in which a creative teacher serves God to reach pupils with His truth."[86]

Fourth, with this qualification in mind, Homrighausen commends the use of creative and experiential teaching methods as championed by the Religious Education movement, as long as they are "christened" to Christian purposes.[87] Accordingly, he would moderate the Reformed tradition's overriding emphasis on the spoken word, which too often results in an overemphasis on the lecture and discussion methods of teaching. He argues that "the Word may not only be spoken, but painted, printed, dramatized, symbolized, sung, portrayed, [and] lived."[88] Moreover, there should be ample room for contemporary experience in Christian teaching, especially the sort of experience "induced by the Word invading life through faith and Spirit."[89] Such experiences are the outgrowth of regeneration at the personal level and participation in community of faith at the corporate level.

Summary and Concluding Reflections

John Mackay's presidency at PTS marked an important transition in the seminary, a movement beyond the conflict of the early decades of the twentieth century toward a more ecumenical and missional Reformed theological identity. Elmer Homrighausen represents well many of the currents reshaping the seminary during this period, especially its heavy emphasis on neo-Reformation theology, its continued commitment to a learned ministry in which both piety and learning are taken seriously, and its commitment to both the academy and the church. In many ways, PTS was far more similar to other seminaries and divinity schools during this period than the first decades of the twentieth century when the seminary curriculum was shaped by the theological assumptions of Reformed orthodoxy. Homrighausen's practical theology of the church and Christian nurture was deeply Reformed but in a far different way than was the theology of Gresham Machen or B. B. Warfield.

Within the field of practical theology Homrighausen's most important contribution was his affirmation of the role of theology in guiding and reforming the life of the church. If the Religious Education Movement had

---

[85] Homrighausen, "The Task of Christian Education in a Theological Seminary," 18.
[86] Ibid.
[87] Ibid., 13.
[88] Ibid., 16.
[89] Ibid., 19.

imbibed the naturalistic assumptions of philosophical pragmatism and the Clinical Pastoral Education Movement in some of its forms had adopted the assumptions of therapeutic psychology, Homrighausen offered a clear affirmation of *theology as central to the identity of practical theology as field.* This is one of his strengths and, indeed, one of the strengths of practical theology at PTS generally. However, there are at least two dimensions of the Religious Education and CPE Movements that Homrighausen failed to engage with sufficient depth.

First, he never articulated an explicit interdisciplinary method with which to bring theology into conversation with education, history, philosophy, psychology, and other fields. It is not enough to write this off as one more example of the way Barth short-circuits interdisciplinary work. It is unclear whether this is really true of Barth. But it *is* true that while Homrighausen was open to dialogue with the natural and human sciences, he failed to engage the interdisciplinary task in a methodologically self conscious way.

Second, Homrighausen failed to fully appropriate pedagogically the importance of reflective practice as a context for theological education. This had been a very important innovation of both the Religious Education and Clinical Pastoral Education movements. While Homrighausen did use case studies and "task groups" in some of his courses, his pedagogy primarily utilized the lecture method, aided by discussion groups. For several decades, the Religious Education Movement had taught through lab schools, and the CPE movement through supervised ministry in clinical settings. Yet Homrighausen and PTS generally did not fully appropriate the significance of reflective practice as a focal point of teaching throughout the Mackay years. This would begin to change when Seward Hiltner joined the PTS faculty in 1961, as we will see in the following chapter.

Chapter 5
The Flowering of Practical Theology During the McCord and Gillespie Years

The department of practical theology had gathered for its monthly meeting in the stately Board Room of Speer Library. Seward Hiltner and Charles Bartow were seated in solid wooden chairs around a long, rectangular table. During the monthly meetings of the entire faculty, the seats at the table were occupied by senior faculty, and junior faculty were relegated to folding chairs nestled together at one end of the room. The agenda reached the point when new course proposals were to be discussed. James Loder, a relatively new, junior member of the faculty, circulated a sheet of paper describing a new course on the developmental psychologist Jean Piaget. A few faculty offered inconsequential comments. Then Hiltner raised a pointed question: "Who are the other psychologists you'll cover in the course?" Loder responded, "Piaget is a complex figure and important enough to be the focus of the entire course." Hiltner pressed him further: "But how will students be able to locate Piaget in the broader context of psychology and theology? They won't grasp the strengths and limitations of his perspective if you only teach him." Loder responded, "I am dealing with Piaget in terms of the larger philosophical background of his theory. They'll gain perspective on his assumptions that way."

The two went back and forth with a slowly increasing note of emotion in their voices. Anxiety was palpable among the junior faculty. Hiltner appeared to be quite comfortable escalating the conflict, but Loder refused to back down, a rare occurrence among junior faculty in the face of one of Hiltner's interrogations. The exchange continued for a while longer until Hiltner finally gave a hint of a smile and said, "Well, Jim, I guess a course on Piaget is something you'll just have to teach." The Department quickly voted to approve Loder's new course.

An eyewitness shared this story with Osmer many years after it occurred.[1] While the exchange between Hiltner and Loder may not be an exact reproduction of their original wording, it captures the gist of what was said. A note of conflict and tension is apparent, and this would be a part of the relationship between Loder and Hiltner over the years. But this does not signal a department torn apart by deep divisions. Rather, it marks the beginning of a new stage in which the members of the department would begin to engage one another intellectually with a new seriousness. Indeed, it is an early sign of the flowering of practical theology during the years in which James McCord (1959-1983) and Thomas Gillespie (1983-2004) were the presidents of the seminary.

It is no accident that Hiltner and Loder would lead the way. Hiltner joined the Princeton Theological Seminary faculty in 1961 and was followed by Loder the next year. The two had met at the Menninger Clinic where both received clinical training. Hiltner actively supported Loder's appointment in Christian Education, though their relationship was often conflictual at PTS. It is to Campbell Wyckoff's credit that he supported Loder's appointment as well, in spite of the fact that Loder led a group of students in criticizing one of Wyckoff's courses in Christian education as lacking "philosophical depth" during Loder's senior year at PTS.[2]

In an interview for this chapter, a former academic dean of the seminary characterized the department of practical theology as largely an "administrative convenience" when Hiltner and Loder joined the faculty. Each area had its "own little fiefdom." Under Wyckoff's leadership, the School of Christian Education had its own degree programs, suite of offices, and staff. Wyckoff also served as director of the summer school. Donald Macleod stood at the center of preaching. An accomplished scholar in New Testament studies and literature, he drew on these fields more commonly than theology in his teaching or writing. W. J. Beeners was Professor and Director of Speech. The Speech Department had its own staff and studios on the third floor of Stuart Hall, commonly known across the

---

[1] This chapter draws on interviews of former students and colleagues of Hiltner, Loder, and Bartow, who are featured.
[2] This incident is reported in *Redemptive Transformation in Practical Theology: Essays in Honor of James E. Loder, Jr.*, eds., Dana R. Wright and John D. Kuentze Rapids: Eerdmans, 2004), 13.

campus as "Beenersville." Beeners appointed all full-time speech teachers with the approval of the seminary president. These teachers were accorded faculty voice and vote but were not given faculty rank. The speech and preaching faculty worked together in a required preaching course, and much animosity sprang up between Beeners and Macleod after the preaching professors tried unsuccessfully to remove the speech professors from the course. Pastoral theology, too, had its own courses and special relationships with programs in Clinical Pastoral Education. Hiltner played a key role in establishing the Doctor of Ministry degree in 1971 and remained a dominant figure in this program until his retirement.

Thus, in the early 1960s, when Hiltner and Loder joined the faculty, the department of practical theology was largely a patchwork of separate areas. Each viewed itself as having proprietary rights over its own part of the curriculum. Within the department, very little attention was given to the nature of practical theology as a discipline or the sort of pedagogies appropriate to it as a distinct field. Hiltner, Loder, James Lapsley, and others would encourage the department to explore the shared responsibilities, pedagogies, and discourse running across the specialized areas of speech, preaching, pastoral care, and Christian education. The department would gradually become a confederation, a differentiated unity of specialized areas with overlapping methods and pedagogies. The tension between specialization and commonality has remained a focal point of ongoing conversation in practical theology to the present, not only at PTS but also in the field as a whole.

The New Discussion of Practical Theology: 1960-2000

Princeton's story is no different than that of other departments in the "practical field" during the early 1960s. The specialized fields of religious education, preaching, and pastoral care and counseling were dominant. Each area had its own guild and journals, and structured course offerings around the competencies of its own specialization. A counter-voice to this pattern of specialization began to emerge in practical theology during the 1960s and developed significant momentum in the decades that followed.

In the 1980s, the American Association of Practical Theology began to attract prominent figures from many different areas of practical theology, including Don Browning, James Fowler, Mary Elizabeth and Allen Moore, and James Poling. In recent decades, APT has gained significant strength as an academic guild, and several of its leading members organized a working group at the American Academy of

Religion.[3] New guilds in practical theology were established around the world. The Société Internationale de Théologie Pratique was founded in 1992, the International Academy of Practical Theology in 1997, and the International Society of Empirical Research in Theology in 2002. New journals and book series began to appear, like the *International Journal of Practical Theology,* the *Journal of Empirical Theology*, and international series in practical theology sponsored by Lit Verlag, Eerdmans, Peter Lang, and other publishing houses.

Several social and intellectual trends led to the flowering of practical theology between 1960 and 2000, not just at PTS, but also more broadly. The most comprehensive trend was the emergence of global institutions and communications media. From the economy to international law to global media to popular culture, globalization reshaped many features of contemporary life. It is no accident that international academies and publications emerged during this period.

One of the most globally significant events in religion during this period was the Second Vatican Council, which opened up new thinking about the Roman Catholic Church's pastoral mission. In the wake of Vatican II, Catholic scholars in Europe and North America began to explore what pastoral and practical theology might look like in the Catholic tradition, sparking a new ecumenical spirit in these fields. Protestants learned from Catholics like Thomas Groome, James and Evelyn Whitehead, Robert Schreiter, Robert Kinast, Bernard Lee, Johannes van der Ven, Claire Wolfteich, and Kathleen Cahalan, to name a few. During this period, moreover, the one major systematic theologian to give a prominent place to practical theology in his writings was the Roman Catholic scholar David Tracy. At the same time, Catholics learned from Protestants like James Fowler, Don Browning, Bonnie Miller-McLemore, Rebecca Chopp, James Poling, and Daniel Schipani, among others. After Vatican II, the field of practical theology in the United States became one of the richest arenas of ecumenical conversation in the world.

A second global trend in religion to have a major impact on the new discussion of practical theology was a "turn" to praxis. This was sparked by South American liberation theology, European political theology, international feminist theology, and various indigenous theologies. The resulting interest in praxis was strengthened in the United States by the

---

[3] In 2005, Bonnie Miller-McLemore, Jim Nieman, and Gordon Mikoski submitted a successful proposal that established the Practical Theology working group within the academy.

emergence of the neo-pragmatism of Richard Rorty, Jeffrey Stout, Cornel West, and Robert Brandom. In this context, practical theology no longer had to apologize for its longstanding interest in praxis/practice. It was well situated to make an important contribution to this discussion, as seen in Don Browning and Charles Foster's writings on theological education.

These broad global trends were interconnected with trends taking place in religion in the United States. One of the most important of these was the decline of denominationalism as the primary structuring force in American religion.[4] While many American seminaries and divinity schools retained some sort of denominational affiliation throughout this period, their student bodies became far more diverse. They included more women, second career students, non-denominational students, and greater racial, ethnic, and international diversity. These changes in the student bodies of theological schools reflect additional national trends during this period: the entry of large numbers of women into higher education and the work force, as well as the increased diversity of American religion.

From the 1960s to the present, theological schools have experimented with a variety of curricular patterns to respond to the challenges these trends present, though no single pattern has become dominant. Theological schools have had to ask a series of novel questions. How might schools of theology teach students from different cultural and ecclesial backgrounds and of different races, genders, and ages? How might they teach students who will carry out ministries in remarkably different contexts? How might they prepare students to engage other religions and other fields beyond the theological disciplines? A least part of the reason practical theology flowered during this period had to do with its readiness to engage these questions. For almost a century, Protestant practical theologians had grappled with contextuality, interdisciplinarity, and the relationship between theory and practice, issues that theological education as a whole began to face during this period. Roman Catholic practical theologians have joined them in these efforts and have made their own important contributions to the new discussion of practical theology.

Practical Theology during the McCord and Gillespie Years

As the new discussion of practical theology emerged around the world, it also flowered at PTS. In the remainder of this chapter, we will

---

[4] For an account of this trend, see Wuthnow, *The Restructuring of American Religion*, cited in chapter three.

examine models of practical theology developed by prominent figures in each area of the department of practical theology: Seward Hiltner in pastoral theology, James Loder in Christian education, and Charles Bartow in preaching, speech communication in ministry, and worship. It is significant that faculty in each departmental area published material explicitly framing their specialized field in terms of practical theology. It is noteworthy that other members of the department did so as well.[5] This is an important indication that the older pattern of separate "fiefdoms" was being modified in the direction of a common intellectual discourse about the nature and pedagogies of practical theology. During this period, the department also began to accept responsibility for shared tasks like course planning and approval, admissions of PhD students, and teaching a required doctoral seminar in practical theology, even as it continued to affirm the importance of specialized areas.

The department truly flowered during the McCord and Gillespie years. It became larger and more diverse. It is hard to overstate the importance of the support of the two presidents during this period. Both were strongly committed to a vision of theological education at PTS that affirmed high academic and intellectual standards, on the one hand, and strong connections to the church, on the other. The seminary, they believed, was in a unique position in American theological education. Like university-related divinity schools, it sponsored a doctoral program and supported a high level of scholarship among the faculty. Like denominationally-related seminaries, it was committed to the education of pastors, missionaries, Christian educators, and pastoral counselors. While committed to the Presbyterian Church, it attracted students from other denominations and, more recently, non-denominational congregations. It was also committed to attracting a substantial number of international students.

A key part of the leadership of McCord and Gillespie was their ability to strengthen the financial resources of the seminary. They invested this money in the seminary's programs, physical plant, financial aid, faculty, administrative staff, and new initiatives—all with an eye to strengthening its mission. When McCord began his presidency in 1959, the seminary was operating on a deficit budget. In a budget of less than

---

[5] These include Conrad Massa, Campbell Wyckoff, James Lapsley, Craig Dykstra, Thomas Long, Nora Tubbs Tisdale, as well as a variety of people who have been members of the department since 2000. Indeed, the number of departmental members who describe their specialized field in the context of practical theology has increased markedly over the past decade.

$2 million, its accumulated deficits were $800,000.[6] The endowment had a market value of $6.76 million. By 1992, nearly half way into the Gillespie presidency, the operating budget was $24 million and the endowment had a market value of over $400 million. When Gillespie retired, the endowment stood at $801.2 million. It reached a high of $1.13 billion on September 30, 2007. In addition to the leadership of the presidents, the financial strength of the seminary rested on a combination of the long bull market from the 1980s and the wise investment strategies of the Board of Trustees.

The department of practical theology benefited from the vision and financial resources marshaled by McCord and Gillespie. During these years, for example, the seminary established the Joe R. Engle Institute for Preaching and the Institute for Youth Ministry, and regularized the status and compensation of all teachers in the Speech Department upon their integration into the department of practical theology as ranked faculty. Gillespie raised financial resources that allowed the founding members of the International Academy of Practical Theology to gather at PTS for an organizational meeting in 1996. PTS hosted the first meeting of the Academy the following year. Scholarship in the service of the church lay at the heart of McCord's and Gillespie's vision of the seminary's mission.

When Seward Hiltner challenged Jim Loder to clarify the assumptions of his course proposal, it was a sign of a new level of intellectual engagement of the issues surrounding practical theology in the department. But it also was a sign of the new discussion of practical theology emerging around the world between 1960 and 2000. In order to flesh out the framework of this new discussion, we will listen to its echoes in the lives of three PTS scholars. We begin with Seward Hiltner.

Seward Hiltner: Perspectival Practical Theology
Biography

Seward Hilter was born in Tyrone, Pennsylvania in 1909. He graduated from Lafayette College in Easton, Pennsylvania in 1931, having majored in English and minored in psychology. He entered the University of Chicago Divinity School the following fall. During this period of his life, Hiltner began his involvement in what was later known as the Clinical Pastoral Education Movement, while completing a

---

[6] William Selden, *Princeton Theological Seminary: A Narrative History—1812-1992* (Princeton: Princeton University Press, 1992), 148.

Bachelor of Divinity and starting a Ph.D. at Chicago.[7] During his first year at Chicago, he attended a seminar by Anton Boisen on "Summer Clinical Training" and spent the next two summers in clinical programs in Pittsburg and Worcester, supervised by Donald Beatty and Carroll Wise, respectively.[8] He successfully passed the comprehensive exams for his doctorate during his fourth year at Chicago.

Before writing his dissertation, Hiltner took a lengthy occupational detour. Helen Flanders Dunbar invited him to join the staff of the Council for Clinical Training for Theological Students, and he served as the executive secretary from 1935 to 1938. One of his primary responsibilities was to persuade seminaries of the value of clinical training and to help establish standards for clinical programs.[9] In 1938, Hiltner moved to the Federal Council of Churches to serve as the director of the Commission on Religion and Health.[10] In this position, he organized the first meeting of representatives of all groups and seminaries involved in clinical training in 1945, an important step toward the eventual adoption of national standards in 1953.[11]

Throughout this period, intense debate arose among different programs and leaders about the role of theology in clinical training. Hiltner argued that clinical training for future pastors should be theological at its core, even as it also should include clinical, empirical, and psychological components. This was a position that would later come to expression in books like *A Preface to Pastoral Theology* and *Theological Dynamics*. Hiltner joined the faculty of the University of Chicago Divinity School as Professor of Pastoral Theology in 1950 and finally completed his doctoral dissertation two years later. In 1961, he moved to PTS as professor of theology and personality, a position he held until his retirement in 1980.

Hiltner was a complex figure at PTS. He was a gifted teacher who made extensive use of verbatims and case studies in his classes and the

---

[7] Originally, this movement was known as Clinical Pastoral Training. It officially became Clinical Pastoral Education after the merger of various training organizations in 1967.
[8] John McDonough Cassem, *An Analysis of Seward Hiltner's Systematic Pastoral Theology and Its Value and Application to Contemporary American Catholic Pastoral Theology* (Washington: STD Thesis, Catholic University, 1974),10. Additional biographical information can also be found in James Lapsley, "Pastoral Psychology: Editorial – Seward Hiltner, 1909-1984," in *Pastoral Psychology*, 34:1, 3-8.
[9] Cassem, *Hiltner*, 12-4.
[10] Hiltner also served as the executive secretary of the Department of Pastoral Services in the Federal Council, as well as the Commission on Ministry in Institutions.
[11] Hiltner wrote up the minutes of this meeting, which were subsequently published as *Clinical Pastoral Training* by the Commission on Religion and Health in 1945.

Doctor of Ministry program. As chair, he is remembered as pressing the department toward "greater intellectual coherence and theological integrity," in the words of one interviewee. This is apparent in Hiltner's contribution to a student-faculty seminar for PhD students in 1963, "Introduction to Practical Theology as a Theological Discipline." He outlined what it means to have a doctoral program in practical theology as part of a larger discussion of the field:

> Our Department does bear this name, and we find it of value to have a theory about "practical theology" especially in relation to inquiry, research, and doctoral studies. For doctoral students the following general implications may be seen to follow from the preceding analysis: 1. The doctoral student...whatever his area of specialization, has some obligation toward the larger discipline. 2. The student's specialized study, whatever its content, should contain theological dimensions...and implications, which he is capable of articulating critically and constructively. 3. The student should strive for competence in relating theory and practice.[12]

Yet Hiltner's former students and colleagues also shared stories of a more demanding and, in the words of some, even a "dark" side to Hiltner. Doctoral students sometimes felt that he used his clinical skills in ways that left them feeling exposed before their peers. He was described by a former colleague as getting his way in departmental meetings "by ratcheting up the level of conflict until others dropped out." As department chair, he sent lengthy memos to members of the department whose classroom performance, in his view, lacked intellectual depth.[13] During Hiltner's years at PTS, moreover, he experienced personal tragedy and suffering. His son committed suicide, and his daughter suffered from severe mental illness. Hiltner himself developed a drinking problem. Herbert Anderson characterizes Hiltner's theological anthropology as

---

[12] Seward Hiltner, "Introduction to Practical Theology as a Theological Discipline," Seward Hiltner Collection, Special Collections, Princeton Theological Seminary Library.

[13] This is mentioned in the tribute to Hiltner immediately following his death: "Seward Hiltner was exacting of himself and others, and when either failed to measure up to high standards, his temper could flare along with the bluntness of communication, which did not always achieve the result he desired. His extended memos to colleagues about matters in which he perceived their performance to be less than adequate are a part of 'Hiltneriana' at Princeton." See, "Seward Hiltner (1909-1984)," *The Princeton Seminary Bulletin,* 7:1 (1986), 76-8.

pointing to "the ambiguities of the human situation" and "the paradoxes of humanness."[14] Perhaps this is an apt description not only of Hiltner's understanding of humanity, but also of the man himself.

The Constructive Contribution of Practical Theology

Seward Hiltner's most important contribution to the new discussion of practical theology at PTS and in the field was to challenge the idea that the so called practical fields have no constructive contribution to make to the larger theological enterprise. This notion is deeply entrenched in the Western philosophical tradition, which commonly has portrayed the "practical arts" as making no contribution to fundamental knowledge. Hiltner challenged this position by developing a perspectival model of practical theology.[15] If approached from a theological perspective and interrogated theologically, reflection on the concrete practice of ministry yields theological knowledge that cannot be gained in any other way. Rodney Hunter summarizes:

> Hiltner's basic thesis...is that pastoral theology can and ought to be conceived, not as a secondary professional or academic enterprise in which theology is somehow "applied" to practical work...but as a fundamental form of theological inquiry—basic research, as it were—that is focused on the empirical data of pastoral experience.[16]

---

[14] Herbert Anderson, "Toward a Constructive Anthropology: Hiltner's Paradoxical View of Persons," *The Journal of Psychology and Christianity*, 4:4 (1985), 54.

[15] The interpretation of Hiltner's understanding of practical and pastoral theology offered here is deeply informed by Rodney Hunter, Emeritus Professor of Pastoral Theology at Candler School of Theology Emory University. Hunter was a student of Hiltner at PTS in both the Masters of Divinity and PhD programs. While a doctoral student at Emory, Osmer had the good fortunate to take classes from Hunter, who was on his dissertation committee. Osmer even had the opportunity to meet Hiltner in one of Hunter's classes. This section draws on Hunter's published writings, as well as interviews and correspondence. Some of Hunter's most important articles and chapters on Hiltner are: "A Perspectival Pastoral Theology," in *Turning Points in Pastoral Care: The Legacy of Anton Boisen and Seward Hiltner*, eds., LeRoy Aden and Harold Ellens (Grand Rapids: Baker Book House, 1990), 53-79; "The Future of Pastoral Theology," in *Pastoral Psychology* 29 (1980), 58-69; "Moltmann's Theology of the Cross and the Dilemma of Contemporary Pastoral Care," in *Jürgen Moltmann: Hope for the World*, ed., Theodore Runyon (Nashville: Abingdon, 1979), 75-92. The description of Hiltner as offering a perspective practical theology is a play on the title of the first article cited above, though the intention here is to focus on Hiltner's broader understanding of practical theology and not his definition of pastoral theology.

[16] Hunter, "Perspectival Pastoral Theology," 56.

Hunter believes that Hiltner learned this from Anton Boisen. As we saw in the previous chapter, Boison believed that the study of "living human documents" is just as important as the study of sacred texts and doctrines.[17] Inquiry into ministerial practice yields theological knowledge that is different from, but as important as, the knowledge generated by other forms of theological inquiry.

One of the strategies Hiltner used to describe the constructive contribution of the practical fields was to locate them within a broader description of the task of theology as a whole. Drawing on Anselm's classical definition of theology as faith seeking understanding, he portrayed the task of theology in terms of "fidelity" and "relevance."[18] All forms of theology must take account of God's "final revelation" in Jesus Christ, but must also keep "faith and religion in touch with the changing social and personal forms of life."[19] In *Preface*, Hiltner made this point with William Temple's description of revelation as the "coincidence of event and appreciation":

> The revelation in Jesus Christ is final in that no further basic clue needs to be given or new type of work needs to be done by God for the salvation of man. But the assimilation and understanding of the revelation by man is never final, nor is that work of God ever done that attempts to help man receive the revelation.[20]

Revelation does not stifle theological reflection; rather, it evokes "the most discriminating inquiry that can be made."[21] In short, theology deepens the understanding of faith by relating God's final revelation in Jesus Christ to new cultural, historical, and personal contexts.[22]

---

[17] As Hunter observes: "Hiltner's claim is the more ambitious one of Boisen—that the encounter with human nature in the practical experience of ministry can contribute to the church's basic theological understanding." Ibid., 57.

[18] Seward Hiltner, *Theological Dynamics* (Nashville: Abingdon, 1972), 185-9. Hiltner also describes "relevance" with the concept of "communicability."

[19] Ibid., 187.

[20] Seward Hiltner, *Preface to Pastoral Theology* (New York: Abingdon, 1958), 221, n17. See also his comments on the following page about the importance of "future-oriented inquiry."

[21] Ibid., 22.

[22] Hiltner gave perhaps his clearest and most extensive discussion of this understanding of theology in *Theological Dynamics*, Chapter 9, in which he also appealed to John Calvin's portrait of the inextricable and necessary relationship between the knowledge of God and the knowledge of humanity to ground the importance of interdisciplinary work. See 198-201.

Practical theology contributes to this task in different ways from the other theological disciplines. In *Preface*, Hiltner described this in terms of the distinction between "operation-centered" and "logic-centered" fields.[23] All of the practical fields are operation-centered. Hiltner identified three operation-centered fields, based on what he calls the shepherding, communicating, and organizing perspectives. The logic-centered fields of theology include traditional areas like biblical studies, dogmatic theology, and church history, as well as new areas like aesthetical and comparative theology.[24] Hiltner illustrated what he meant by logic-centered in the following description of dogmatic theology: "The study of doctrine is organized systematically and logically around the relation of doctrines to one another and their mutually reinforcing capacity to give testimony to the total faith."[25] In contrast, an operation-centered field like pastoral theology "organizes theological reflection around the themes and issues presented by concrete, real-life, ongoing pastoral practice."[26]

The distinction between operation-centered and logic-centered is not without difficulties. At one point, Hiltner wrote: "Every theological discipline must be systematic," including the operation-centered fields.[27] Presumably, this means they too organize their material in a rational and logical manner. What, then, is the basis of Hiltner's distinction, if logic-centered and operation-centered fields both produce rational, systematic knowledge? The difference between the two appears to reside in their different subject matters and modes of inquiry.[28] Operation-centered fields seek to understand intentional human actions and practices with an eye to deepening and reformulating theological principles, themes, and theories that can guide them more effectively and faithfully in the future. They are inductive in the sense of being grounded in, studying, constructing knowledge out of, and shaping practice (operations). Logic-centered fields do not approach their subject matter from the standpoint of practical human actions aimed at achieving particular ends. Rather, they study texts, historical events, and doctrines in order to explain their organizing structures and principles in a logical manner.

---

[23] He borrowed the term "operations" from John Dewey. See, Hunter, "Perspectival Pastoral Theology," 56.
[24] These examples come from the chart in *Preface*, 28 and conclude with "Etc." Hiltner was clearly moving away from the older fourfold approach of the theological encyclopedia.
[25] Hiltner, *Preface*, 21.
[26] Hunter, "Perspectival Pastoral Theology," 56.
[27] Hiltner, *Preface*, 219, endnote 15.
[28] The following discussion draws on personal correspondence with Rod Hunter.

The Perspectives of Practical Theology

It may well be that Hiltner's attempt to divide all of theology into operation-centered and logic-centered fields was not fully adequate. More important to his proposal is the description of operation-centered fields as reflecting on intentional human actions and practices and constructing theological knowledge that both learns from and guides such actions and practices. This is the heart of his model of practical theology. Within this model, Hiltner identified three operation-centered theological fields. Each is oriented around a different perspective. Pastoral theology is oriented around the shepherding perspective; ecclesiastical theology, the organizing perspective; and educational/evangelistic theology, the communicating perspective. Each perspective addresses a different dimension of the church's ministry at a different level of its life:[29]

> *Shepherding* – tender solicitous concern toward individuals or small groups of persons who are experiencing some form of suffering or other personal needs, including existential questions of faith and practice; here, persons are addressed in their individuality.
>
> *Organizing* – building up the church as a living fellowship with various internal structures and relationships and with various external relationships to the wider community; here the church as an organization with social and institutional needs is addressed.
>
> *Communicating* – communicating saving truth through the articulation of the gospel in various ways; here, the cultural and symbolic dimension of the church and world are addressed, the need for meaning, truth, and moral vision.

Hiltner also argued that different "aspects" may be distinguished within each perspective. In *Preface*, for example, he described the shepherding perspective as including the aspects of healing, sustaining, and guiding. Healing orients pastors toward situations in which some restoration and recovery is possible. Sustaining, in contrast, orients them toward situations in which healing is not an immediate possibility or

---

[29] This summary of these perspectives draws on Hunter, "Perspectival Pastoral Theology," 61.

possibility at all (e.g., a person dying of cancer) but a sustaining pastoral presence may be offered. Guiding orients pastors toward situations in which moral and spiritual guidance is needed but must be "educed" (drawn out, not prescribed) in order to promote the growth of the parties involved.

Hiltner's perspectival model of practical theology was highly creative and deserves more serious attention than it has received. It represents an alternative to the long tradition of practical theology that focuses on the specialized competencies of preaching, teaching, pastoral care, and other activities carried out by the minister.[30] In Hiltner's model, perspectives, not conventional roles or tasks, provide the organizing principle of practical theological reflection. In complex, concrete situations, pastoral leaders must discern the perspective most needed. In a confirmation class, for example, a pastor or youth leader might need to set aside a well-crafted lesson plan and bring the shepherding perspective to bear upon a young person who is experiencing some form of suffering. Likewise, in a pastoral counseling relationship, a pastor might need to bring the communicating perspective to bear on a counselee who needs to receive a straightforward and clear presentation of the gospel. Roles, tasks, and settings alone do not determine the sort of actions that should be taken. Rather, actions are organized around the perspective best suited to the objective needs of the situation and the subjective judgment of the pastor.[31]

In Hiltner's teaching and writing much attention was given to helping ministers learn how to read the particularities of a situation and to discern which perspective could guide their actions. His approach was typically inductive, starting with cases or critical incidents and only gradually moving to theories appropriate to a particular perspective. A perspective, however, provides an important theoretical and interdisciplinary orientation to the situation at hand. The shepherding perspective, for example, marshals the resources of therapeutic psychology and theological reflection on human caring in order to direct healing, sustaining, or guiding. The communicating perspective, likewise, marshals the resources of communication theory, performance studies, educational theory, and developmental psychology, as they illuminate a particular situation.

To summarize, Hiltner's perspectival model of practical theology brought together a description of the operation-centered fields and a description of three distinct perspectives. Operation-centered fields are

---

[30] This way of organizing the field was found in the writing of Charles Erdman, examined in Chapter 3. Erdman followed the standard literature of practical theology in dividing the field into homiletics, liturgics, ecclesiastics, poimenics, catechetics, archagics, and alieutics.
[31] Hunter, "Perspectival Pastoral Theology," 59.

distinguished from other forms of theology in the way they reflect on intentional human actions in which moral and theological aims are at stake. The three perspectives bring into focus different dimensions of the church's ministry at a different level of its life: shepherding, communicating, and organizing. In his writings and in his leadership of the PTS department of practical theology, this model offered a powerful way of affirming both the unity and the specialization of practical theology as a field.[32] In retrospect, Hiltner may be judged as making important contributions, not only to the PTS department of practical theology and the pastoral care and counseling movement, but also to the new discussion of practical theology.

---

[32] At times, Hiltner emphasized the *distinctiveness* of pastoral, ecclesiastical, and educational/evangelistic theology, which are coordinate with the shepherding, organizing, and communicating perspectives, respectively. He described them as distinct fields, as different from one another as biblical studies is from dogmatic theology. This, perhaps, is most evident in the chart given in *Preface,* on page 28. On the same page, he warned against reducing these perspectives and their respective forms of theology to a single "master discipline." See also, his comments in *Preface*, on page 24, where he was critical of older attempts in nineteenth century theological encyclopedias to define practical theology as a single discipline "coordinate with biblical theology, doctrinal theology, and historical theology, and seen in the same series." He can be interpreted here as critiquing the "tree and branch" metaphor of the older theological encyclopedias, which draw on a common understanding of science (tree) in order to differentiate the four branches of theology. This model makes all forms of theology of "the same series," that is, drawing on the same model of science. This, of course, would eliminate Hiltner's concern for the distinctiveness of the practical arts and, thus, he rejects this way of conceptualizing theology. Cf., ibid. 218, n12, where he was critical of the term, "theological science." Yet there are many places where Hiltner underscored points of commonality and overlap across the three perspectives. This is evident in his description of the education of doctoral students in practical theology at PTS, where he claimed that such students have an "obligation toward the larger discipline" beyond their particular areas of specialization. Moreover, in *Preface* and "The Teaching of Practical Theology in the United States during the Twentieth Century" in *The Princeton Seminary Bulletin*, 61:1 (1977), 61-75, Hiltner offers historical overviews of practical theology, along with pastoral theology. Most important of all, the two most fundamental concepts in *Preface* that are used to describe the operation-centered fields—*operations* and *perspectives*—are not just used to characterize pastoral theology but ecclesiastical theology and educational/evangelistic theology, as well. At points, Hiltner offered a comprehensive definition of practical theology in which its organizing principle is "functional rather than logical." Practical theology as a whole is oriented to the "proper study of functions with resulting systematization of knowledge" which "leads to a body of knowledge and not merely to skill or technique." See, *Preface*, 218, nn12 and 13. In short, Hiltner's model of perspectival practical theology described *both* the unity and the specialization of the field.

James Loder: Fundamental Practical Theology
Biography

James Loder was born in Lincoln, Nebraska in 1931.[33] He had a sister, affectionately known as Francey Kay, who died as a young adult from complications related to diabetes. Loder's father, Edwin, was a high school principle. His mother, Frances, was interested in drama and literature and, for part of her life, was on the faculty of the University of Texas in speech and drama. Neither of Loder's parents participated in organized religion, though they supported their son when he began attending church on his own as a child. Loder attended high school in Kansas City, Missouri, where his family moved, and Carleton College in Northfield, Minnesota, where he majored in philosophy. After graduating from Carleton in 1953, he entered Princeton Theological Seminary and received a Bachelor of Divinity degree in 1957.

In an interview with one of his former students, Dana Wright, Loder shared a significant experience that took place during his first year of seminary.[34] His father was diagnosed as having brain cancer and died fairly quickly. At home and in deep grief, Loder grew seriously ill and was confined to bed. He called out to God, "Do something!" To his surprise, his body was enveloped by a "warming presence," leading him to get up out of bed and begin singing, "Blessed Assurance, Jesus is Mine." He started reading one of his seminary textbooks, Emil Brunner's *The Scandal of Christianity*, and recognized it as testifying to the truth he had just experienced. Loder later shared this experience with Hans Hofmann, a Swiss theologian who had studied with Brunner. Hofmann directed him to the writing of Søren Kierkegaard to help him process this mysterious experience of God after his father's death. Thus began Loder's lifelong passion for Kierkegaard. His dissertation and first book were on Kierkegaard (and Sigmund Freud), and he drew on Kierkegaard in virtually all of his published writings. Throughout his years as a professor at PTS, he offered a limited-enrollment, upper level seminar on Kierkegaard, which often served as a training ground for future doctoral students.

---

[33] This biographical sketch of Loder's life draws on Freda Gardner, "James Edwin Loder, Jr.: A Tribute," *The Princeton Seminary Bulletin*, 23:2 (2002), 188-94 and Dana Wright, "Are You There? Comedic Interrogation in the Life and Witness of James E. Loder," in Wright and Kuentzel, *Redemptive Transformation*, 1-40, and "James E. Loder, Jr," *Christian Educators of the 21st Century*, Talbot School of Theology database, www.talbot.edu/ceacademic. See also, Kenneth E. Kovacs, *The Relational Theology of James E. Loder: Encounter and Conviction*, (New York: Peter Lang, 2011).

[34] Wright and Kuentzel, *Redemptive Transformation*, 13.

After graduating from PTS, Loder joined Hofmann at Harvard where he worked as an assistant on Hofmann's interdisciplinary research project. This period proved critical to Loder's early formation as a scholar. He received a ThM from Harvard Divinity School (1958) and a PhD in the History and Philosophy of Religion from Harvard's Graduate School of Arts and Sciences (1962). While completing work on his dissertation, he was a Danforth scholar at the Menninger Foundation in Topeka, Kansas, where he worked with Seward Hiltner and Paul Pruyser. As Wright notes, Loder's time at Harvard afforded him the opportunity to study with some of the greatest scholars of his era: Talcott Parsons, David McClelland, Paul Tillich, James Luther Adams, Paul Lehmann, and Robert Bellah.[35]

Upon completing his PhD, Loder was invited to return to PTS as Instructor in Christian Education in 1962 and was later appointed as the Mary D. Synnott Professor of the Philosophy of Christian Education in 1982. The word "philosophy" in the title of this chair was significant, for he often drew on philosophy in his courses and writings. Loder loved teaching what he often described as "foundational" courses in Christian education and practical theology. He turned out to be a brilliant teacher in spite of the extremely demanding, academic nature of his courses. His introductory course in Christian education soon had the largest student enrollment of any non-required Masters of Divinity course in the seminary curriculum. Loder also became one of the key contributors to the doctoral program in practical theology. He regularly taught the departmental seminar, attracted a steady pool of exceptionally strong doctoral students in Christian education, served on the dissertation committees of students in other areas, and was a long-time member of the PhD Studies Committee. Loder was also a regular participant in the Doctor of Ministry program.

In addition to his faculty responsibilities at PTS, Loder regularly offered "spiritual counseling" to students and members of the Princeton community. Trained in psychodynamics at the Menninger Clinic, yet awakened to the power of the Holy Spirit through a close encounter with death, Loder's counseling was something different than pastoral counseling or spiritual direction. His untimely death in 2001 kept him from writing about this practice; but, in his teaching and writing he often told stories emerging out of his spiritual counseling.

In his book *The Transforming Moment*, Loder recounted the life shaping experience noted earlier in this chapter. The Loder family was driving to Toronto and stopped to help an elderly couple on the side of

---

[35] Ibid.,14.

the highway. A passing motorist who had fallen asleep ran into the Loders' car, flipping it over, dragging Jim for some distance, and trapping him under the car. Staring death in the face, Loder experienced what he later would call a "transforming moment," an intense and deeply personal experience of God's presence. This episode proved to be lifechanging. In Loder's own words, it "raised countless new questions, disturbed several personal relationships, and forced me to reenvision the spiritual center of my vocation."[36] In an interview with Dana Wright, Loder shared the ways his academic work changed after this experience:

> Before 1970, I was doing all of my teaching within a basic psychoanalytic model, that conflict learning is basic to psychoanalysis...After 1970 I realized it was the Spirit of God who creates the problem and guides us into truth. And the whole convictional picture in four dimensions began to become a way for me to talk about what I know had happened, and what could happen. And so, it was still conflictual, but now it had shifted into a much bigger perspective. And the dynamics involved were not just limited to the human spirit but also to the divine redemption in action.[37]

This comment clarifies why Loder's contribution to practical theology is not always easy to grasp. His writings are complex. But, perhaps even more importantly, the four-dimensional understanding of transformation articulated in the comment above challenges many of the assumptions that readers bring to Loder's work. It also challenges many of the assumptions embedded in contemporary practical theology.

Loder is sometimes described as developing a four-dimensional, *transformational paradigm* of practical theology. Human knowing, he argues, includes four dimensions: (1) lived experience, which encompasses the human construction of a meaningful "world;" (2) the self, the active agent in world construction who has the capacity to transcend lived experience through self-reflection and self-relatedness; (3) the void, the experience of the negation of being in which the lived world is ruptured; (4) the Holy, the eruption of new being in the face of non-being, the negation of the negation through which the self discovers

---

[36] James Loder, *The Transforming Moment: Understanding Convictional Experiences* (San Francisco: Harper & Row, 1981), 6.
[37] Wright and Kuentzel, *Redemptive Transformation*, 15-16.

meaning and new life beyond the void's rupture of lived experience and self.[38] Loder contended that much of human life is lived on a two-dimensional plane. It remains within the patterns of lived experience as these are shaped by socialization and appropriated by the human self. When the void is experienced through suffering and other disruptions of the social world, the common human response is to minimize such experiences and repair the patterns of everyday life as quickly as possible. Genuine transformation, in contrast, enters the void and discovers the contingency of finite existence. It discovers a new grounding point in the Holy beyond a two-dimensional world, which opens up the possibility of new forms of being, acting, and relating.

An important part of Loder's project involved describing the way this transformational paradigm is potentially present in all of life. But the heart of his project as a practical theologian was articulating the way human transformation is itself transformed through the Holy Spirit who joins human beings to the redemptive transformation of Christ. Early in his career, he described this as convictional knowing: "Convictional knowing is the patterned process by which the Holy Spirit transforms all transformations of the human spirit. This is a four-dimensional, knowing event initiated, mediated, and concluded by Christ."[39] It is important to keep this four-dimensional understanding in mind as this discussion now turns to Loder's formal description of practical theology and, then, to the substantive theological claims that articulate his constructive position.

Fundamental Practical Theology

Near the end of his life, Loder wrote two articles that developed his formal description of practical theology as a field: "Normativity and Context in Practical Theology: The Interdisciplinary Issue" and "The Place of Science in Practical Theology: The Human Factor."[40] These articles, like his other published writings, were not written for a broad reading public. They addressed academic specialists in practical theology and other fields.[41] Moreover, they were the fruit of decades of reflection. In a very

---

[38] Loder, *Transforming Moment*, Chapter 3.
[39] Ibid., 92.
[40] James Loder, "Normativity and Context in Practical Theology: The Interdisciplinary Issue," in *Practical Theology—International Perspectives*, eds., F. Schweitzer and J. van der Ven, and "The Place of Science in Practical Theology: The Human Factor," in *The International Journal of Practical Theology*, 4 (2000), 22-41.
[41] "Normativity and Context," was originally an address to the Academy and "Science in Practical Theology," published in the *Journal of the Academy*.

real sense, Loder did practical theology for many years before standing back and reflecting methodologically on what he had done. To use his own way of putting it, we might say he "indwelled" the subject matter of practical theology in order to allow the patterns of its relationships and intelligibility to disclose themselves.[42] Articulating the fundamental disciplinary issues of practical theology was one of Loder's strengths. He believed that focusing primarily on practical models and techniques ultimately eviscerated the constructive contribution of the field. As Loder often put it, there is nothing more practical than a good theory.

Perhaps, the best way of describing Loder's contribution is to portray him as writing fundamental practical theology.[43] Don Browning was probably the first practical theologian to use this term to describe his own work.[44] It is an appropriate way of characterizing Loder as well, as long as it is recognized that Browning's goal was to describe all of theology as practical and Loder's to identify the core problematic of the specific field of practical theology. Both Browning and Loder address basic theoretical issues and view "how to" methods and programs as grounded in fundamental practical theological reflection.

In his two articles on practical theology, Loder attempted to describe what he calls the "generative problematic" of this discipline. He argued that this encompasses three defining features: (1) practical theology's focus on action, more exactly, theories of divine and human action, (2) its commitment to interdisciplinary thinking and dialogue, and (3) the self-implication of the practical theologian in his or her investigation of the subject matter of the field. Loder began by asking a basic question: What is the nature of a discipline? He answered by defining a discipline as "a communal tradition of procedures and techniques for dealing with

---

[42] James Loder, *The Knight's Move: The Relational Logic of the Spirit in Theology and Science* (Colorado Springs: Helmer & Howard, 1992), 90-2.

[43] The first person to refer to Loder's work as fundamental practical theological science was Dana Wright. See, *Redemptive Transformation*, 416-20.

[44] Don Browning, *A Fundamental Practical Theology* (Minneapolis: Fortress, 1991), 7-8. Drawing on the recent turn to "practical philosophy" in Gadamer, Ricoeur, and Habermas, Browning outlined a proposal in which *all* fields of theology are portrayed as integrated "subspecialties of the larger and more encompassing discipline called fundamental practical theology." He did not focus exclusively on the field of practical theology. In this description of Loder's work as fundamental practical theology, the focus zeroes in on this field alone and to the core features of its generative problematic. Dana Wright is correct in describing Loder as developing a "fundamental practical theological science" in *Redemptive Transformation*, 416.

theoretical or practical problems."[45] A discipline, he argued, grows static unless it continues to engage its "generative problematic," which enables it "to transcend the enculturated structure of the discipline and invent new paradigms which depart from, but are nevertheless legitimate heirs of, what has gone before."[46] He described the core features of the generative problematic of practical theology as follows:

> In practical theology, the core of the discipline is not its operations, procedures, practices, roles, congregations, and the like. Rather, its core problematic resides in why these must be studied; why these are a problem…The fundamental problematic implied in this question, and what drives this discipline forward and generates its issues, is that such phenomena or events combine two incongruent, qualitatively distinct realities, the Divine and the human, in apparently congruent forms of action. Because this field requires an inclusive theory of action, even the methodology for approaching this problematic cannot itself be detached from its claims about action in the field at large. The methodology that attempts to come to terms with this problematic, and to bring it…into a form that can guide and govern the field as a whole, is the centerpiece of practical theology as a discipline.[47]

This passage provides insight into Loder's claim that *action* is a core dimension of practical theology. Unlike Hiltner, Loder did not believe that reflection on concrete actions or practices is the grounding point of the field. Rather, he argued that articulating an "inclusive theory of action" is more important. Pastoral actions and practices assume such theories, and a key task of practical theology is to identify these assumptions and to examine them critically. Otherwise, practical theology will simply reinforce the conventional patterns of church life in a particular social context or merely reiterate the taken-for-granted disciplinary patterns into which practical theologians are "enculturated." If practical theologians, for example, were simply to focus on how to teach well in a Sunday School class or how to offer pastoral care along the lines of psychotherapy, they would never question the assumptions guiding such actions. Practice is

---

[45] Loder, "Normativity and Context," 374, n2.
[46] Ibid.
[47] Ibid., 374-5, n2.

theory laden, as Loder sometimes put it. It is the task of fundamental practical theology to identify and evaluate these implicit "theories" of action as part of the broader task of constructing a comprehensive theory of divine and human action. Otherwise, pastors and practical theologians will remain trapped in a two-dimensional world.

In the passage above, Loder pointed to this dimension of practical theology's generative problematic when he described it as investigating events that "combine two incongruent, qualitatively distinct realities, the Divine and the human, in apparently congruent forms of action." Here, Loder affirmed the theological task of the field and the possibilities of redemptive transformation. Practical theology views individual and social actions as encompassing more than human action alone. They also involve God's action, the source of redemptive transformation. A key task of fundamental practical theology, thus, is articulating a comprehensive theological theory of divine and human action in which these qualitatively different realities—God and humanity—are both involved. Ultimately, such theories may be quite helpful in assessing and guiding concrete actions in particular situations and, even more importantly, in spotting the possibilities of redemptive transformation opened up through the present action of the Holy Spirit.

While Loder strongly upheld the theological task of practical theology, he also affirmed interdisciplinary thinking and dialogue as a second dimension of the generative problematic of this discipline. "Addressing this problematic requires an interdisciplinary methodology that systematically establishes a relationship between theology and the human sciences" in a manner that is "nonreductionistic, mutually illuminating, and constructive for both sides of the relationality."[48] Over the course of his work, Loder would expand this to include the natural sciences.

Why must practical theology engage the natural and human sciences? In a number of his writings, Loder offered a contextual reason: the challenge of an all-encompassing scientific and technological culture.[49] In this context, practical theology needs to learn from science; but science needs to learn from practical theology and other normative fields as well. Loder argued that science is the most important way modernity understands and explains the world. Practical theology must learn from science as part of a larger quest to grasp the intelligibility and relationality

---

[48] Loder, "Normativity and Context," 359.
[49] See, for example, Loder, "Science in Practical Theology," and the opening chapters of *The Knight's Move*.

of God's creation. The findings of sciences like psychology, anthropology, evolutionary biology, neuroscience, and sociology throw a great deal of light on human action and are particularly helpful to practical theology.

But science also needs to learn from practical theology and other normative fields. Loder believed this is the case because science is distorted in the present context. It has become the servant of technological innovation, reducing its purpose to the manipulation of reality for material advantage. It needs to learn from disciplines that raise questions of the meaning and purpose of life if it is to serve as more than the research base of an endless stream of trivial consumer novelties or, even worse, of technologies that ultimately destroy planet earth. It especially needs to become open to the possibilities of redemptive transformation in Jesus Christ, which point to the reordering and healing of a creation wounded by the technological juggernaut unleashed by science.

This brings us to the third dimension of Loder's understanding of the generative problematic of practical theology: the self-involvement of the practical theologian in the subject matter of the field. This is not unique to practical theology, he believes, but it has important implications for this field. Drawing on Michael Polanyi and Søren Kierkegaard, Loder argued that the self-involvement of knowers in the discovery and construction of knowledge is a dimension of all theology and science.[50] Knowers and the known are mutually implicated. Knowers cannot investigate an object or field without influencing it. Nor can they truly understand an object or field unless their tacit and explicit knowing are shaped by the object or field under investigation. As Loder often explained, knowers must "indwell" the subject matter, allowing its intelligible patterns and relationships to impact their constructions in order that true knowledge may emerge.

Loder believed it is especially important to acknowledge the self-involvement of the knower in theology, for its primary subject matter is God and the world in relationship to God. In part, this is because human beings have turned away from God in sin and must rely on God-as-Subject to shape their knowledge. They must allow the assumptions of their two-dimensional world to pass through the void of not knowing for new knowledge to emerge. Loder unpacked the practical theological implications of the self-involvement of the knower along three lines.

---

[50] One of the clearest brief descriptions of his perspective is found in "Science in Practical Theology," 28-30.

First, practical theologians must carry out their work with "fiduciary passion," from the stance of a committed and trusting relationship of faith in the God revealed in Jesus Christ through the Holy Spirit. Their posture must be one of passion, in Kierkegaard's sense. In interviews of his former doctoral students and teaching fellows, Loder was described as embodying this passion in his teaching. His lectures were filled with stories, moments of prayer, and, sometimes even tears, as they explored highly intellectual matters. In seminars, Loder shared his own engagement of the subject matter and evoked personal, spiritual, and intellectual responses to the material from students. He did not expect them to agree with his perspective, but he did expect them to engage the material with passion.

Second, and closely related, the self-involvement of practical theologians means they should approach their work as theologians who are a part of a particular religious community that takes its bearings from God's self revelation in Jesus Christ. Too often in the twentieth century, practical theologians turned to other fields, like social science or psychology, to construct their theories. To claim the mantle of scientific respectability, they bracketed out their self-involvement in the subject matter they were investigating: God's action in Jesus Christ and continuing action in the Holy Spirit in the contemporary world. As we have seen, Loder was fully committed to practical theology's dialogue with other fields. But the starting point in this dialogue is theological, a commitment to theos-logos, intellectual discourse about the God in whom Christian theologians believe as part of a community of believers.

Third, the self-involvement of practical theologians entails creative engagement of their subject matter. They must transcend the "enculturated structure of the discipline" and invent "new paradigms which depart from, but are nevertheless legitimate heirs of, what has gone before," as Loder wrote in a quotation offered above. It is, perhaps, at this point that Loder's understanding of transformation was most apparent. It is not enough for practical theologians to merely repeat the reigning assumptions of their field at a given time. They must engage them with criticism and creativity, opening up the possibility of new insights and perspectives that may transform the dominant paradigms of the field. For Christian practical theologians, this represents one of the ways they participate in the Holy Spirit's transformation of the human spirit.

A Constructive Framework of Practical Theology

Thus far, this chapter has provided an overview of Loder's formal description of practical theology as a discipline, though it is obvious that his substantive theological commitments shape his perspective. The next section turns to his constructive contribution to this field. What sort of comprehensive theory of divine and human action did he develop? How did he portray interdisciplinary work in practical theology? How did he describe his involvement in the subject matter he was investigating as a practical theologian? Loder's answers to these questions are complex and were developed over many decades. Moreover, previous sections have outlined already key components of his transformational paradigm. The purpose of the following discussion is to provide a brief overview of other themes important to his constructive framework.

Relationality as the Key to Divine and Human Action. The theme of relationality runs through all of Loder's writings. Along with redemptive transformation, it is the most important concept he used to develop a comprehensive theory of divine and human action. The theme of relationality was present in his depiction of the Trinity, the inner nature of Christ, the Holy Spirit, the human spirit's relationship to the Holy Spirit, and the relationship of the contingent order of creation to the Creator. Loder's use of this theme reflected a broader turn to relationality. Across the modern period, a variety of philosophers, theologians, and scientists have criticized substance theory and granted ontological priority to relationality in their accounts of being. To put it simply, beings do not merely have relationships, they are their relationships. They are constituted in and through relationality. LeRon Shults and others have traced the development of this theme across modernity, and there is no need to rehearse their accounts here.[51] The present task is to summarize Loder's understanding of relationality and how he used it to construct a comprehensive theory of divine and human action.

Loder realized that many different types of relationships exist in the world. He was primarily interested in relationality that takes the form of an asymmetrical, bipolar-relational unity.[52] Among Loder's

---

[51] See, F. LeRon Shults, "The Philosophic Turn to Relationality and the Responsibility of Practical Theology," in Wright and Kuentzel, *Redemptive Transformation*, 325-46.

[52] Loder offered one the most succinct discussions of his understanding of this form of relationality in *Knight's Move*, 55, where he wrote: "Bipolar-relationality understandings arise when inquiry into a situation or object discloses that its nature is manifested in two very different, contextually incompatible (mutually exclusive) perceptual levels—both of which are required in order to gain a comprehensive understanding of the situation or object under investigation. For instance, the nature of light manifests itself as both particle and wave in empirical investigation. When the observed phenomenon must be understood as consisting of two conceptually distinct levels in hierarchical relationship, it constitutes what we are calling an asymmetrical, bipolar-relational unity."

interpretators, this is sometimes called the "strange loop" or "Möbius band" model because Loder often illustrated asymmetrical bipolar-relational unity with a picture of M.C. Escher's Möbius Strip II.[53] The model describes an object or situation that may be accounted for in two incompatible ways, both of which are required to gain a comprehensive understanding of the object or situation. An example Loder often used was modern physics' description of light as both particle and wave. One might also think of the relationship between human bodies and minds or individual family members and a family system.

In each case, two poles can be identified. Each is conceptually distinct, and they may even appear to be mutually exclusive. How can we affirm the free agency of individual family members and the power of family systems? Is it not a matter of either/or? Loder argued that both poles are necessary and are best conceptualized as standing in a bipolar relational unity in which each influences the other. Unless both poles are affirmed, one pole ends up being explained in terms of the other. We see this kind of reductionism, for example, in accounts of the human mind that explain it exclusively in terms of the structures and processes of the body, most commonly the central nervous system. A similar reductionism is at work in family systems theories that eliminate altogether the histories, personalities, and unique capacities of individual family members.

Loder was quite critical of this sort of reductionism, for he believed that both poles are necessary to understand families, light, or the human mind. Yet he did believe that in many instances of bipolar relationality, one pole exerts "marginal control" over the other. He described this as follows: "Marginal control represents a condition in which the bipolar structure's 'lower' level is controlled by the laws governing its constituent components, but is also controlled by being subject through its boundary conditions to determination by the laws regulating the 'higher' level."[54]

In the home, for example, the family system exerts marginal control over family members, though the agency of individuals is not eradicated. Likewise, the human mind exerts marginal control over the human body, even though it is clear that bodily conditions impact the functioning of the mind. The poles stand in a bipolar relational unity that is asymmetrical, with one pole exerting marginal control over the other.

Loder believed this model of relationality is applicable to many areas of life. He also believed that it has been articulated along somewhat

---

[53] See, for example, ibid., 41.
[54] Ibid., 54.

different lines in various disciplines. He examined, for example, the thinking of the developmental psychologist Jean Piaget and of the physicist Niels Bohr, in terms of the strange loop model of relationality. He argued, however, that the quintessential expression of this model is found in theology, particularly, the writings of Søren Kierkegaard, Karl Barth, and T. F. Torrance. He drew on their writings to construct his own comprehensive theory of divine and human action. Though he focused his attention primarily on Jesus Christ and the Holy Spirit, he did so in the context of a description of the relationality of the Trinity.

In Loder's view, the Trinity is the ultimate expression—indeed, the grounds—of bipolar relational unity: one God in three Persons. In *The Knight's Move*, he traced the discussion of the Trinity in the fourth century, during which theologians posited the full and distinct personal reality of the divine persons along with their inseparable unity. He found the concept of perichoresis as developed by the Cappadocian theologians particularly helpful. They affirm the distinct personhood of each member of the Trinity and the unity of the Godhead in terms of their mutual interpenetration and reciprocity. As Loder put it: "Perichoresis, then, takes on an inherently relational quality in the writings of the Cappadocian fathers. Thus, the unity of the Trinity is the relationality, and the relationality is the unity. Further, each one implies all three yet the distinction of each from the others is not lost."[55] The oneness and threeness of the Triune God is the quintessential form of bipolar-relational unity.

The Chalcedonian Paradigm as the Key to Interdisciplinary Method. Loder further developed this understanding of relationality in his account of divine and human action in Jesus Christ. While the present focus is Loder's interdisciplinary method, it is important to note from the outset that his Christological reflections have implications for all of life. As Loder put it: "Relationality is revealed to us definitely in the inner nature of Jesus Christ. In Christ's nature as fully God and fully human, we have the definition of relationship through which all other expressions of personal, social, and cultural relatedness are to be viewed."[56] Interdisciplinary thinking and dialogue, thus, are only one area of life that can be understood in terms of his Christological model of asymmetrical bipolar-relational unity. He described his model as a Chalcedonian paradigm of relationality.

---

[55] Ibid., 23.
[56] Ibid., 13.

Drawing on the writings of Karl Barth and T. F. Torrance, Loder argued that the Council of Chalcedon (451) provided three rules that describe the asymmetrical bipolar-relational unity of Christ's two natures.[57] First, in Christ the human and divine are differentiated, coexisting without the reduction of one to the other. Jesus is not merely a very good human being with certain godlike qualities; nor is he a god who only appears to be human. He is both human and divine, two poles that must remain differentiated. Second, the divine and the human coinhere in an inseparable unity. As the mediator of the relationship between God and humanity, Christ is necessarily both human and divine. He brings salvation to the world as the true human being before God and as the true God with human beings. Third, the relationship of the human and divine follows an asymmetrical order. The divine has ontological priority over the human. Jesus does not become God's Son by virtue of his of faith and obedience. He is God's Son who enters fully into finite existence as the incarnate Word of God. In short, the Chalcedonian paradigm describes the humanity and divinity of Christ as an asymmetrical bipolar-relational unity.

This is the key to Loder's approach to interdisciplinary thinking and dialogue. He developed has been called a "transformational" model, which made use of the three rules described above to describe the relationship between theology and the human and natural sciences.[58] The knowledge given to faith is unique and not to be confused with other forms of human knowledge. Theology, thus, must be differentiated from the natural and human sciences. Yet theology cannot carry out its work without engaging these sciences. They are inseparably joined in a bipolar unity. In constructive theological work, theology maintains marginal control over other fields. It listens to and learns from other fields but it transforms their insights when they are appropriated for theological purposes.

Transformation as the Key to the Holy Spirit's Relationship to the Human Spirit. As noted above, Loder portrayed the generative problematic of practical theology as including the self-implication of the practical theologian in the subject matter of the field. It involves the creativity inherent to transcending the "enculturated structure" of practical theology and inventing "new paradigms" in the field. This is a form of participation in the Holy Spirit's transformation of the human

---

[57] See Richard Osmer, *Practical Theology: An Introduction* (Grand Rapids: Eerdmans, 2008), 169-70.
[58] Ibid.

spirit. Thus it is to Loder's depiction of this theme during the last part of his career that this section turns.

Loder's thinking about this theme was an extension of his understanding of the Chalcedonian paradigm and the strange loop model of relationality. When the human spirit is open to the transformative power of Holy Spirit, the human spirit and the Holy Spirit stand in an asymmetrical bipolar-relational unity. The result is the christomorphic reshaping of the human spirit, which is transformed toward the likeness of Christ. To grasp this core feature of Loder's thinking, what he means by the human spirit, the Holy Spirit, and redemptive transformation needs to be further explored.

The human spirit and the Holy Spirit are both portrayed along the lines of the strange loop model. Two dimensions of relationality characterize the human spirit.[59] What Loder called the "view from below" drew on philosophy, neuroscience, evolutionary science, and other fields to portray the self-relatedness of human beings. Human beings are exocentric, that is, they are open to the world, transcending the drives of the animal world and the adaptational demands of the immediate environment. They rely on culture and their own personal interactions with the world to form knowledge. Moreover, there is an "I" in this knowing, a self that develops over time. Self-relatedness—a knower and the activity of knowing—stands at the very heart of the human spirit. This is the result of a long evolutionary process in which the exocentricity and transcendence of the human spirit emerged from an unfolding universe.[60]

Loder also described the human spirit from what he calls the "view from above." Here, theology comes to the fore. Loder drew on T. F. Torrance's portrait of the world as both a divine and contingent order. Loder unpacked the implications of this perspective for his understanding of the human spirit: "Human development and its reciprocity with the unfolding of the universe through time is the created and therefore contingent order. It has its own life and inherent lawfulness, but it is contingent on the undergirding, intervening, recreative, and redemptive order of God's action in creation."[61] The human spirit, he continued, "has a measure of constructive power, but

---

[59] While the relationality of human spirit and Holy Spirit is treated in virtually all of Loder's writings, this section draws on *The Logic of the Spirit: Human Development in Theological Perspective* (San Francisco: Jossey-Bass, 1998).

[60] This portrait of Loder lends support to Kovac's description of his work as best located in the personalist-relational tradition. See Kovacs, *Encounter and Conviction*, Chapter 1.

[61] Loder, *Logic of the Spirit*, 10.

without its proper ground, it becomes a loose canon of creativity." This is particularly the case in the face of human experiences of the void, the nothingness of death and experiences of suffering and vulnerability that threaten the human spirit. In the face of the void, human beings turn away from the ultimate ground of their existence, the God who created the world and entered it in Jesus Christ. The result is various forms of sin by which human beings set up false gods in the true God's place and attempt to secure their existence in the face of the void.

Loder, thus, explicated the human spirit in terms of two poles: humans are exocentric, self-transcending beings who have emerged from an unfolding evolutionary process *and* they are participants in God's creation, who long for God but have turned away from God in sin in response to experiences of the void. These two poles stand in an asymmetrical bipolar-relational unity. The view from below and the view from above are both needed. In his writings on the latter, Loder gave greatest attention to the Holy Spirit, whom he also explicated in terms of relationality.[62] While he affirms the centrality of the saving work of God in Christ, he rarely developed this extensively. Instead, he focused his attention on the ways the Holy Spirit mediates Christ's work through redemptive transformation of the human spirit. In the 1980s, Loder commonly described this in terms of a "transformational logic," which includes conflict, interlude for scanning, a constructive act of the imagination, a release of energy and greater openness, and a new interpretation of one's self and world.[63] Near the end of his life, he described the Spirit's transformation of the human spirit in terms of awakening, purgation, illumination, and unification.

Two "transforming moments" in Loder's life story initiated a journey that shaped his teaching, research, and writing as a practical theologian. To say that he was self-implicated in the subject matter of practical theology would be an understatement; he viewed it as the redemptive transformation found in Christ through the power of the Holy Spirit. He engaged this subject matter with passion, bringing together his personal, spiritual, and intellectual journey at the deepest level. In his view, this sort of passionate engagement of the subject matter, involving creativity and transformation,

---

[62] See, for example, *The Knight's Move*, 22-8.
[63] For his account of the logic of transformation, see Loder, *The Transforming Moment*, Chapter 2 and "Transformation in Christian Education," in *The Princeton Seminary Bulletin*, 3:1 (1980), 11-25. The second perspective is found in *Logic of the Spirit*, Chapter 3.

is not merely an optional or idiosyncratic feature of his model of practical theology. It is fundamental to this field as a form of theology.

Charles Bartow
Biography

Charles Bartow was born in Raritan, New Jersey in 1937 and raised nearby in Middlesex. He graduated from high school in 1955. From an early age, he was identified as gifted musically and, by the age of twelve, was invited to join the chancel choir of the local Presbyterian Church. He enrolled at Michigan State University in 1955, and upon his graduation three years later, immediately began work on a Masters degree in Television Broadcasting at MSU. Among the courses he took for this degree were courses on the oral interpretation of literature and mass communications, both of which would later become important to his work as a professor of speech communication in ministry.

Prior to completing his Master's thesis, Bartow enrolled at PTS in 1960, where he took courses from Conrad Massa and Donald Macleod in preaching and W. J. Beeners in speech. The single most important event this time occurred during his final year when he preached his senior sermon.[64] This was required of all students, and they were given feedback by one of the preaching professors. In Bartow's case, the respondent was the great Lutheran preacher, Paul Scherer, who was a visiting professor at the seminary. Scherer's comments, in Bartow's own words, were "devastating, describing the sermon as sub-Christian, as completely failing to communicate grace and the manifest action of Christ." He continues, "I was furious when the session was over, and it took me two weeks before I finally realized that he was right. I had given a clever address and little more. It was a kind of Damascus Road experience for me, which brought me out of the 'dark woods' of moralistic preaching. This started me on my long journey toward an adequate theology of proclamation."[65]

Immediately following his graduation from PTS, Bartow was invited to begin teaching full time in the speech department by Beeners. During his first year of teaching, he completed his masters thesis and received his masters degree from Michigan State. Three years later, he began doctoral work at New York University, which culminated in a dissertation in which he drew on the writings of the English theologian, H. H. Farmer, to

---

[64] Personal Interview, August, 2010.
[65] Ibid.

develop criteria for evaluating the content and delivery of sermons.[66] Upon his graduation in 1971, Bartow began teaching in the speech and theatre department at Mansfield State College in Mansfield, Pennsylvania, where he offered courses in speech and the oral interpretation of literature. He also established a degree emphasis in broadcasting. He then served as pastor of the Deep Run Presbyterian Church in Bucks County, Pennsylvania from 1974-80. In 1980, he was invited to join the faculty of San Francisco Theological Seminary, where he served as Professor of Speech Communication and Homiletics. He also served as "convener" of the doctoral program in Religion, Theology, and the Arts at the Graduate Theological Union. In 1991, after eleven years at SFTS, he joined the PTS faculty as the Carl and Helen Egner Professor of Speech Communication in Ministry. Appointed to the chair previously held by W. J. Beeners, Bartow joined the faculty the year the speech department was integrated into the department of practical theology. In addition to his primary work in the area of speech, he taught courses in homiletics and worship, was an active participant in the PhD program in practical theology, and served as chair of the department from 1993-1998. He retired in 2009, though he continues to teach speech courses at the seminary.

God's Human Speech: A Practical Theology of Speech and Homiletics
Of Bartow's numerous books and articles, the most important for this study is *God's Human Speech: A Practical Theology of Proclamation*. It advances our argument that prominent faculty members in all the areas of the department developed a model of practical theology to frame their specialized fields. This is particularly noteworthy with regard to speech, which was not fully integrated into the department until 1991.[67] Written in the years immediately after this institutional shift and published in 1997, *God's Human Speech* represents the first publication by a speech professor to articulate what it means to view this area as a form of practical theology. This trajectory was carried forward by Bartow's younger colleague, Nancy Lammers Gross in *If You Cannot Preach Like Paul*.[68]

---

[66] The dissertation title was: "An Evaluation of Student Preaching in the Basic Homiletics Courses at Princeton Theological Seminary: A Farmerian Approach to Homiletical Criticism."
[67] Bartow, "In Service to the Servants of the Word: Teaching Speech at Princeton Theological Seminary," *Princeton Seminary Bulletin* 13:2 (1992), 277, n12. Speech was once "integrated" into the department via Beeners himself who held the position of Professor and Director of Speech. Other speech faculty, however, were "teaching administrative appointments." Though they had voice and vote in the faculty and department, none held rank or were tenure track.
[68] Nancy Lammers Gross, *If You Cannot Preach Like Paul* (Grand Rapids: Eerdmans, 2002).

God's Human Speech is an important book in its own right. It is a splendid example of practical theology deeply rooted in the Reformed tradition. In a field that has often been dominated by rhetoric or poetics, it provides a striking example of interdisciplinary dialogue in which the perspective of practical theology remains primary, even as it is brought into conversation with rhetoric, performance studies, oral interpretation of literature, and other fields. Perhaps, most important of all, *God's Human Speech* carries out constructive work in practical theology, transposing the Reformed tradition's threefold understanding of the Word of God into a theory of divine and human action that can guide the preaching of pastors. This constructive contribution lies at the very heart of Bartow's book.

A Model of Practical Theology

At the outset of *God's Human Speech*, Bartow describes the purpose of the book as writing a "practical theology of the spoken word, that is, of proclamation."[69] Its goal is "to serve the servants of the Word," to help ministers reflect on and strengthen their preaching.[70] Practical theology has a special contribution to make to preaching by virtue of the distinctive way it carries out the theological task. Bartow describes this as follows: Practical theology "is always and of necessity local and performative, inductive and interdisciplinary."[71]

By local and performative, Bartow has in mind the way practical theology deals with specific forms of praxis, concrete actions like worship, preaching, teaching, and care-giving. As activities that are performed, they typically involve elements of choice, calculation and commitment. They are also public; that is, they draw on socially shared meanings and roles and are performed in the context of "audiences" and "co-actors." Such activities are local in the sense of being conducted in particular times and places, in contexts with histories. Bartow comments on these two elements: "Practical theology in its descriptive, constructive, and critical moves always starts with concrete, performative acts, and it sticks with them. Even in its most theoretical moments those acts are kept in focus."[72]

Bartow portrays practical theology as characterized by two additional elements. It is inductive and interdisciplinary. It is inductive in seeking the significance of the performative acts being studied. As Bartow puts it:

---

[69] Charles Bartow, *God's Human Speech: A Practical Theology of Proclamation* (Grand Rapids: Eerdmans, 1997), 1.
[70] See Bartow's inaugural lecture, "In Service to the Servants of the Word," cited above.
[71] Bartow, *God's Human Speech*, 1.
[72] Ibid.

"Since those acts are usually public and calculated and a function of commitment, it may be assumed that they hold significance for those engaged in them—and perhaps for others as well. Practical theology seeks to explicate that significance, hold it up to scrutiny, and construct theory that may serve as a guide to further practice."[73] The critical study of such acts is necessarily interdisciplinary, Bartow goes on to argue. The significance of performative acts is complex and multidimensional and requires the critical scrutiny of various fields. Understanding the significance of particular acts of Scripture reading and preaching, for example, requires a theological lens. But these acts may also be helpfully explored with the perspectives of fields like "the semiotics of language and vocal and physical gesture, literary theory and rhetoric, even aesthetics."[74]

While Bartow does not explicitly state the interdisciplinary method informing his work, in an interview, he acknowledges that his method is akin to Hans Frei's *ad hoc* correlational method.[75] Informed by Karl Barth, Frei argued that theology necessarily engages other fields of scholarship, but when it appropriates them for its own purposes it should not do so at the level of a system. Rather, their insights are integrated in an *ad hoc* manner, placed in the service of theology. This is what Bartow does in *God's Human Speech*. Drawing on knowledge of fields such as rhetoric and performance studies, as well as his reflective practice as a preacher and teacher of preaching, he appropriates in an ad hoc manner the insights of a variety of fields in the service of a practical theology of proclamation.

Bartow's understanding of practical theology overlaps Hiltner's in certain ways. Both argue that the field is oriented toward concrete practice. Both also believe that fundamental theological knowledge can emerge from reflection on such practice, knowledge as basic and as important as that found in other branches of theology. Near the end of *God's Human Speech*, Bartow offers several of his sermons as examples of the homiletical theory articulated in the book. He introduces them by writing:

> These sermons may fail to measure up to the criteria for homiletical criticism explicated in the preceding chapter. On the other hand…the theory may fail to measure up to the practice. In other words, there is always the chance that the

---

[73] Ibid., 2.
[74] Ibid., 2-3.
[75] For an overview and references to Frei's interdisciplinary approach, see Osmer, *Practical Theology: An Introduction*, 169-70.

practice of preaching—itself being theory laden—will reform constructive homiletical thought and criticism.[76]

The inductive examination of local, performative acts may yield theological insights that cannot be gained any other way. Practice grounds theory in practical theology and has the potential of transforming it.

Bartow also argues that practical theology's contribution to fundamental theological knowledge is evident in what it "adds" to the preacher's interpretation of biblical texts. He affirms the preacher's use of the critical methods of biblical studies in studying a particular text, as well as knowledge of a text's interpretation across history and theology, as found in church history and dogmatic theology. But he argues that a carefully crafted performance of a text, as well as its study through performance analysis, affords knowledge not offered by the other theological disciplines. Having offered a performance analysis of Psalm 27 to illustrate this approach, he underscores the fundamental knowledge that emerges from this way of approaching the Psalm:

> Performance is not just an act of technical virtuosity following upon scholarly analyses of the work and totally dependent upon them. Instead, it is a type of public criticism that brings fresh understanding to the work, and so contributes to the body of knowledge concerning it.[77]

As preachers explore how to perform a text in their sermon preparation and in their actual preaching, they acquire certain knowledge that cannot be gained merely by studying it as literature or a historical artifact. Bartow, thus, shares with Hiltner the belief that practical theology's orientation toward concrete ministerial practice yields knowledge that is fundamental to the theological enterprise as a whole. His model of practical theology also shares certain features with Loder's approach. Like Loder, he believes that practical theology has the responsibility of articulating a theory of divine and human action that

---

[76] Bartow, *God's Human Speech*, 147.

[77] Ibid., 90. In a similar fashion, on page 91, he writes: "Categories of performance analysis are brought into play not only upon completion of one's preparation of the text for public reading, but as part of that preparation. Performance analyses are undertaken along with, and not just after, historical-critical, form-critical, generic, stylistic, and thematic analyses." Cf., "Who Says the Song? Practical Hermeneutics as Humble Performance," *The Princeton Seminary Bulletin,* 17:2 (1996), 143-53.

frames the entire practical theological enterprise. In Bartow's case, this is found in his portrait of the threefold Word of God with the concepts *actio divina* and *homo performans*.

The Threefold Word of God

In the Reformed tradition, dogmatic theology has often portrayed the interrelation of Jesus Christ, sacred Scripture, and the living proclamation of the church as three forms of God's Word.[78] This can be summarized in the following way: God's Word, the Logos, incarnate in Jesus Christ, is attested in Scripture and proclaimed today in the verbal communication of the gospel.

The first form of the Word, Jesus Christ, is granted theological priority over the other forms. Christ not only uses human words to announce God's salvation of the world, but also *is* God's Word who accomplishes this salvation through his life, death, and resurrection. The second form of the Word, Scripture, derives its authority and status from its witness to Christ in the context of God's election of Israel. As a witness, the words of the Bible and the Word of God do not stand in a mechanical or one-to-one relationship. Rather, Scripture is God's Word in the sense that God uses it as an instrument or medium to address the church.[79]

The third form of the Word is proclamation. It is the announcement of the gospel, based on the interpretation of Scripture, in ways that fit the situation of the hearers. God remains the true Subject of proclamation, not merely in the sense that it is about God, but also, that it is of God. God uses human words to render the gospel real and efficacious in the lives of particular hearers through the power of the Holy Spirit. In the Reformed tradition, proclamation includes more than pulpit discourse. Any human discourse that bears witness to the gospel is a form of proclamation. But Reformed theologians have typically viewed preaching in the context of worship as a divinely appointed means of the Word's continuing self communication. Moreover, preaching holds before the church its task as a witnessing community. It is called into being to serve as an ambassador of the gospel through whom God is making God's appeal.

God's Human Speech builds on this Reformed theology of the threefold Word of God. Bartow does not merely reiterate this theology along the lines of dogmatic theology or, even, "applied" dogmatics.

---

[78] For an excellent discussion, see James Kay, *Preaching and Theology*, Preaching and Its Partners (St. Louis, Missouri: Chalice Press, 2007), Chapter 1.
[79] See ibid., 15.

Rather, in a highly creative fashion, he explicates the interrelationship of the three forms of the Word in a manner appropriate to practical theology. Preachers are offered a framework with which to approach the public reading of Scripture and the preaching of sermons as performances of God's Word. They are taught how to engage biblical texts, attend to the particularity of local contexts, and make use of the resources of fields like rhetoric, performance studies, and oral interpretation of literature with an eye to their primary task: the proclamation of God's Word in preaching.

Actio divina and *homo performans* are the key theological concepts of the framework Bartow develops to articulate his theory of divine and human action in preaching. *Actio divina* describes God's self-performance in Jesus Christ, the interpretation of Scripture, and the living proclamation of the church. *Homo performans* describes human actions that are responsive to God's action in each form of the Word. Bartow develops these concepts with a theological version of critical realism.[80] Near the beginning of the book, he introduces this perspective in general terms: "Objectively we are addressed by God and claimed by God in Jesus Christ from without. Subjectively, we appropriate that address and claim through an act of faith, which is the work of God's own Spirit within us."[81]

In philosophy and social science, critical realism is a position that affirms the reality of a world independent of the human mind without lapsing into the naive correspondence theories of older forms of realism.[82] It recognizes that human understanding of the objective world is always fallible because it is shaped by language and interpretive patterns. It takes the hermeneutical dimension of science and human knowing seriously. It resists the idea that human knowledge is nothing but a form of social construction. For example, the shape of the world did not change when people abandoned a "flat earth" theory. What changed was their understanding of the world, a world that is independent of their prior interpretive framework. In critical realism, disciplined inquiry attempts to offer the best account possible of mechanisms and properties to explain some feature of the objective world, though such accounts remain subject to future revision.

---

[80] References to critical realism are scattered throughout *God's Human Speech,* but see especially 61-3, where he draws on the work of Violet B. Ketels and Wentzel van Huyssteen.
[81] Ibid., 22.
[82] For an overview, see Christian Smith, *What Is a Person?* (Chicago: University of Chicago Press, 2010) and William Outhwaite, *New Philosophies of Social Science: Realism, Hermeneutics, and Critical Theology* (New York: St. Martin's Press, 1987).

In *God's Human Speech*, Bartow develops a theological version of critical realism that focuses on God's Word. The objectivity of God's self-performance (*actio divina*) is portrayed in ways that are appropriate to each form of the Word. God is truly present in the Word. This divine objectivity, however, is unlike that of any phenomenon or object of the created world. God is immanent and transcendent, fully revealed in the incarnation of Jesus Christ and yet still being revealed in human experience through the Holy Spirit. In describing this objectivity as *actio divina*, Bartow points to the nature of the divine object as active subject.

Homo performans points to the subjectivity of human responsiveness to God's Word. Bartow affirms a robust role for human experience and action in preaching while resisting the idea that preaching is nothing but a human activity. God remains the objective, self performing Word in Jesus Christ, Scripture, and proclamation. The task facing preachers is to allow this objectivity to guide their subjectivity, broadly understood—their interpretation and public reading of biblical texts and their composition and performance of sermons. Subjectivity, as used here, does not refer to the internal states of individuals. Rather, it refers to the way human subjects are shaped by their transactions with the objective world, including God. In the theological inquiry of preachers and practical theologians, it refers to the way their methods, hermeneutical strategies, and performances are shaped by the divine "object" they are investigating.

One of the most striking examples of this perspective is Bartow's discussion of three figures of speech: oxymoron, metaphor, and metonymy.[83] An oxymoron is a figure of speech that combines terms that are normally contradictory: a virgin mother, a sound of sheer silence, a burning bush that is not consumed. A metaphor is an analogy between two fields in which the more familiar is used to describe certain features of the unfamiliar field: the kingdom of heaven is like treasure hidden in a field, a merchant in search of fine pearls, or a net thrown into the sea. Metonymy employs a term closely related to a larger reality to refer to that reality: Christ's work of reconciliation is indicated by singing about the cross, Golgotha, or his broken body.

This sort of figurative speech is found throughout Scripture and Christian discourse, and Bartow argues that each figure articulates a different dimension of the human experience of divine self performance.[84]

---

[83] The discussion of figurative speech begins in Chapter 2 of *God's Human Speech*. See especially 25-6.
[84] A nice summary is found in ibid., 144-5.

Oxymoronic figures of speech focus on the discontinuities experienced in divine self disclosure. Metaphoric tropes express this discontinuity in terms of the familiar, signaling difference in sameness and continuity. Metonyms signal transcendence in immanence.

Figurative language of this sort in Christian discourse is a kind of test case of Bartow's theological account of critical realism. Obviously, such language is fashioned by human beings in acts of great creativity. But even figurative speech is referential, Bartow argues, drawing on the thinking of Violet Ketels.[85] It brings to expression human experiences of the divine actor who enters into but remains beyond their experience. As Bartow explains: "In their use of heightened figures of speech, such as oxymoron and metaphor, biblical authors…are not simply emoting. They are gesturing toward what is there, acting on the biblical authors, causing them joy, anguish, hope, despair." [86]

Proclamation and Jesus Christ: The First Form of the Word

What is the significance of Jesus Christ, the first form of the Word, for the public reading of Scripture and the preaching of sermons? Bartow answers this question by transposing the Chalcedonian formulation—Jesus Christ is fully divine and fully human—into a pattern of divine and human action that can guide proclamation. He insists: "Jesus Christ therefore is not only the definitive locus of *actio divina*. He is also the locus of *homo performans*."[87] This has implications for proclamation along three lines.

First, it portrays Jesus Christ as the objective, definitive reference point of God's self revelation and reconciliation of the world. Ultimately, Christian proclamation is based on and points to the one true object of faith, Jesus Christ. In Bartow's view, this means that narrative has a certain priority in preaching, for it is uniquely suited to tell the story of the kerygma, of the life, death, and resurrection of Jesus Christ.[88] But something even more important is at stake. The object of proclamation is not merely the story of a dead man of the past. Jesus Christ is the living Lord who was raised from the dead and reigns at the right hand of the Father. He continues to address the church and the world through his Spirit. Bartow articulates the dynamic quality of the object of preaching by describing Jesus Christ as the locus of *actio divina*, God's self-performance. The one Word of God, incarnate in Jesus, remains the

---

[85] Ibid., 61-3.
[86] Ibid., 62.
[87] Ibid., 95.
[88] Ibid., 100, 104.

active subject of divine self performance. Preaching and Scripture reading are authorized sites of this continuing, divine self-performance. They are God's human speech, human performances which Christ may appropriate to address the church and world today.

Second, this characterization of the object of preaching as Jesus Christ's continuing self performance through the Spirit is coupled with a description of the appropriate human response, the *homo performans* that preaching seeks to evoke. Here again, Jesus Christ provides the normative pattern. Jesus preached the Kingdom of God and embodied God's kingly rule. He formed a community of disciples who lived within God's reign. Ultimately, this is the appropriate, subjective response to God's Word today, just as it was during Jesus' earthly ministry. Bartow exhorts: "Let the church discover what it means for God to reign over the church; then the church will know what part it is to play in the plan of God."[89]

Third, Bartow uses the theme of divine accommodation to ground the particularity and contextuality of preaching in the first form of the Word. He takes the theme of accommodation from John Calvin, who borrowed it from rhetoric. In rhetoric, it describes the way a rhetor must adapt a speech to the audience's capacities and the particulars of an occasion and setting. Calvin used it to describe God's gracious accommodation to human beings' finite condition and their entanglement in the reality of sin, an accommodation that occurs supremely in the incarnation of Jesus Christ.

Building on this understanding of divine accommodation, Bartow points to the scandal of particularity in Jesus Christ, born a Jewish male in a particular time and place.[90] This provides a warrant for the particularity inherent to every act of preaching. He elaborates: "God's own eternal Word is protean in its power to accommodate itself to humanity's poor necessity…God does this specifically, contextually, definitively—and not provisionally—in every epoch of cosmic and human history, and among all sorts and conditions of humanity, that men and women of all times and places might hear the Word that stands forever."[91]

Proclamation and Scripture: The Second Form of the Word

Bartow also uses the concepts of *actio divina* and *homo performans* to describe the second form of the Word, sacred Scripture. His proposal is highly original and represents an important contribution to practical

---

[89] Ibid., 59.
[90] See especially ibid., 26-34.
[91] Ibid., 35-6.

theology. The heart of his account is a portrait of the dynamic objectivity of Scripture as an "arrested performance." A written text in the Bible "is a happening about to happen again, not as a mere repetition of what has happened before, but as a fresh, new happening, discernibly related to, but not completely determined by other, earlier performances of the work."[92]

Several analogies may explain what Bartow has in mind. Scripture is like a score of music. The notes on a page can hardly be considered the work itself. As Bartow observes: "Bach's 'Magnificat' is not sitting there on the page when the conductor opens the score. Magnificat is in the music about to happen."[93] The same is true of the script for a play or movie. The actual performance of a play in the theater or movie on the screen is the realization of the work. So too, the God of whom Scripture speaks has promised to continue speaking through its human words into the concrete lives of readers and hearers. Scripture is an arrested performance, a happening that may happen again whenever it is engaged.

Bartow argues that this way of conceptualizing the second form of the Word is consistent with the sort of "object" the Bible is as "a record of human experience of God."[94] He draws on the New Testament scholar, G. B. Caird, to explain what this means:

> All such experience would be illusory, however, unless it was accompanied by a rational confidence in the objective reality of that which occasioned it; it must be grounded in the existence of something which is independent of the experience itself.[95]

The contents of Scripture, thus, reflect human experiences in different times and places occasioned by God's self performance. They represent the record of the varied ways God has born "faithful witness to himself with the words of prophets and apostles."[96]

By describing Scripture as an arrested performance, Bartow indicates that contemporary human beings play a part in its continuing performance. While this is true of all Christians who read the Bible, he is particularly interested in describing the sort of "subjectivity" of *homo performans* of those who read and preach Scripture in the context of

---

[92] Ibid., 64.
[93] Ibid.
[94] Ibid., 58.
[95] Ibid.
[96] Ibid., 45.

public worship. In many ways, this leads us into a discussion of the third form of the Word, proclamation. Yet two characteristics of Scripture set the stage for its continuing performance.

First, like a musical score or written script, biblical texts offer "cues" in how they are to be performed. The careful interpreter will thus pay close attention to a text's historical context, intertextuality, phrasing, literary setting, and other features. These provide cues that constrain and enable a performance that has integrity and is not merely a matter of impulse or caprice. Such performances allow "form to come through," that is, they "give an account of the rule of God in Christ in the life of the church and world in light of what a biblical text, as performed work, says and does, asserts and signifies."[97] They heed the cues of the biblical text in rendering a fresh performance. Especially important in this regard is the preacher's attempt to establish the persona, or particular speaking voice, of the text, the voice that he or she will take up as his or her own.[98]

Second, readers and preachers of Scripture must take into account the "plural attestation" of the second form of the Word. The canon speaks with many voices, some "profoundly in conflict with each other."[99] The task is not to ignore this pluralism but to acknowledge it as a form of divine accommodation, an echo of the way God has used fresh words, perspectives, and cultural forms to address God's people in different times and places. This should inspire confidence that God will continue to speak afresh in new performances of the Word.

Proclamation and Preaching: The Third Form of the Word

To a large extent, this chapter has already covered the "objectivity" of the third form of the Word in its discussion of the first two forms. Preaching is grounded in Jesus Christ, who is both the primary subject matter and active subject in contemporary proclamation. Preaching is also grounded in Scripture, which provides a record of human experiences occasioned by God's self performance in the past and may occasion new performances in the present. In light of this account, how does a preacher remain a faithful servant of the Word? Bartow answers this question in a variety of ways.

One of Bartow's most important affirmations is that preachers never control God's self performance through their human words. God takes and

---

[97] Ibid., 100. For "form coming through," see, ibid., 70 and 22, n13.
[98] Ibid., 79, 90-1.
[99] Ibid., 66.

uses these words when and where God will. Preachers must never attempt to manipulate their hearers but must leave them free to find the meaning that God would have them find. Moreover, they must never confuse their interpretation of a biblical text with the one, true and final interpretation, as if they alone have the God's eye view. Every "interpretive performance" of a text communicates only part of its meaning. Bartow aphorizes: "Meaning is always more than what was meant."[100] God, moreover, remains free to evoke new meanings in future performances.

Bartow describes his theory of proclamation as transactional. Just as Scripture is the record of human experience occasioned by God, so too, contemporary preaching strives to serve God's self performance in the present within the particularities of human experience. Within this transaction, preachers can only proclaim God's Word if they take their audience's experience seriously. A sermon is a Word fitly spoken only when addressed to particular people in a concrete congregation and cultural setting at a concrete moment in time. This has four implications.

First, there is a place for preachers' own experiences in their transactions with the text. They approach the text as persons who are "in Christ" and bear witness in their sermons to what they have "seen, heard, tasted, felt, and been led to understand of God."[101] Preaching begins and is sustained in prayer. Second, there is a place for the experience of the historic community, brought to expression in the creeds and confessions of the church. In addition to the narrative proclamation of the kerygma, teaching also has a role in preaching, discursive and expository explication of "the Christian message as expressed in its classical documents."[102] While preachers must draw on their experience, they also have a responsibility "to know and tell something quite beyond [their] own experience. The teaching in preaching is ecclesial, not individual.[103]

Third, preaching must be pastoral, which speaks to the broader relationship of preachers to their congregations. They must be aware of the effects of their sermons on the listeners and must attempt to speak into their personal lives. This kind of sensitivity can only be gained if preachers are a part of the Christian friendship (*adelphoi*) that binds the congregation together as a fellowship in Christ. As Bartow puts it: "No preaching can be truly prophetic…that is not thus pastoral, personal, and

---

[100] Ibid., 96-97.
[101] Ibid., 95.
[102] Ibid., 106. Bartow is quoting John Baillie.
[103] Ibid., 107.

profoundly filial. Preachers do not only speak to their congregants, they speak with them on their behalf, and as one of them."[104]

Fourth, preachers must move beyond the bonds of fellowship in order to "exegete" their congregation and local community with the tools of cultural anthropology and congregational studies. Rather than preaching abstract sermons to a generic humanity, they must become familiar with the language, cultural practices, and ongoing needs of their particular community. Bartow links the significance of this understanding to the theme of accommodation: "To accommodate one's preaching to one's congregants, therefore is not a betrayal of the gospel. It is instead a mark of fidelity to the gospel. Sermon design, diction, and delivery are undertaken to facilitate congregants' hearing of God's Word. Consequently they cannot be undertaken without sensitivity to how congregants actually listen."

In short, proclamation, the third form of the Word, takes seriously its grounding in Jesus Christ and sacred Scripture, while attending to matters that allow the preacher to communicate the Word in a manner that is fitting to a particular audience, setting, and context. Divine self-performance (*actio divina*) meets human performance (*homo performans*) in preaching. This returns us to the grounding point of practical theology: local and performative acts of ministry that are studied both inductively and through the perspectives of diverse fields. In Bartow's case, theology remains primary. He develops a theory of the threefold Word of God in a manner appropriate to a practical theology of proclamation.

Summary and Concluding Reflections

In this chapter, we have examined models of practical theology found in the writings of a prominent faculty member in each area of the department of practical theology in the latter half of the twentieth century. The writings of Hiltner, Loder, and Bartow are substantial and represent important contributions to the larger field of practical theology. In the context of PTS, they point to the flowering of this field during the McCord and Gillespie years. Area "fiefdoms" began to loosen their grip on the department and a common intellectual discourse about the nature and pedagogies of practical theology began to be engaged. Others in the department have carried this discourse forward and, in many ways, it has become an even more prominent conversation at PTS today than in the past.

---

[104] Ibid., 114.

Chapter 6
A Continuing Conversation

Social commentators commonly portray the 1960s as a watershed in American history.[1] This decade was not only a time of political and cultural turmoil, but also the beginning of the transformation of long-standing institutional patterns of work, family, religion, education, sexual identity, and the nation-state. A variety of social movements arose during this period: the civil rights movement, the feminist movement, the ecological movement, the anti-war movement, and the gay and lesbian movement. These were followed by the resurgence of evangelicalism, Pentecostalism, and the Religious Right during the 1970s. The landscape of American religion was altered, with important implications for theological education and practical theology. During this period larger numbers of women and second career students began entering mainline seminaries. Student bodies also began to include greater racial, ethnic, denominational, and international diversity.

From the 1960s to the present, theological schools have experimented with a variety of curricular patterns in order to respond to changes in the composition of their student bodies and the changing landscape of American religion. No single pattern has emerged as dominant. Indeed, seminary faculty and administrators are, perhaps, more aware than ever that theological education today must develop

---

[1] Robert Wuthnow, *The Restructuring of American Religion* (Princeton, NJ: Princeton University Press, 1988). Robert Putnam and David Campbell, *American Grace: How Religion Divides and Unites Us* (New York: Simon & Schuster, 2010).

patterns that are highly contextual. They must take account of the particularities of a seminary's denominational history, the diverse needs of its students, and the challenges its congregations face in social contexts that continue to change.

During this period, Princeton Theological Seminary continued to attract very strong faculty to the department of practical theology. This included people like Craig Dykstra, Thomas Long, Nora Tubbs Tisdale, John Stewart, James Kay, and Donald Capps, all of whom made important contributions to their fields. Members of the department and students studying in the doctoral program were participants in a generative conversation in practical theology and, sometimes, made their most important contributions to this conversation after leaving PTS.

Craig Dykstra, for example, attended PTS as an MDiv and PhD student and, after teaching at Louisville Theological Seminary, joined the PTS faculty in the area of Christian education. In *Vision and Character* and *Growing in the Life of Faith*, Dykstra offered a penetrating critique of theories of moral and faith development, which were rooted in the cognitive psychology of Jean Piaget.[2] Perhaps more importantly, he began to lay the foundations for one of the most significant subject areas of recent theology: the discussion of Christian practices. This discussion has been particularly generative in American practical theology.[3] The influence of Alasdair MacIntyre, Edward Farley, and Iris Murdoch are readily apparent in Dykstra's work. Less apparent is the implicit dialogue that Dykstra is carrying on with two of his colleagues at PTS: Seward Hiltner and James Loder. His emphasis on practices shifts the focus away from the centrality of the pastoral leader in Hiltner's writings to the community of faith as a whole. It is here that faith formation and transformation take place as fundamental human needs are reshaped toward the purposes of God for the world. While Dykstra studied Kierkegaard with Loder as a doctoral student, he implicitly is critical of Loder's focus on individual transformation. He emphasizes the Holy Spirit's formative activity in and through the shared practices of congregations and in the practices of everyday life. After leaving PTS to

---

[2] Craig Dykstra, *Vision and Character: A Christian Educator's Alternative to Kohlberg* (New York: Paulist Press, 1981) and *Growing in the Life of Faith: Education and Christian Practices* (Louisville, KY: Geneva Press, 1999).

[3] The influence of the practices discussion can be seen in a wide variety of writings. For a nice introduction to its impact on practical theology, see *For Life Abundant: Practical Theology, Theological Education, and Christian Ministry*, eds. Dorothy C. Bass and Craig Dykstra (Grand Rapids: Eerdmans, 2008).

become senior vice president of religion at the Lilly Endowment, Dykstra has generated wide interest in these seminal ideas, which have proven especially important in practical theology. He illustrates nicely the way many PTS faculty and doctoral students have engaged the practical theology discussion while at the seminary and gone on to make major contributions to this field after leaving this institution.

Between 1960 and the present, one the elements of continuity has been the strength of the faculty and PhD program in the department of practical theology, which have supported a generative conversation about the purpose, methods, and pedagogies of this field. But this period is also one of change and discontinuity. Especially important are changes in composition of the student body faculty, and department, which gradually grew more diverse in terms of race, gender, and denominational affiliation. At least in part, this reflected the shift away from denominationalism as the dominant structuring force in American Christianity.[4] This was closely related to the decline of mainline Protestantism during the second half of the twentieth century, including the Presbyterian Church (USA). PTS maintained its commitment to an inclusive Reformed identity initiated during the Mackay years, even as it struggled to become more ecumenical, broadly understood. Its student body gradually included more students from a variety of denominational and non-denominational backgrounds. It also included more women, international students, and racial-ethnic minorities. Today, its student body remains one of the youngest in the United States. Yet many of its international and racial-ethnic students have worked in congregations and even served as pastors prior to entering the seminary.

The pages that follow trace some of the ways PTS has responded to changes taking place in the second half of the twentieth century— changes that are continuing to unfold. As the title of this chapter indicates, the conversation surrounding practical theology and theological education must continue alongside these changes.

Broadening the Conversation: Diversity in the Department of Practical Theology

> **PTS Alum**: I was here during the late sixties when the Vietnam War was going on. There were a lot of students who were at PTS because they didn't want to get drafted. This was

---

[4] Wuthnow, *The Restructuring of American Religion*.

before the national draft lottery, and you could still get out of the draft if you were in seminary. It was an interesting time to be here. A lot was going on at the university, especially the Black Power movement. And there were things going on at PTS. I remember that a group of students locked the Board of Trustees in the Board Room. I think they wanted them to make a public statement about the war. Of course, they were very polite about it. They did let them out to go to the bathroom. (laughs)

Osmer: Were social issues addressed in the classroom?

PTS Alum: Well some people addressed them. Dr. Shaull certainly did. But a lot of professors who were sympathetic with the anti-war movement kept their heads buried in their books. They didn't really teach about it in their classes. I remember Princeton as being pretty conservative pedagogically. Mostly lectures. Mostly academic study of their particular subjects.

Osmer: Who were your favorite teachers?

PTS Alum: Freda Gardner was head and shoulders above everyone else. Her teaching really imprinted on me. For one, while she lectured sometimes, most of the time she used highly creative teaching methods. Discussion, group projects, experiential pedagogies. She *modeled* creative teaching. Then we read about it and then tried to teach this way ourselves in the class or in our field education placements. Then we reflected on it. Then the whole process would start all over again. There was a constant flow of practice, reading, practice, and reflection. Even today, I still teach out of what I learned from Freda.[5]

Freda Gardner joined the faculty of Princeton Theological Seminary in 1961. While Gardner was not the first woman to teach at PTS, she and Katharine Doob Sakenfeld (Old Testament) were the first two women

---

[5] Personal interview conducted by the authors.

faculty members to receive tenure and serve as professors for many years.⁶ She later became the Director of the School of Christian Education and retired as the Thomas W. Synnott Professor of Christian Education. Prior to coming to PTS she taught sixth grade in public schools, and after further study at the Presbyterian School of Christian Education, was the director of Christian education at the Crescent Avenue Presbyterian Church in Plainsboro, New Jersey. Throughout her time at PTS, she was constantly involved in the church at the congregational, Presbytery, and denominational level. She served as Moderator of the General Assembly of the Presbyterian Church (USA) in 1999-2000.

As the above comments by a PTS alum make clear, Gardner is remembered by her former students as an exceptional teacher, someone who pushed the boundaries of pedagogy at PTS. A course she taught with Katharine Sakenfeld, "The Bible as Liberating Word," became one of the most popular courses at the seminary. Gardner is also remembered as a mentor of women students and as an effective advocate of their issues in the church and seminary in response to the Women's Movement, or "Second Wave" feminism, which emerged in the early 1960s and continued through the 1970s. In the decades that followed, feminism sparked a veritable intellectual and cultural revolution in the United States. In 1960, the year before Gardner was appointed to the faculty, just under 40% of women of all ages worked in the labor market. By 1990, this had risen to nearly 60%. Between 1960 and 2000, the percentage of bachelor's degrees awarded to women rose from 37% to 57%. Of all degrees conferred in higher education in 2009, nearly 60% were awarded to women.⁷ In challenging PTS to begin addressing women's issues, Gardner was an important voice for change on the seminary faculty.

---

⁶ Virginia Damon began serving as visiting lecturer in speech in 1964 and in 1968 became assistant director of speech. She is listed under administration, not faculty, in the biographical catalogue. Jean Cassat Christman was the first woman hired as an instructor in Christian education. She was followed by Harriet Prichard who taught Christian education for four years, including two at the rank of assistant professor. For a brief history of women at PTS, see Ingrid Meyer and Barbara Chaapel, "Years of Courage: Looking Back—and Forward—to Women at Princeton," *inSpire* (Spring 1997), 12-6.

⁷ See *Digest of Statistics*, U.S. Department of Education, which offered the following summary: *Associate's Degrees:* 167 for women for every 100 for men; *Bachelor's Degrees*: 142 for women for every 100 for men; *Master's Degrees*: 159 for women for every 100 for men; *Professional Degrees*: 104 for women for every 100 for men; *Doctoral Degrees*: 107 for women for every 100 for men.
http://nces.ed.gov/programs/digest/d07/tables/dt07_258.asp. Accessed, February, 2010.

Edler Garnett Hawkins was part of the regular PTS Faculty in the years 1971-9 as Coordinator of the Black Studies program and Professor of Practical Theology.[8] For several years prior to this appointment, he had served as an adjunct professor in the area of preaching. As a full time member of the faculty, his courses were offered in the areas of preaching and church administration, though they stretched far beyond the normal perceptions of the latter.[9] For thirty-one years, Hawkins had served as the minister of St. Augustine Presbyterian Church in the Bronx, New York. As a pastor, he was an important force for social change, promoting involvement in the Civil Rights Movement. He was also a force in the church. He was elected moderator of 176th General Assembly of the United Presbyterian Church in the USA and served on the Central Committee of the World Council of Churches.

Hawkins has been characterized as representing the "best of the 'holiness' tradition characteristic of, but not unique to, black religiosity," a tradition in which personal spirituality deeply rooted in the worshiping community and a strong commitment to social transformation go hand in hand.[10] His teaching "rested on the authority of his own personal witness. He had paid his dues."[11] This made him especially effective during an era when many seminarians had been involved in the Civil Rights and anti-war movements. It also allowed him to serve as a generous mentor to African American students. Courses like "Preaching in the Urban Crisis" and "Ministry in Urban Settings" challenged students to wrestle with issues of race, poverty, and authentic congregational witness. Under his guidance, African American students persuaded PTS to establish a program in which one visiting African American scholar would offer a course every semester. This allowed them to fulfill over 25% of their required courses in classes taught by outstanding African American scholars.[12]

One of Hawkins most important gifts to the seminary was the value he placed on the ministry of the church. In a setting that sometimes prized too highly the life of the mind and doctoral studies, he constantly

---

[8] African American Registry, available on-line at http://www.aaregistry.org/historic_events/view/edler-hawkins-civil-activist-his-ministry. Accessed March, 2011. See also, "The Harmonies of Struggle and Light: The African American Experience at PTS," *inSpire* (Summer 1998), no. 3
[9] Geddes (Guy) W. Hanson, "Edler G. Hawkins: The Princeton Years," *Church and Society* (November/December 1987), 74-81.
[10] Ibid., 75.
[11] Ibid., 76.
[12] Ibid., 76-7.

lifted up the high calling of the ministry of the church. As one of his former students put it, "It was like being struck repeatedly with a velvet hammer."[13] Hawkins embodied this high calling in his own person, and his students found him "available, unpretentious and wise."[14] At the time of his death in 1977, several of his PTS colleagues characterized his ministry at the seminary and in the church in the following way:

> Edler Hawkins was an eloquent and persuasive Christian interpreter of the Black experience in this country. In part, his ministry was the nurturing of younger Blacks who struggled, each in a unique way, to come to a creative response to that condition. Perhaps because he was so sure who he was, he was able to mix his life meaningfully with so many other lives very different from his own. His quiet and humane intervention in the lives of Asians, Africans, Europeans, and white American men and women certified to many of them the reality of forgiveness and the possibility of reconciliation.[15]

Geddes W. Hanson joined the PTS faculty in 1969 as an instructor in practical theology. He was eventually promoted to the rank of full professor and appointed as the Charlotte W. Newcombe Professor of Congregational Ministry. Prior to coming to the seminary, he served as the assistant pastor of the St. Augustine Presbyterian Church while Edler was pastor. He subsequently served churches in Philadelphia and Indianapolis. He remained deeply involved in the church while at PTS, serving on the General Assembly Mission Council of the United Presbyterian Church and on the Executive Committee of the World Alliance of Reformed Churches, as well as many other denominational committees and boards.

In addition to his teaching responsibilities, Hanson served as the assistant and associate director of professional studies from 1970-7. He played a key role in the Doctor of Ministry program, serving as the chair of this committee for many years. He also provided leadership for the establishment of an area in the department of practical theology,

---

[13] Ibid., 77.
[14] Freda Gardner, Daniel Migliore, and Geddes Hanson. "Memorial Minute of The Faculty of Princeton Theological Seminary," *The Princeton Seminary Bulletin*, 2:1 (1978), 28-9. See also, "Eulogy," James Hasting Nichols, ibid., 26-7.
[15] Gardner et al., "Memorial Minute," 28

congregational ministry, which focused on congregational studies, leadership, and organizational analysis. In his words, "I am satisfied with my ministry at the Seminary to the degree that ordained and unordained people are motivated to focus on Christians in community and to learn the skills to evoke, empower, and enable the faithful and effective witness of those communities."[16] He is the author of numerous articles, book chapters, and published sermons.

Students who took Hanson's courses remember him as using a practical theological pedagogy that constantly brought theory and practice, reflection and action into conversation. As one former student recollected:

> He introduced me to the whole fields of congregational studies and organizational theory. We worked in teams to carry out research on a congregation and its context. He was especially good at teaching us the kinds of questions we need to ask if we want to understand what is going on in a church. And he modeled this for us in class. His method was dialogical; he was really good at leading a discussion. He also assigned us activities that were simulations of the work of a pastor. I remember one, I think it was called the In Box. Dr. Hanson would give us a pile of stuff made up of the kind of things that would appear in a minister's in box. There was way more than any pastor could do. So we had to prioritize them and give a rationale that explained why some things were done before others. We also used case studies in class.[17]

Slowly, the PTS faculty and department of practical theology became more diverse in terms of race and gender. Sandra Brown taught in the area of pastoral care from 1975-1987, Christie Cozal Neugar, from 1987-1992, and Deborah Hunsinger from 1994 to the present. Janet Weathers taught in the area of Speech from 1994-2001, and Nancy Lammers Gross, from 2001 to the present. Christine Smith taught in the area of Homiletics from 1986-1991 and Nora Tubbs Tisdale, 1993-2001. Two African Americans were appointed in Homiletics, Cleophus J. LaRue in 1996 and Luke Powery in 2007. Sally Brown joined this area in 2001. All three continue as members of the faculty. Carol Lakey Hess taught in the area of Christian education from 1992-1999. Currently teaching in this area are

---

[16] *The Faculty: Princeton Theological Seminary.* (Princeton, NJ : The Seminary, 1999), 44.
[17] Personal Interview.

Kenda Creasy Dean, who joined the faculty in 1996, and Bo Karen Lee, who was appointed in 2007. Dean is the first professor of Youth, Church, and Culture; Lee is the first full-time Asian American woman in the department and the first professor of Spirituality and Historical Theology.

A Conversation among Women in the Department of Practical Theology

The following is the edited transcript of a conversation among Sally Brown (preaching), Kenda Dean (education and formation), Nancy Gross (speech), and Deborah Hunsinger (pastoral care). All of these women are tenured members of the department of practical theology. The conversation was moderated by the authors and took place in December, 2010. The participants were asked to reflect together on the perennial tension between specialization and commonality in practical theology, their pedagogies, and the unique nature of practical theology as a field. Unprompted, the theme of change in theological education emerged as an important issue.

Gordon Mikoski: In looking at the history of practical theology as a field in the United States is there an integrating principle to the different component disciplines of practical theology? How do you see the practical theology department at PTS? Is it a department or a confederation of areas? If it is the former, what is the logic that holds the pieces together into a whole?

Sally Brown: I would see it as a confederation that is becoming self aware as a department, so a department on the way to arriving at a shared self identity. I really do think that if we are honest, the construction of the department has been pragmatic and driven by the fourfold division of the curriculum. But as we have been in conversation with theory in our fields and with each other, and through the practices that we are obligated to as a department, particularly around PhD students, I think that our shared theoretical commitments have started to emerge, although I do not see us as uniform in that regard. I think we have a variety of ways of brokering the relationship between theology and cognate fields in the secular disciplines, as well as practical theology and our own particular theological fields, like preaching, Christian education, and pastoral care. But we all seem to agree that some such brokering does go on and that how it's done, matters.

Kenda Dean: I was going to answer that question as a "both/and" also. I suppose, historically, I think Sally is probably right. My hunch is that we are a confederation in part because we are not all of one mind that we should be a department. So to keep peace in the family, we allow ourselves to be a confederation. I would call what binds us together as a department of practical theology "the epistemological priority of practice." People "know" differently when they "do" things: participation yields a form of understanding that is distinct from just reading or talking about participating. Theologically speaking, I'm willing to link performative knowing in the church with revelation. God not only reveals who God is and what God is up to in the texts and traditions of the church, but also in the practices that give rise to those texts and traditions. Practices that honored God were prior to theologizing about what those practices meant. Yes, Christians "do things" in faith practices—but through these practices, God does things as well. God uses them to change us, and through these practices, God uses us to change the world. So God acts in the world through people who participate in the practices of the Christian community. Practical theology focuses on the interplay between "knowing" and "doing." When we "do" the practices of Christian life, we have access to part of the divine life that remains hidden when all we do is talk about it. So this is what I mean by the "epistemological priority of practice." There are just some things you can't know about Christ until you set out to imitate him. Locating God's action in the daily acts of Christian life gives practical theologians their distinctive reflective angle.

Deborah Hunsinger: I believe that functionally we are a confederation. We organize ourselves according to our sub-areas to discuss PhD candidates, to decide on courses, to think about PhD program requirements and so forth. Whenever we take the time to talk together across our various areas about how we organize our courses and why, I find it quite exciting. While we are each focusing on describing our particular practice—whether preaching, teaching or pastoral care—there is a kind of cross fertilization that takes place that is quite rich. I learn more about why I teach the way I do as I hear how each of my colleagues approaches their particular subdiscipline. It feeds my imagination and makes me long for more such conversation.

Nancy Gross: I do not think many of us imagine a phrase as elegant as Kenda's "epistemological priority of practice" when we contemplate what binds us together as a department. I would say we are bound together by the "so what." We aren't who we are, we don't do what we do, if we are not always learning through practice and dealing with the "so what." If we don't go to the "so what," we have probably failed in our practical theological task. You can be deeply theoretical and deeply theological and deeply philosophical but if you don't bring it to the level of the "so what," you're probably not going to be in our department. Perhaps, we behave more departmentally at the PhD level. We have this fundamental commitment to thinking about practical theology and methodology. So when we go to a dissertation defense of someone in another area of our department, we still recognize a common language and commitments. We can see where this person worked with some kind of a methodological approach that we all understand. So, in that sense I think we are a department, especially at the doctoral level. Obviously we are more of a confederation at the MDiv level, teaching our more specialized classes. Still, again, I love being able to say to my speech classes, "I know that education and formation will support me in this. We don't like object lessons. You can't really tell children that sin is like the moss hanging in a South Carolina tree, with bugs in it. (laughter). It is so beautiful hanging from the tree that I put some in my trunk. But at the end of the trip, there are bugs infesting my whole trunk. That's like sin growing in you. (laughter). Actually, I have pretty strong roots in Christian education through my relationship with Jim Loder, but haven't traversed as much ground in pastoral theology. But I have the sense that we have common ground and I rely on that; I actually rely on that in the classroom.

Gordon Mikoski: Recently, at one of the orientation sessions for new students, I identified seven markers of practical theology. To continue our conversation, perhaps, you could react to this idea. These aren't in any particular order: theory/practice orientation … performance oriented … priority of practice (like Kenda was saying) … contextuality … one that we haven't mentioned but that I think is important to us is embodiment—that we have bodies … interdisciplinarity, familiarity with the social sciences … change and formation-oriented. So, what do you make of those seven markers? We mentioned some of them already. Are they all inclusive or is something missing?

Kenda Dean: Can you just clarify what you mean by performance oriented and the priority of practice. How are you distinguishing those?

Gordon Mikoski: Well, there is certain performance involved in preaching and teaching and in care. That is not the same as practice...like the practice of prayer. They overlap but they are not the same.

Sally Brown: What of the striving toward excellence, the how and the quality of the doing? That's important to all of us. I see those as helpful aspects of performance.

Gordon Mikoski: Maybe we should say we are also conversational.

Sally Brown: We *are* conversational, an ongoing conversation. We are a particular kind of discourse that goes on inside the theological institution. But we have enough difference and enough overlap in terms of what's at stake, that is, in terms of the "so what," that the conversation continues and stays lively. We don't work on parallel tracks; we are often engaged. We can easily be engaged with each other in a common discourse about excellence, about context, about any one of those seven.

Rick Osmer: Let's focus on several of these markers in particular. What about contextuality?

Deborah Hunsinger: All pastoral care is contextual. Everything that we do takes place in a specific situation, in a particular culture, whether it is offering pastoral care to an individual in a hospital bed, working with a family or offering pastoral leadership with an entire congregation. All the issues that we think of as contextual—gender, race, class, ethnicity—are of fundamental importance and worthy of reflection. But our context is not simply outside of us, an environment that surrounds us. It is "the total environment in which we are and which is in us," as Han van den Blink once wrote. The environment that we have internalized and carry with us interacts with the external environment in which we find ourselves. Our context is therefore incredibly complex because the inner and the outer are inextricably related, and usually lie outside our conscious awareness. We can no more opt out of the context than we can choose to leave our bodies temporarily.

A great deal of my teaching therefore focuses on helping students to become aware of the people and events that have given fundamental shape to their identity. For example, in my class on marriage and family, I use family systems theory to help them become aware of the relational patterns they have internalized from their families of origin. Those patterns drastically affect how they will function in ministry. We are simply not able to do ministry without taking our personal baggage with us. So it behooves us to know what precisely is in that baggage, what the contexts are that are part of the water that we swim in, the attitudes and norms that we take for granted. They are also worthy of reflection.

Sally Brown: That segues right into preaching and speech performance. We're so aware that every student who comes into a classroom already "knows" how to preach, because they've heard a lot of preaching. So they have some fairly well formed ideas of what it sounds like to preach, what content is, what the cadence is, what kind of use of body authenticates preaching, what a successful sermon sounds like. So unless you take that seriously from the get-go, you are just rowing against the stream. The question is how to make previous experience productive rather than an excuse for not learning anything. We ask them to examine that and to listen to themselves, and to listen in ways that allow their assumptions to come out. Sometimes those are very disabling assumptions—for example, if they were exposed only to preaching by men and they are female. A female pulpit-speaker person is an oxymoron in their experience. They are dealing with shaming and a sort of a "de-selfing" dynamic. They may avoid the space of the pulpit. I have seen that happen, the physical inability to center the body behind the pulpit because that is forbidden space. They get there, and then they slide side to side to a safer zone. So, previous formation impacts the body and impacts voice; it impacts interpretation; it impacts their ability to imagine new contexts or to take seriously the one in front of them. So I can't say enough about contextuality and the way it figures into homiletical theory, as well as the way it impacts the concrete practice of teaching and the practice of risking speech as a preacher.

Nancy Gross: I'd like to tag on to that since Sally and I are in the same area. That student who Sally has in mind, who can hardly bear to be behind the pulpit, has already been through a year of speech where we have worked with that person to help her claim her home space. If she's had me in class, this was addressed very specifically, including an individual conference that helps her explore what makes it difficult to claim her space behind the lectern. Contextuality has to do with a wide range of dynamics. It includes the ways African Americans learned to read scripture, simply by growing up in an African American church. It has to do with the Korean woman who knows in the core of her being that her voice should not be elevated above a man's. It has to be quieter, and when a woman speaks in the presence of men, her language is more formal than when she's speaking with women in the kitchen. Those are extremely important contextual dimensions of speech and preaching. There also is the whole physical dynamic of it: how she feels about her body. That too impacts her ability to work behind the lectern. The vocational discernment piece is important as well. What does it mean for me to be one who proclaims the Good News of Jesus Christ and Him crucified? All of these contextual factors are entangled in socio-cultural, family, and ecclesial dynamics. And they impact vocal production—from how I stand in the pulpit to what I am saying. It is not just about demographics; it goes deeper. Speech is one of the places in our curriculum where the *individual* gets the opportunity to become aware of and begin dealing with these issues at a very deep level. It is labor intensive because it takes account of each person as an individual.

Kenda Dean: I often talk about youth ministry as radically contextualized ministry. The big secret of youth ministry is that it's just ministry—but like all good ministry, it must be contextualized for a particular flock. In other words, what makes youth ministry distinct is not its form, but its flock. The prerequisites for every successful pastoral minister are the desire and ability to know one's flock. In studying youth ministry, the hope is that by focusing very sharply on one window into the lifecycle, students will gain skills and pastoral intuition that can be transferred elsewhere.

Deborah Hunsinger: Can you give an example for youth ministry?

Kenda Dean: For years I have had students write a spiritual autobiography of their own adolescence. I don't grade their stories, but I do grade their ability to put those stories in conversation with James Fowler's *Stages of Faith* and one other developmental theorist of their choice.

Deborah Hunsinger: So by means of these two different theories you have them lift up certain kinds of contextual themes?

Kenda Dean: Well, part of what they have to wrestle with is the way they have been shaped by their contexts, by their place in the developmental lifecycle. It looks different for every student. The lens is the developmental theory, and they have to look at other surrounding elements that tint that lens. The whole exercise was designed to give them the tools they need to know their flocks, regardless of age. It's very much intended to underscore Nora Tisdale's thesis from her dissertation: that every congregation has a local theology.

Sally Brown: I can give another concrete example right out of Nora Tisdale's work. For example, when students tackle the assignment of preaching a sermon that engages a public issue for a particular context, they need to work out what's going on in that congregational context with respect to this issue. But they need to exegete the issue on a broader scale, and then they also need to exegete themselves in relationship to the context. They need to be self aware about their own angst, rage, or whatever it might be with respect to the issue. Part of proclaiming responsibly is to be aware of that. Then they choose a text to be in conversation with the context, and they do exegesis of the text. So we talk about a four-way exegesis: self, text, issue, and congregational context. That's pretty complex but that's what practical theology is about. It has multi-dimentionality. Maybe that's something we all share.

Kenda Dean: I'm adding a footnote on to this because of Gordon's list of markers. The marker that jumps out at me is embodiment. When Nancy, in her role as Dean of Students, puts me in front of students, and I have to explain what practical theology is, my shorthand is to explain our various academic departments by dividing them up according to our primary sacred texts. In practical theology, the text is the Christian life and all of the things that come with that. It's situated; it's embodied; it's performed. That's a different kind of text than is studied in church history, or in biblical studies, or systematic theology. So practical theology requires a different skill set than our sister disciplines. In practical theology, the self and the pastoral situation become texts that we must exegete.

Gordon Mikoski: I want you to think about practice in your teaching. Nicholas Lobkowicz has a book called *Theory and Practice*.[18] It's an interesting treatment of the *theory* of theory and practice. He's quite clear from the beginning that this is not the *practice* of theory and practice; this is the *theory* of theory and practice. It's actually rather difficult to talk about practice and not have it be colonized by theory. I can teach a class, for example, in which I *talk* about the idea of teaching, but it really

---

[18] Nicholas Lobkowicz, *Theory and Practice: History of a Concept from Aristotle to Marx*, (Notre Dame, IN: Notre Dame, 1967).

doesn't make much sense to teach without, as Katherine Turpin says, "teaching about teaching by teaching." So, how do you use practice or what role does practice play in your teaching? Not just as a theoretical marker, but the actual *doing* of some practice.

Nancy Gross: At the pedagogical level in speech, we practice. That is, we have very little theoretical conversation at first in speech. Our whole theoretical structure is backgrounded. All of us as instructors know this theoretical background, and it's informing our teaching, but our focus is on *practice*. The students get up; they speak; we give them feedback; then they speak again. If they haven't gotten it at all, we might give them more feedback, and they speak yet again. First year students get almost nothing in the way of theory until second semester when some of us might offer more of that having to do with the oral interpretation of texts and hermeneutical theory. We could begin by talking about vocal performance or rhetoric, but it wouldn't hit home. We stay grounded in *practice*. For some students, we're challenging them at a very deep level because this is the way they've always spoken or heard others speak. We evoke their thinking: Have you asked questions about what that means, or how that comes across, or if you would be able to go into a different context without reading it and making some sorts of adjustments in your communication? Would you take what you're yelling into every context and just yell? In other speech classes and speech-preaching classes, it's different. In Word and Act, for example, we practice, but we also talk a lot more about the theological meanings of the act. We help our students bring their theology and practice together, including what they do with their eyes, hands, and bodies.

Sally Brown: I think a preaching class is a conscious and deliberate jumping onto a moving train pretty much, by the instructor and the students. We're all involved in the practice of preaching already. And, having been listeners to it, with a lot of them already having preached, the practice of preaching isn't my solitary engagement with the text; it is the practice of a gathered community listening and speaking. So the listener side of the act of preaching is something that everyone is involved in, all the time, so we activate all of that in the practice of preaching. Certainly it becomes your turn to do the talking, but part of training in the practice of preaching is homiletically teaching people to listen more effectively and communicate the effect of the preaching experience on them back to the preacher in a helpful way. So it's activating the listener in preaching as well as activating the preacher. Our pedagogy certainly reflects that understanding of preaching as a shared project of congregation and preacher.

Deborah Hunsinger: Meaning that in the class you are activating the listeners to the sermon in a certain way and you are asking them to…

Sally Brown: We pray for the preacher, and we pray for the listeners, for example. So it is a very deliberate process of feedback that takes the *different* hearings of the sermon seriously.

Deborah Hunsinger: And does this go into their thinking about how they function as a preacher in their actual congregations? Do you help them like try to elicit feedback from their congregants?

Sally Brown: Well, we suggest it; we can't demand it. I have taught in other settings where that was incorporated, where there was a trained cadre of listeners in their field education, and they were accountable for that in the preaching course. You can't always count on having a Field Ed. setting that's open, willing and able to provide that. At any rate I contend that the practice is not only the interpretive act of utterance in response to interpretation of the Word on behalf of these folks, but it is a shared practice that includes the hearers. One needs to be trained in the listening and the feedback as well as the preaching.

Kenda Dean: I wonder if I understand what you are getting at, Gordon. I'm hyper-aware every single minute that I am teaching about teaching. I mean every minute. I'll look at a syllabus and say, okay, the content is here but that alone won't teach them. I have to somehow model that which I am teaching about. We teach the way were taught, inside the classroom and especially outside of it. So I'm learning how to cultivate both the explicit and implicit curricula more intentionally. I get a lot of joy out of that, but it's not a pure relationship because I am also conscious all the time that every interaction is a teaching moment, for good or for ill. If I have students in my home, I am teaching them something about Christian hospitality, something about how to be a leader in a group situation. The teaching identity is always, always there. And so it creates a kind of barrier, a healthy one I hope, but it means I can't ever completely just let go because I am modeling something about what it looks like to be a Christian who is an educator. It is a mantle I wear gladly—I think I signed up for that when I got into this business—but it makes me constantly aware that practical theological education is so much more than what happens in class. I'm increasingly won to the kind of education that happens informally. My hunch is that—in the same way they say that music is what happens in between the notes—Christian formation is what happens in the community of faith in and around the formal curriculum.

Sally Brown: Can I raise a question around the table. What do you think is the significance of practice as a point of integration of the curriculum?

Nancy Gross: What is the significance?

Sally Brown: The significance of practice. It's *a* point of integration. I'm becoming more and more aware of the significance of practice as integrative.

Gordon Mikoski: For the whole curriculum.

Sally Brown: Absolutely! For the whole curriculum.

Kenda Dean: I always have trouble when they ask us which courses are "integration" courses. Duh. Aren't all of them?

Sally Brown: It's interesting that that's kind of a non-question for us. (laughter) By the end of the semester it's interesting how many of them are saying, "I'm getting it…I'm getting it, I understand why these things matter."

Gordon Mikoski: That's a very interesting comment in light of reevaluations of Ed Farley's analysis of theological education and how practical theology has been reduced to clericalism and the idea that everybody else does the heavy lifting, and we just apply their insights. We've spent how many years reacting against that characterization. That's not what we do. We're not just the appliers of other people's ideas. But by pushing so far away from that, we may have missed something. This is part of what's going on in the wider conversation about practical theology, at least in the US. Bonnie McLemore-Miller has been key in raising this. We don't want to throw the baby out with the bathwater in reacting against the notion that we're just the appliers or just the practitioners. Maybe we are also the integrators. Don't we teach people how to do ministerial stuff? Anyway, I think that's really fascinating to think about.

Deborah Hunsinger: I am interested in what Kenda was saying about teaching our students about teaching as we are teaching. I resonate with that in terms of pastoral care. I try to get as much mileage as I can out of simple practices that I repeat in class. There are certain practices that I have adapted from my pastoral counseling training, for example, that work well in the classroom. For example, one psychotherapeutic practice is to reflect together on what happened that day in therapy, i.e. what was especially significant or brought about a shift in their thinking. It is a kind of metacommunication about the communication that has taken place. A simple practice of asking for feedback about the class at the end of every class helps all of us to reflect on what has occurred and why it is significant.

The ability to speak directly about what is happening in the present moment is a key skill in pastoral care, but it also makes pastors much more effective when they make it a habit of mind. You do something together, then you reflect together on what you have just done. I imagine Session meetings becoming far more effective if pastors knew how to reflect aloud on the process of the meetings. I am very intentional about reflecting on process in class and also helping our students to feel comfortable in reflecting together about our process. It not only deepens the sense of connection to others in the community, but at the same time, it deepens our connection to the subject matter we are studying. The learning that takes place is taken more deeply to heart because it is embodied in our relationships to one another.

Rick Osmer: As we reach the end of our time, I think it is important for us to talk a bit about the future of our school, PTS. I mean our department.

Nancy Gross: I have to comment on what might be seen as a Freudian slip, when you said, "What do we see as the future of our school," and then "the future of the department." They are not unrelated. We are keenly aware in speech that we are probably the most vulnerable area of our department to being seen as expendable. Rather than valuing speech by affirming, "This is the only school in the country with this kind of a commitment to sacred rhetoric, or the oral interpretation of texts, for the sake of the church," it often is viewed as a relic and at least implied: "You are the last one to give it up." But I truly believe that as goes practical theology so goes the school. How committed are we to the Church? I mean the church, not just the PC(USA), especially the local congregations and the practice of Christian living, being a witness in the world. If that doesn't remain a priority, then we as a department don't remain a priority. So its not just speech that's vulnerable. The rest of our department is right behind, and the character of the school is right behind. So I found it interesting that you sort of misspoke the question.

Sally Brown: I do see something really interesting in what you are pointing to, what some of us have been calling the implications of the shift to this multi-tasking, multi-dimensional, digitalized, virtualized, new self. It is something in which students are well-practiced, far better than we are. This has implications, not only for what many see as increasingly irrelevant practices of education, but for practices of the church. I think there is a big question mark in a lot of people's minds whether one voice speaking in the presence of real bodies with real ears and whether listening itself is being eclipsed. I want to stake my hope for the future on the idea that it is *not* being eclipsed by virtual communities and by visual communication.

It's interesting to me that texting is the preferred way of using phones, for example. You can present an alternative self. But you've got to bring your naked self to ministry. You can't disguise very much of who you are when you are standing in front of people preaching, or reading Scripture, or sitting with a couple or a family in an intense unveiling of who they are. I don't know, we may be at risk for a time. It depends on whether we are willing to be countercultural. I think that practical theology practices are countercultural, and a lot will depend on whether the infrastructures of this and other schools are willing to take the risk that a countercultural way of human beings being together is essential and worth gambling on and worth investing in. I do see it as at risk. You never used to get the question in the Introductory Preaching class: "Why do we still bother to preach?" But you do get it now.

Kenda Dean: I'm trying to untangle the school versus department. It's really helpful to hear you say that. I think our stake in the ground in a post-Christian culture is to form people to become countercultural, so they can help other people become countercultural. I have a particular kind of countercultural in mind. To be conformed to Christ would be, in my mind, the countercultural norm. That may be what keeps the church alive. We want to be current, but our purpose is not really to be relevant. The gospel needs to have meaning in our particular contexts, but our *purpose* is to stay faithful to what Christ has called the church to be. I have to fight the urge to throw everything out and start over.

Deborah Hunsinger: You want to throw everything out?

Kenda Dean: Well, that would be a mistake, of course—and yet: yes, I want to start over on the way we do most theological education right now. I'd like to make practical theology the centerpiece of theological education and not an afterthought—the hub of the wheel with lots of theological spokes. How would you do that except to be in a context where you are trying to engage in practices of ministry? Placing practical theology at the hub of the wheel suddenly makes all the spokes necessary. When you are holding the mother of this child who has died, suddenly scripture is necessary to water your soul, suddenly church history matters to give you some tracks to follow, suddenly all those theological encyclopedia pieces matter because they are grounded in the practices of ministry. The way we do theological education today feels completely upside down to me. I'm probably overstating it, but discouragement looms large in me right now. And I think it might be because the assumptions I bring to the table as a practical theologian suggest that the way we are going about theological education is just ass-backwards. Quote that! (laughter)

Nancy Gross: Sally and Kenda and I were together in another meeting a couple of weeks ago where we were talking about these kinds of things. I shared a little about my experience of reforming the curriculum of Palmer Seminary back in '96. We started to build a brand new curriculum, very intentionally starting from scratch. The very first thing entering students did was go into Philadelphia and become immersed in some ministry context. Then they began asking questions: What are the issues and what do we need to address these issues—that sort of thing. It's interesting to me that even in a small school, the size of a tugboat that can turn pretty quickly, it took five years. There's not a PhD program there; it's fully committed to preparing pastors for the Church and people for other ministries in the public sphere. That doesn't mean it is anti-theory. Our theologians and historians and biblical scholars were all on board. Of course, they were all church people too and that made a big difference. There was a very high degree of integration and interaction between theory and practice in the curriculum. That's harder to achieve at PTS. For example, in our preaching practicum, students have the assignment of a public issue sermon and they have to draw on theology. Sometimes, they say, "Oh! I have to talk about theology again? I thought I was done with those courses!" It is almost as if they are going to the library and reading theology because they have to check off a box. They haven't gotten it! It's not embedded in what they do.

Sally Brown: It hasn't yet become a critically important question for them, which happens when they are immersed in ministry.

Deborah Hunsinger: As I have been listening to all of you today, I am filled with a sense of longing for more conversations like this one. I would like for us to be less of a confederation and more integrated as a department. I love the kind of intentionality that you in Education and Formation have in designing a fall retreat with your doctoral students, for example. The way that you bring them on board as junior colleagues from day one, I find inspiring. I wish that we did a retreat for our whole department and not just one area of the department, especially now when the cohort of students gets smaller with the tough economic climate. The integrative vision we have for the ministry of the church is shared by some of our colleagues in other departments, I believe, but it is one of the real strengths that our department in particular has to offer the seminary as a whole.

Sally Brown: I would like to see us able to initiate more and not just react. We'd be leaving out an important part of our history if we didn't note that between 2003 and 2010 our numbers have been reduced by better than one-third as a department. That makes a huge difference in the amount of the load of just introductory courses and departmental work that each of us is carrying. And that tends to suppress free conversation, and it tends to suppress inter-area creativity. A subject that would be interesting for us to just press forward into this faculty is Practical Ecclesiology. We make vague assumptions that we understand what the present and future church is and does, and then theorize about what kind of a community it is and what it is up to. But I think that we have a lot to say about that, a lot of creative thinking about that which could also cause us to call into question the present organization of the curriculum and the way we envision preparing leaders for such a church. I emphasize Practical Ecclesiology, the church as a community of particular practices that take place through bodies and particular places rather than theoretical and purely theological treatment of ecclesiology, because it has everything to do with how you envision education.

Gordon Mikoski: I think that is really key, because it seems to me like Protestant denominations are collapsing by stages, and the denominational structures can't provide the leadership for thinking about the future. The theological schools will have to do that, at least the ones who are still standing after all the financial stress plays out. We'll still be standing. Maybe, we ought to think about making it our business to look at what is the future of the churches and what ought to be our approach to education and formation and so on, because it's not going to come from anywhere else, except for entrepreneurial people out there. We have the resources and the intellectual capacities and tools. We have our colleagues from other departments that we can draw into that or make that a thematized priority discussion. Otherwise, what will be the future of the school? Already we are feeling the effects of the diminishment of the pool of Presbyterian candidates, and we still have a lot of candidates…I mean…applicants because it is Princeton Seminary. But maybe that will even change too. So, anyway, I think what you are saying is really key. I would like to see us take on the challenge of asking: What is the future of the church and what ought to be leadership for that and how can we strategize to help bring it about? I don't mean just turning out pastors. How can the church be vital in the future? We have the capacity to do that, to have that conversation, and to be catalyst internally with our colleagues and maybe even beyond.

Nancy Gross: Could I just say one more word about the future of the department? We've kind of been speaking about theological education and that sort of thing. I think our department needs personal transformation. This has to do with authenticity, genuineness, and integrity. In some ways, the future of the department does not depend on whether we get another professor here or another professor there, or how many PhD students we have. I think it really depends more on whether we are willing to work together toward a common goal that's anchored in the church. How we can best serve the church is more important than pushing my particular approach to practical theology or who gets an adjunct. This takes a certain amount of selfless, and most faculty I know aren't really about this. My brother describes the university where he teaches as all about "grabbing"…getting as much as you can because the more you can grab, the more you get. Our department can sometimes be like this, too; though I also believe we are capable of functioning at a very high level. We can be collegial and caring about one another with a sense of the group as a whole. But if we're going to become more like this, then there needs to be transformation, transformation at the personal level that leads to greater authenticity, genuineness, and integrity.

Rick Osmer: I think this has been a remarkable conversation. I want to thank all of you for taking the time for this right before Christmas when everybody is so busy. I think it says a lot about who you are. So thank you for doing this.

* * *

In a very real sense, this conversation underscores the importance of further conversation in the PTS department of practical theology, the broader seminary community, and the field as a whole. This chapter ends, thus, with talking points for the ongoing conversation that is practical theology at Princeton Theological Seminary.

Talking points

1. How does practical theology handle the tension between *specialized* areas like education and formation, pastoral care, and preaching, on the one hand, and the *shared* responsibilities, pedagogies, and discourse of the department and field, on the other?

2. Does practical theology have a *distinct epistemological orientation* grounded in praxis, practice, or performance? Is there necessarily a political dimension to this orientation in light of the influence of power and socialization on students and professors?

3. In what ways is practical theology's knowing-by-doing properly construed as a form of participation in the life of God? Does this mean that *spiritual formation* is always a component of the pedagogies of practical theology? What implications might this have for the mentoring dimension of professors' relationships with students?

4. In light of differences in theology, methods, pedagogies, and focal practices, why is *ongoing conversation* important in practical theology? How is this supported or subverted in different contexts like faculty departments and guilds?

5. What are the varied meanings of *context* in practical theology? How do they impact the pedagogies of this field?

6. In light of the centrality of performance in the pedagogies of practical theology (learning by observing, participating, and doing), how are *theories and research* practices best taught in this field? Is this totally different at the Masters and PhD levels?

7. What are some of the characteristics of the present context that make teaching a young and diverse student body so challenging? What kinds of pedagogical changes might need to be made in courses in the department of practical theology and in other seminary departments?

8. How do we interpret the fact that departments of practical theology are growing smaller in many schools of theology, including PTS? Does this simply reflect the economic realities of the recent recession or does it represent an undervaluing of the contributions of this field? What actions might guilds and departments take to counter this trend?

Epilogue

What Have We Learned about Practical Theology at PTS?
A bicentennial retrospective on the theory and practice of practical theology at PTS has yielded several important insights. Throughout its history, practical theology at PTS has consistently emphasized that its ultimate purpose is threefold: glorification of God; edification of the church; and transformation of society in the direction of the Reign of God. These interrelated aims reflect the core ethos of the Reformed tradition. To greater and lesser degrees, each era of practical theology at PTS has affirmed this threefold *telos*. In this sense, practical theology has operated in harmony with the mission of the seminary as a whole.

In service to this Reformed teleology, the long line of practical theologians at PTS has held that a dynamic, differentiated unity of "piety and learning" forms the core operative principle for practical theology. James Loder's language of an asymmetrical, bipolar unity (Ch 5) captures well the PTS approach to the relationship between piety and learning. Genuine and deep piety—understood as a response of committed gratitude to the grace of God made known in and through Jesus Christ by the power of the Holy Spirit—provides the anchor for the entire project of practical theology at PTS. The relationship between piety and learning tends to encourage PTS practical theologians to move in the direction of faithful Christian humanism, in which cultural engagement and a learned faith are inherent parts of the theological task.

At the heart of such piety and learning in the tradition of practical theology at PTS lies a strong commitment to the priority and normativity of biblical revelation. PTS practical theologians have consistently operated with a high view of Scripture and revelation in accordance with the Reformed tradition. In the nineteenth century, this led to a unidirectional application of text to context and, at times, a defensive reaction to critical approaches to Scripture. In the twentieth century, PTS practical theologians developed increasingly sophisticated understandings of the complex relationship between sacred texts and lived contexts, while maintaining a high view of Scripture—even when that meant standing in tension with dominant paradigms in the field of practical theology and its various guilds.

PTS practical theologians have also demonstrated a strong commitment to the theological dimension of practical theology. In every chapter of the seminary's history, they have lifted up the importance of theological reflection upon practice, performance, and context. They have asked searching questions about the presence and work of God in the midst of the vicissitudes of human experience. Such emphasis on theology has been—and still is—a key dimension of the distinctive profile of practical theology at PTS, especially as the social sciences grew more central to this field during the twentieth century.

These commitments to the centrality of biblical revelation and robust theological reflection have strengths, but they also have key limitations. While practical theology at PTS has always been concerned with practice and context, the epistemic status of practice and the shaping power of context as sources of theological knowledge have not always received the sort of attention they have received elsewhere in practical theology. From a contemporary practical theological perspective, the most glaring failure to fully engage the social context came in the form of attempts by nineteenth century PTS practical theologians to deal with matters of slavery and race. Rather than letting engagement with social context challenge their theological convictions, they attempted to deal with the social evil of slavery through strategies of moderation, gradualism, and colonization. While twentieth century PTS practical theologians such as Charles Erdman and Elmer Homrighausen recognized the importance of context, they did not reflect on its methodological status in theological construction. The predominant trend was rather the unilateral application of biblical and theological concepts to context. The main exception to this trend at PTS is Seward Hiltner, who very explicitly argued along the lines of Anton Boison that the study of living human documents yields knowledge as fundamental as that found in the other fields. Arguably, Hiltner developed this appreciation of context while at the University of Chicago Divinity School and brought it with him to PTS. The history of PTS practical theology highlights the need to perpetually struggle to give context sustained attention while also affirming biblical revelation's central claims.

PTS practical theologians in the twentieth century engaged matters of context with increasing sophistication as they began to discover and use the tools of the social sciences. Interdisciplinary work with fields like psychology, sociology, rhetoric, and performance studies has helped to make the interplay between text and context much more complicated, textured, and exciting. Yet it cannot merely adopt the assumptions and procedures of the arts and sciences without a critical appraisal from the perspective of Christian theology—a conviction firmly held by PTS practical theologians throughout the seminary's history. Equally as important, however, is the increased diversity of the department, faculty, and student body in terms of race, ethnicity, and gender. As never before, this has made it clear that PTS practical theology cannot and should not ignore context. It is present in the practical theologian's presuppositions. It is present in the backgrounds and diverse ministry settings of students. The underdevelopment of contextuality among PTS practical theologians, at least in part, is due to the white and male context they took for granted. The increased diversity of the department is thus a welcome development at PTS. It must be preserved and enhanced, not only within department of practical theology but also in the seminary community as a whole. This remains an unfinished project and, therefore, a perpetual summons to PTS practical theologians. If PTS practical theology is to remain faithful to its historic, distinctive Christian identity, and if it is to work in service to God and to the church, then in its dialogue with the arts and sciences, it must not ignore either the voice of context or the voice of theology grounded in Scripture and living tradition.

This study of the history of practical theology at PTS has also shown the perpetually provisional character of the nomenclature, taxonomy, and institutional structure of the field of practical theology as practiced internally at the seminary. In the seminary's earliest days, the entire curriculum was understood to be a form of "pastoral theology," in the widest sense of the term. The patriarchs of the seminary also used that term in a more limited or restricted sense to cover the entire range of issues pertinent to the calling, practices, and lifestyle of congregational clergy. At midcentury, under the sway of Alexander McGill's theoretical vision, pastoral theology became one component within the much larger rubric of "practical theology." By the early years of the twentieth century, the latter term became normative and functioned as a key part of the framework for reorganizing the academic departments along the lines of the traditional fourfold pattern of knowledge in the theological school curriculum.[1]

Different eras in this history witness to some variation on the theme of what academic areas and specializations should function under the rubric of practical theology. The patriarchs had no trouble seeing mission as an integral part of this area, alongside such foci as preaching, speech, catechetics and education, pastoral care, and pastoral leadership. They also saw a compelling logic in holding together church history, ecclesiology, and practical ecclesiology in one larger conversation. McGill envisioned six areas: pastoral theology, homiletics, catechetics, liturgics, ecclesiology, and ecclesiastical law and discipline. In the last decades of the nineteenth century, "Christian social science" took place in the curriculum of the theology department. Hiltner argued for three areas: shepherding, organizing, and communicating. The current instantiation of the department of practical theology at PTS branches out into three areas: preaching and speech communication for ministry; pastoral care and specialized ministries; and education and formation. These taxonomical and organizational variations indicate that, at least at PTS, the disciplinary boundaries for practical theology are somewhat open to revision, both internally and in relation to the organization of the theological curriculum as a whole. One could make a case, for example, that subjects like missiology or practical ecclesiology, certain areas of church history, and even ethics could function dynamically together with the more traditional areas of preaching and speech, pastoral care, and education and formation.

Regardless of curricular configuration, all of the areas of practical theology per se and their near disciplinary partners share certain key characteristics. Any areas of the theological curriculum that have to do with focal concerns pertinent to the Christian life, theory and practice, action, performance, contextuality, embodiment, interdisciplinarity, leadership, and strategic intervention for change will have a natural affinity with the department of practical theology at PTS, regardless of where they happen to fall on an organizational chart. Practical theology at PTS has distinguished itself from other PTS departments by foregrounding, emphasizing, and giving priority to such focal concerns.

Pedagogical practices have also played a key role in defining the character of practical theology at PTS. PTS practical theologians have

---

[1] In the contemporary PTS practical theology department, the MDiv level "pastoral care and specialized ministries" area is designated as "pastoral theology" at the PhD level. The use of the latter term likely expresses a strand of long institutional memory.

consistently expressed ambivalence about the role of practice and experience in construction and reconstruction of theological knowledge. However, it is important not to overstate such ambivalence, because PTS practical theologians have historically given and presently give attention to performance in pedagogy. Yet only Seward Hiltner and Charles Bartow themetized performance as a distinctive source of knowledge and, accordingly, designed pedagogies that linked performance, practice, and reflective learning. Others used case studies, research projects, and reflection on field education. Yet they seldom explicitly attended to the distinctive pedagogies of practical theology. While the contemporary practical theology department focuses on this task much more than its forebears, the department still has a long way to go toward embracing pedagogical practices appropriate to and expressive of the subject matter and distinctive epistemologies operative in the field. The challenge of balancing the teaching of the theory with the teaching of the practice of "theory and practice" remains a dynamic challenge for the department.

This study has also yielded insight on the central importance of oral communication in ministry and of preaching for the long enterprise of practical theology at PTS. A careful examination of lecture notes from Archibald Alexander and Samuel Miller make clear that there has never been an academic year at PTS when the teaching of preaching and speech have not been central to the curriculum. For two hundred years, PTS faculty members have emphasized the tremendous importance of oral communication in all forms of ministry. Because pastors, teachers, and other ministry leaders speak for a living God, the PTS curriculum has always emphasized the importance of developing the ability to communicate effectively. Similarly, PTS has always taken the apostle Paul's teaching about the central importance of the preached Word in Rom 10.14-17 as of paramount importance. In the long sweep of its history, any impartial observer would affirm that PTS produces men and women who can proclaim the Good News of Jesus Christ with clarity, persuasiveness, and relevance. More than anything else, oral proclamation of the gospel message has given the seminary as a whole its *raison d'etre* and its most effective principle of curricular integration.

Practical theologians have at times played an important role in leadership and even reform of the seminary. This is certainly true of Erdman, who played a key part in the break with "Old Princeton." Homrighausen as dean of the faculty and department chair, Hiltner as founder of the DMin program, and Loder as a key player in the doctoral program all impacted the seminary curriculum. However, much of the change driven by practical theologians has been "departmentalized," that is, limited to specific parts of the curriculum like field education, the DMin program, and the department of practical theology. Practical theologians have had a more limited role in the curriculum of PTS as a whole, which remains driven by the longstanding theory-practice separation initially formed in the theological encyclopedia. Today, more than ever, PTS needs a new, post-encyclopedic paradigm for theological education—one that would emphasize the kinds of concerns and questions that have been central to the history of practical theology at the seminary. Perhaps practical theology can lead the way. The kinds of ideas pointed to in the transcript of Chapter Six gesture in this direction.

Looking to the Future

Learning about the history of practical theology at PTS has stimulated our thinking about future possibilities and challenges. In closing, we offer some thoughts about possible directions for practical theology in our own institutional context and in the wider field.

Practical theology at PTS needs to continue to strengthen its work with a robust and nuanced hermeneutical perspective in order to maintain an optimally generative tension between its deep commitment to scriptural revelation and its engagement with contexts. Developments in the twentieth century moved in this direction and significant work along these lines continues today. This history of practical theology, however, would seem to suggest that practical theologians at PTS face a perpetual challenge to take contextual matters as seriously as they take the Bible and theology. Our greatest strengths often point toward our biggest challenges.

The wider field of practical theology may need to correct in the opposite direction. As PTS practical theologians have often noted since the early part of the twentieth century, much of the field has moved increasingly toward vigorous engagement with contexts and the complexities of human experience through sophisticated use of the social sciences—often, perhaps, at the expense of equally sophisticated biblical and theological reflection. In our judgment, the wider conversation needs to strengthen and deepen its engagement with sacred texts and theological normativity.

The tension between specialized areas and the entire field of practical theology continues to be an issue, not only at PTS, but also more broadly. In part, this reflects the modern pattern of the theological encyclopedia, in which specialization of the fields of theology and specialization within these fields has dominated. This emphasis on discrete fields is highly questionable today for many reasons. It renders the inner logic of theological education invisible, as students are left to sort out for themselves how the courses in different fields fit together. It also fails to acknowledge the interdisciplinary nature of modern research, from the human genome project to urban planning. With regard to practical theology, specialized courses in discrete subareas like preaching, pastoral care, and Christian education fail to address the ways ministry hangs together in congregational contexts. Pastoral issues impact preaching; educational deficits do as well. Ministry is never just a set of discrete, highly specialized activities, though it is true that acquiring expertise in any particular practice involves specialized learning, practice, supervision, and reading. How practical theology in the future handles the tension between specialization and overlapping theories, pedagogies, and skills will say much about this field's contribution to a new paradigm of theology and theological education at the end of the theological encyclopedia.

This question is closely related to practical theology's distinctive relationship to culture and living practice. Because this field necessarily pays close attention to developments in society and culture, it always has an open ended and provisional or even ad hoc quality. This means that the institutional shape of the field can vary considerably over time, even while maintaining commitment to core issues like theory-practice interplay, embodiment, action, practice, performance, and the like. While ministerial functions like preaching, care, and education have remained central to the work of practical theology at PTS over a considerable period of time, areas like missiology, ecclesiastical history, polity, and congregational studies have either dropped away or migrated into other departments. Areas of study like liturgics and liturgical theology have maintained a consistent but relatively low profile in the PTS conversation. In principle, this means that the institutional instantiation of the practical theology department can change in order to accommodate new developments or theoretical frameworks. Perhaps it means, too, that the practical theology department at PTS should work more proactively to build curricular and pedagogical bridges with areas and faculty in other departments that have overlapping interests, concerns, and methods.

The wider field of practical theology also exists in some degree of perpetual flux. At best, the boundaries for the field function as a highly permeable membrane. While disciplinary boundaries do exist, they are flexible and can be revised as necessary. For example, in recent years the field has seen a growing interest in and commitment to inclusion of scholars who work in the area of spirituality and spiritual formation. Because the logic of the field is derived in part from attentiveness to currents in culture and the vicissitudes of human experience, practical theologians should perpetually embrace a certain degree of boundary blurring and shape shifting. It goes with the territory. Yet as our predecessors at PTS would be quick to add, this willingness to cross and blur disciplinary boundaries must be done with a careful eye toward the church's mission as found in Scripture, embodied in tradition, and reflected on by theology.

A critically underdeveloped piece of the PTS discussion and of the broader discussion in practical theology today involves the nature and procedures of practical theological reason. A dynamic model of practical theological reason must account for the way this form of rationality is related to the sources of theology, to practice, and to non-theological disciplines. Yet it cannot forget to develop the ways in which practical theological reason represents a unique form of rationality. Several of the people we examined in the twentieth century (Erdman, Bartow, and Hiltner) came close to articulating such a model but did not do so adequately. Further, any such discussion of practical theological reasoning must listen to political and liberation theologies in order to analyze the role of power and change in practical theology. Important as dialogue with philosophy might be, it is not adequate to define practical theology exclusively in terms of an abstract philosophical or theological model, as if rationality does not unfold in specific contexts.

For these reasons, we may need to talk about "practical theologies" in the plural and in terms of family resemblances. The core tasks of practical theology are carried out in very different ways by different practical theologians, all influenced by their commitment to different metatheoretical positions. PTS practical theologians in the twentieth and twenty-first centuries have not and do not always agree on the best ways to approach work in the field. How to affirm the pluralism in practical theology while simultaneously articulating the field's distinctive focus is an important and ongoing issue at PTS and in the wider field.

Future plurality in practical theology is also likely to be driven by the diverse contexts of practical theologians and the issues to which they give attention. In our view, the pressing issues before the field today include: interreligious dialogue, poverty and race, gender and sexual identity, technology and science, and the emergence of global institutions of law, governance, and civil society that can bring global economic institutions and markets under some kind of control. Undoubtedly, other practical theologians would foreground a different set of issues. Focal issues and methodologies are likely to be a source of robust diversity and creative tension in field in the future.

The US and European discussions of practical theology are still far too limited to white, mainline denominations and congregations. They have had little significant contact with Pentecostalism, for example, which is the largest and fastest growing Protestant sector. As PTS moves in the direction of greater diversity in its student body and faculty, so too, practical theology needs to become more than a predominantly white, mainline Protestant discussion. As this continues to happen, exciting new sets of issues and challenges have and will continue to emerge. Along these lines, practical theology at PTS needs to catch up to what practical theologians are doing in other institutional contexts. At the same time, we also have the sense that the larger field of practical theology needs to continue to work on diversification and the inclusion of all voices and perspectives. Moreover, the global context of practical theology needs more explicit attention and support in guilds. This means taking seriously others' local theologies, which are sometimes more conservative or at least have implicit assumptions quite different from those of the guild. In whichever ways practical theology continues to unfold at PTS and in the wider world, it will have to develop a common intellectual discourse out of the richness and self implicating dimensions of particularity.

This means that reconstructing the meaning of piety will become a key task in the future. Our historical case study has placed this much-abused and mistrusted term on the table. The history of practical theology at PTS demonstrates that piety cannot be reduced to fervent religious devotion, but must also involve an integration of ideas, actions, beliefs, and emotions. PTS practical theologians have consistently exhorted ministers to give attention to this integration. They have insisted that ministers of the gospel who do not themselves trust and know God cannot adequately teach the things of God. Our story has uncovered several examples of a failure to integrate beliefs and actions. Slavery was opposed in theory but not in practice. Clinical skills were valued and taught, but then used to intimidate students and colleagues. The legacy of Old Princeton was viewed as a gift then occasionally defended in ways that lacked charity and mutual respect. This historical account has also yielded several examples of piety as authentic integration of belief and action. Practical theologians struggled to reform the seminary in the face of vicious personal attacks. They demonstrated generosity and respect in the classroom toward even the most pugnacious interrogators. They engaged passion as an intellectual topic and taught with a spirit that demonstrated this very passion. In each of these examples, practical theologians lived by their firm convictions so that students both learned their ideas and saw them embodied. They integrated theory and practice both in their thinking and writing, and in their personalities and way of life. They understood that the harmony of these elements cannot be simply urged upon future ministers, but must also be demonstrated. Indeed, in our roundtable interview, all four professors hinted at the need for piety among practical theologians—piety as devotion to the God revealed in Christ, as personal authenticity and transformation, as faith that acknowledges our embodiment and situatedness, and as a vital combination of theory and ongoing practice. Such integration is not extraneous to true piety, but is its truest expression, and, as the four women suggested, continues to be a deep need today.

Finally, practical theologians must also reconsider where to locate the vital connection between this reconstructed piety and the promise of embodied, diverse, contextual learning. Particularly, they should attend to how this connection is embodied not only in individuals, but also in a learning community. Among the many leitmotifs weaving through the various chapters of the PTS story, the theme of community is perhaps the subtlest. Yet we can trace a distinct trajectory from the patriarchs' afternoon conferences and daily worship gatherings to our final roundtable discussion. The dynamic, differentiated unity of piety and learning often finds the source of its oneness when practical theologians come together for simple shared meals, quiet times of intercessory prayer, and joyful acts of corporate worship. If the practical theological conversation is to continue, practical theologians must talk to each other. If the discrete fields of the larger discipline are to negotiate their relationship to each other, those who work in those fields must also forge relationships. If diverse voices are to be heard and celebrated, diverse people must meet each other around a table of fellowship, honesty, and reconciliation.

The future holds much promise for the wider field of practical theology and for those who participate in the work of practical theology at PTS. We hope that our living tradition will continue to bear fruit in the preparation of women and men for the glory of God, the upbuilding of the church, and the transformation of society. We also hope that the work we do at PTS will make further constructive contributions to research and teaching in the broad, diverse, and ever-emerging global field of practical theology. Whatever we might accomplish and contribute in the future, we will strive to do everything in a way that holds together piety and learning.

Bibliography

Adams, Jay E. *The Homiletical Innovations of Andrew W. Blackwood.* Grand Rapids: Baker Books, 1975.

African American Registry. http://aaregistry.org/historic_events/view/edler-hawkins-civil-activist-his-ministry. Accessed March, 2011.

Ahlstrom, Sydney E. "The Scottish Philosophy and American Theology." *Church History*, 24:3 (September 1955): 257-72.

Alexander, Archibald. "Compend of Didactic Theology Lectures." 1822. The Archibald Alexander Manuscript Collection, Special Collections, Princeton Theological Seminary Library, box 2, file 3.

—. *A History of Colonization on the Western Coast of Africa.* Philadelphia: William S. Martien, 1846.

—. "Lectures on Pastoral Theology." Archibald Alexander Manuscript Collection, Special Collections, Princeton Theological Seminary Library, box 7, file 3.

—. "Lectures on Pastoral Theology. Student notes of Allen H. Brown, 1841-42. Archibald Alexander Manuscript Collection, Special Collections, Princeton Theological Seminary Library, box 4, file 3.

—. "Lectures on Pastoral Theology." Student notes of J. Peter Lesley, 1843-44. The Archibald Alexander Manuscript Collection, Special Collections, Princeton Theological Seminary Library, box 3, file 25.

—. "Lectures on Pastoral Theology." Student notes of Thomas B. Markham, 1850. Archibald Alexander Manuscript Collection, Special Collections, Princeton Theological Seminary Library, box 5, file 3.

—. "Pastoral Duty to the Colored Race." The Archibald Alexander Manuscript Collection, Special Collections, Princeton Theological Seminary, box 12, file 55.

—. "Questions on Theology." Student notes of J. Peter Lesley. The Archibald Alexander Manuscript Collection, Special Collections, Princeton Theological Seminary Library, box 3, file 5.

Alexander, James W. *Discourses on Common Topics of Christian Faith and Practice.* New York: Scribner, 1858.

—. *Forty Years' Familiar Letters.* Edited by John Hall, Vols. 1 and 2. New York: Scribner, 1860.

—. *The Life of Archibald Alexander, D.D., First Professor in the Theological Seminary at Princeton, New Jersey.* New York: Scribner, 1854.

—. *The Life of Archibald Alexander.* Harrisonburg, VA: Sprinkle, 1991.

—. "The Value of Church History to the Theologians of our Day: An Inaugural Discourse." In *Discourses at the inauguration of the Rev. James W. Alexander ... as professor of ecclesiastical history and church government in the Theological Seminary at Princeton: delivered at Princeton November 20, 1849 before the Directors of the Seminary.* New York: Robert Carter and Brothers, 1850.

Anderson, Herbert. "Toward a Constructive Anthropology: Hiltner's Paradoxical View of Persons." *The Journal of Psychology and Christianity*, 4:4 (1985): 47-55.

Barth, Karl. *God in Action*. Translated by Elmer Homrighausen and Karl Ernst. New York: Round Table Press, 1936.
—. *God's Search for Man*. Translated by George Richards, Elmer Homrighausen and Karl Ernst. New York: Round Table Press, 1935.
—. *Homiletics*. Louisville, KY: Westminster John Knox, 1991.
Barth, Karl and Eduard Thurneysen. *Come Holy Spirit*. Translated by George Richards, Elmer Homrighausen and Karl Ernst. New York: Round Table Press, 1934.
Bartow, Charles. "An Evaluation of Student Preaching in the Basic Homiletics Courses at Princeton Theological Seminary: A Farmerian Approach to Homiletical Criticism." Ph.D. diss., New York University.
—. *God's Human Speech: A Practical Theology of Proclamation*. Grand Rapids: Eerdmans, 1997.
—. "In Service to the Servants of the Word: Teaching Speech at Princeton Theological Seminary." *The Princeton Seminary Bulletin*, 13:3 (1992): 274-86.
—. "Who Says the Song? Practical Hermeneutics as Humble Performance. "*The Princeton Seminary Bulletin*, 17:2 (1996): 143-53.
Bass, Dorothy C. and Craig Dykstra. *For Life Abundant: Practical Theology, Theological Education, and Christian Ministry*. Grand Rapids: Eerdmans, 2008.
Boisen, Anton Theophilus. *The Exploration of the Inner World: A Study of Mental Disorder and Religious Experience*. Philadelphia: University of Pennsylvania Press, 1936.
Bosch, David. *Transforming Mission: Paradigm Shifts in Theology of Mission*. Maryknoll, NY: Orbis Books, 1991.
Boyer, Paul S., ed. *Oxford Companion to United States History*. New York: Oxford, 2001.
Breckinridge, John. *Controversy between the Rev. John Hughes, of the Roman Catholic Church, and the Rev. John Breckinridge of the Presbyterian Church; relative to the existing differences in the Roman Catholic and Protestant religions*. Philadelphia, PA: Joseph Whetham, 1833.
—. "Lecture X, May 13, 1832." *Spruce Street Lectures by several clergymen. Delivered during the years 1831-32. To which is added a lecture on the importance of creeds and confessions by Samuel Miller*. Philadelphia: Presbyterian Board of Publications, 1840.
Brown, William Adams and Mark May. *The Education of American Ministers*. 2 vols. New York: Institute of Social and Religious Research, 1934.
Browning, Don. *A Fundamental Practical Theology*. Minneapolis: Fortress, 1991.

Calhoun, David B. *Princeton Seminary: Volume 1: Faith and Learning, 1812-1868*. Carlisle, PA: Banner of Truth Trust, 1994.

Cassem, John McDonough. "An Analysis of Seward Hiltner's Systematic Pastoral Theology and Its Value and Application to Contemporary American Catholic Pastoral Theology." Washington: STD Thesis, Catholic University, 1974.

Catalogue 1841-1842. Princeton, NJ: Robert E. Hornor, 1841.

Catalogue 1855-1856. Philadelphia: C. Sherman and Son, 1855 [sic].

Catalogue 1862-1863. Trenton, NJ: Murphy, Betchtel, 1862.

Catalogue 1865-1866. Princeton, NJ: Blanchard, 1866.

Catalogue 1869-1870. Philadelphia: Caxton Press of Sherman and Co., 1874.

Catalogue 1874-1875. Philadelphia: Caxton Press of Sherman and Co., 1874.

Catalogue 1882-1883. Philadelphia: Caxton Press of Sherman and Co., 1882.

Catalogue 1883-1884. Philadelphia: Caxton Press of Sherman and Co., 1883.

Catalogue 1890-1891. Princeton, NJ: Princeton Press, 1890.

Catalogue 1891-1892. Princeton, NJ: Princeton Press, 1891.

Catalogue 1892-1893. Princeton, NJ: Princeton Press, 1892.

Catalogue 1893-1894. Princeton, NJ: Princeton Press, 1893.

Catalogue 1894-1895. Princeton, NJ: Princeton Press, 1894.

Catalogue 1895-1896. Princeton, NJ: Princeton Press, 1895.

Catalogue 1898-1899. Princeton, NJ: C.S. Robinson and Co., 1989.

Catalogue 1902-1903. Not provided: C.S. Robinson, 1902.

Cherry, Conrad. *Hurrying Toward Zion: Universities, Divinity Schools, and American Protestantism*. Bloomington, Indiana: University of Indiana Press, 1996.

Clutter, Ronald T. "The Reorganization of Princeton Theological Seminary Reconsidered." *Grace Theological Journal*, 7:2 (1986): 179-201.

Coe, George Albert. "Religious Education Is in Peril." *International Journal of Religious Education*, 15:5 (January, 1939): 9-10.

Collins, Allen and Richard Halverson. *Rethinking Education in the Age of Technology: The Digital Revolution and Schooling in America*. New York: Teachers College Press, 2009.

Craig, Samuel G. "Developments at Princeton Seminary." *Christianity Today*, 8:7 (November, 1937): 127.

DeWitt, John. "Discourse at the Funeral Service, in the First Presbyterian Church, Princeton, New Jersey, November the Thirtieth, 1904." In *In Memoriam: William Miller Paxton, D.D., LL.D., 1824-1904: Funeral and Memorial Discourses with Appendixes and Notes*. New York: No Publisher, 1905.

Dowey, Edward. *A Commentary on the Confession of 1967 and an Introduction to The Book of Confessions*. Philadelphia: Westminster, 1968.

Dunlavy, Colleen A. "Railroads." In *Oxford Companion*.

Dykstra, Craig. *Growing in the Life of Faith: Education and Christian Practices*. Louisville, KY: Geneva Press, 1999.

—. *Vision and Character: A Christian Educator's Alternative to Kohlberg*. New York: Paulist Press, 1981.

Elliott, Harrison. *Can Religious Education Be Christian?* New York: The Macmillan Company, 1940.

"Elmer G. Homrighausen." *The Princeton Seminary Bulletin*, 4:1 (1983).

Erdman, Charles. "Modern Practical Theology." *The New York Observer*, January 3, 1907. http://digital.library.ptsem.edu/default.xqy?terms=Charles+Erdman, accessed, June, 2008.

—. *The Spirit of Christ: Devotional Studies in the Doctrine of the Holy Spirit*. New York: George H. Doran Company, 1926.

—. *The Work of the Pastor*. Philadelphia: Westminster Press, 1924.

The Faculty: Princeton Theological Seminary. Princeton, NJ: The Seminary, 1999.

Farley, Edward. *Theologia: The Fragmentation and Unity of Theological Education*. Philadelphia: Fortress, 1983.

Gardner, Freda. "James Edwin Loder, Jr.: A Tribute." *The Princeton Seminary Bulletin*, 23:2 (2002): 188-94.

Gardner, Freda, Daniel Migliore and Geddes Hanson. "Memorial Minute of the Faculty of Princeton Theological Seminar. *The Princeton Seminary Bulletin*, 2:1 (1978): 28-9.

Green, W. Henry. "Address at the Funeral of Rev. Alexander Taggart McGill, D.D., LL.D. in Princeton, Jan. 16, 1989." No publisher, 1889.

Gross, Nancy Lammers. *If You Cannot Preach Like Paul*. Grand Rapids: Eerdmans, 2002.

Guelzo, Allen. "Charles Hodge's Antislavery Moment." In *Charles Hodge Revisited: A Critical Appraisal of His Life and Work*. Edited by John W. Stewart and James H. Moorhead. Grand Rapids: Eerdmans, 2002.

Haines, George L. "The Princeton Theological Seminary, 1925-1960." Ph.D. diss., School of Education, New York University, 1966.

Handy, Robert. *A Christian America: Protestant Hopes and Historical Realities*. New York: Oxford University Press, 1971.

Hanson, Geddes W. "Edler G. Hawkins: The Princeton Years." *Church and Society* (November/December 1987): 74-81.

Harris, William O. *Digest of the Minutes of the Board of Directors, 1812-1929*. Unpublished manuscript, 1992.

Hart, Darryl. *Defending the Faith: J. Gresham Machen and the Crisis of American Protestantism in Modern America*. Baltimore: John Hopkins University Press, 1994.

Hiltner, Seward. "Introduction to Practical Theology as a Theological Discipline." Seward Hiltner Collection, Special Collections, Princeton Theological Seminary Library.

—. *Preface to Pastoral Theology*. New York: Abingdon, 1958.

—. "The Teaching of Practical Theology in the United States during the Twentieth Century." *The Princeton Seminary Bulletin*, Vol. 61 No. 1 (1977): 61-75.

Hiltner, Seward. *Theological Dynamics*. Nashville: Abingdon, 1972.

Hodge, Charles. "Introductory Lecture, Delivered in the Theological Seminary, Princeton, N.J. Nov. 7, 1828." *Biblical Repertory: A Journal of Biblical Literature and Theological Science. Conducted by an Association of Gentlemen*. New Series, 5:1 (1829).

—. "Introductory Remarks on *The Life of Kant* by Professor Stapfer of Paris, Translated from the French by the Editor." *Biblical Repertory, A Collection of Tracts in Biblical Literature*, Vol. 4, No. 3 (1828).

Hoffecker, Andrew. *Piety and the Princetonians: Archibald Alexander, Charles Hodge, and Benjamin Warfield*. Phillipsburg, NJ: Presbyterian and Reformed Publishing Co., 1981.

Holifield, E. Brooks. *A History of Pastoral Care in America: From Salvation to Self-Realization*. Nashville: Abingdon Press, 1983.

Homrighausen, Elmer. "Axioms of Evangelism." *The Pastor*, 17:4 (December, 1953): 3-6.

—. "Barthianism and the Kingdom." *The Christian Century*, 48:2 (July 15, 1931): 922-25.

—. "Barth and the American Theological Scene." *Union Seminary Review,* 46 (July 1935): 283-301.

—. "Calm After Storm." Pt. 12 of "How My Mind Has Changed in This Decade." *The Christian Century*, 56:1 (April 12, 1939):477-9.

—. *Choose Ye This Day: A Study of Decision and Commitment in Christian Personality*. Philadelphia: Westminster Press, 1943.

—. "Christian Education After Ten Years of Ecumenical Thinking." *International Journal of Religious Education*, 15:9 (May, 1950): 176-85.

—. *Christianity in America: A Crisis*. New York: Abingdon Press, 1936.

—. "Communicating the Christian Faith." *Theology Today*, 1:4 (January, 1945): 487-504.

—. "Evangelism and Christian Nurture." *The Christian Review*, 8:4 (October, 1939), 271-8.

—. "Evangelism and the Presbyterian Reformed Churches." *Presbyterian World*, 19:2 (June, 1949).

—. "Evangelism in Such a Time." In *The Ecumenical Era in Church and Society: A Symposium in Honor of John A. Mackay*. New York: The Macmillan Company, 1959.

—. "Evangelistic Calling." *Pastoral Psychology,* 7:69 (December, 1956): 55-7.

—. "The Holy Spirit and the Renewal of Witness." *Theology and Life*, 7:1 (Spring 1964): 46-57.

—. *I Believe in the Church*. Nashville; Abingdon Press, 1959.

—. *Let the Church Be the Church*. New York: Abingdon-Cokesbury Press, 1940.

—. "The Minister and Religious Education." *Christian Education* 21:4 (April, 1938): 233-45.

—. "The New Emphasis in Christian Education." *Christendom*, 7:1 (Winter 1942): 81-9.

—. "The Real Problem of Religious Education." *Religious Education* 34:1 (January-March 1939): 10-7.

—. "Religious Education vs. the Church." *The Christian Century* 56:2 (November 29, 1939): 1465-6.

—. "The Salvation of Christian Education." *International Journal of Religious Education*. 15:9 (May, 1939): 12-13, 40.

—. "The Significance of Justin Martyr in the History of Early Christianity, or the Significance of Justin Maryr as a Witness to the State of Christianity in the Middle of the Second Century." S.T.D. diss., University of Dubuque Graduate School of Theology, 1930.

—. "The Task of Christian Education in a Theological Seminary." *The Princeton Seminary Bulletin*, 34:1 (1940): 3-21.

—. "Toward a Pastoral Church." *Princeton Seminary Bulletin*, 48:4 (May, 1955): 10-9.

—. "Wanted: The Recovery of the Christian Paideia." *Religion in Life*, 15:1, 126-36.

—. "What is the Witness of Presbyterianism?" *The Presbyterian World*, 22:4 (December, 1953): 152-8.

—. "A Young Minister's Counter-Revolt." *The Christian Century*, 48:1 (February 18, 1931): 236-8.

Homrighausen, Elmer, Charles T. Fritsch, and Bruce M. Metzger. "In Memoriam: Charles Rosenbury Erdman, July 20 1866-May 10, 1960." *The Princeton Seminary Bulletin,* 54 (November, 1960): 36.

Hunter, Rodney. "The Future of Pastoral Theology." *Pastoral Psychology* 29 (1980): 58-69.

—. "Moltmann's Theology of the Cross and the Dilemma of Contemporary Pastoral Care." In *Jürgen Moltmann: Hope for the World*, edited by Theodore Runyon. Nashville: Abingdon, 1979: 75-92.

—. "A Perspectival Pastoral Theology." In *Turning Points in Pastoral Care: The Legacy of Anton Boisen and Seward Hiltner*, edited by LeRoy Aden and Harold Ellens. Grand Rapids: Baker Book House, 1990: 53-79.

Israel, Paul. "Telegraph." In *Oxford Companion*.

Kay, James. *Preaching and Theology*, Preaching and Its Partners. St. Louis, MO: Chalic Press, 2007.

Kelly, Robert. *Theological Education in America: A Study of One Hundred Sixty-One Theological Schools in the United States and Canada*. New York: George H. Doran Company, 1924.

Kerr, Hugh T., ed. *Sons of the Prophets*. Princeton: Princeton University Press, 1963.

Kovacs, Kenneth E. *The Relational Reality of James E. Loder: Encounter and Conviction*. New York: Peter Lang, 2011.

Lapsley, James. "Pastoral Psychology: Editorial – Seward Hiltner, 1909-1984." In *Pastoral Psychology*, 34:1: 3-8.

"The Late Dr. Alexander." *New York Times,* August 5, 1859.

Leas, Rober. "Anton Theophilus Boisen." http://www.acpe.edu/networks/boisen_bio.htm, 2007.

Link, Arthur, ed. *The First Presbyterian Church of Princeton: Two Centuries of History*. Princeton: Princeton University Press, 1967.

Lobkowicz, Nicholas. *Theory and Practice: History of a Concept from Aristotle to Marx*. Notre Dame, IN: Notre Dame, 1967.

Loder, James. *The Transforming Moment: Understanding Convictional Experiences*. San Francisco: Harper & Row, 1981.

—. "Normativity and Context in Practical Theology: The Interdisciplinary Issue." In *Practical Theology—International Perspectives*, edited by Friederich Schweitzer and Johannes A. van der Ven. New York: Peter Lang, 1999.

—. *The Knight's Move: The Relational Logic of the Spirit in Theology and Science*. Colorado Springs: Helmer and Howard, 1992.

—. *The Logic of the Spirit: Human Development in Theological Perspective*. San Francisco: Jossey-Bass, 1998.

—. "The Place of Science in Practical Theology: The Human Factor." *The International Journal of Practical Theology*, Vol. 4 (2000): 22-41.

—. "Transformation in Christian Education." *The Princeton Seminary Bulletin*, 3:1 (1980): 11-25.

Loetscher, Lefferts A. *Facing the Enlightenment and Pietism: Archibald Alexander and the Founding of Princeton Theological Seminary*. Westport, CT: Greenwood, 1983.

Longfield, Bradley J. *The Presbyterian Controversy: Fundamentalists, Modernists, & Moderates*. New York: Oxford University Press, 1991.

Lovell, Arnold B. "Communicating the Christian Faith: A Study of the Relationship between Education and Evangelism in the Work of Elmer G. Homrighausen." Diss., Presbyterian School of Christian Education, May 1995.

Lynn, Robert Wood. "Notes Toward a History: Theological Encyclopedia and the Evolution of Protestant Seminary Curriculum, 1808-1868." *Theological Education* (Spring 1981): 118-44.

Machen, J. Gresham. *Christianity and Liberalism*. Grand Rapids, Eerdmans, 2009.

—. *Christianity and Liberalism*. Grand Rapids, Eerdmans, 1923.

—. "Christianity and Culture." *The Princeton Theological Review*, 11:1 (1913): 1-15.

—. "The Present Situation in the Presbyterian Church." *Presbyterian*, May 14, 1925: 8.

—. "The Relation of Religion to Science and Philosophy: A Review." *The Princeton Theological Review*, 24:1 (1926): 38-66.

—. "Westminster Theological Seminary: Its Purpose and Plan." In *Selected Shorter Writings*, edited by D.G. Hart. Phillipsburg, NJ: Presbyterian and Reformed Publishing Co., 2004.

Mackay, John. "The Restoration of Theology." *The Princeton Seminary Bulletin*, 31:1 (1937): 7-18.

—. "The Role of Princeton Seminary THE TASK WE ENVISAGE." *The Princeton Seminary Bulletin,* 38:4 (1945): 1-3.

Marsden, George. "Understanding J. Gresham Machen." *The Princeton Seminary Bulletin*, 11:1 (1990): 46-60.

—. "J. Gresham Machen, History, and Truth." *Westminster Theological Journal*, 42:1 (1979): 157-75.

McCord, James. "Tribute to Elmer G. Homrighausen." Memorial Service, Jan. 9, 1982, Miller Chapel, Princeton Theological Seminary. Tape Recording.

McGill, Alexander Taggart. *American Slavery as Viewed and Acted on by the Presbyterian Church in the United States of America*. Philadelphia: Presbyterian Board of Publications, 1865.

—. *Church Government: A Treatise Compiled from his Lectures in Theological Seminaries*. Philadelphia: Presbyterian Board of Publication and Sabbath Work, 1888.

—. *The Hand of God with the Black Race: A Discourse Delivered Before the Pennsylvania Colonization Society*. Philadelphia: William F. Gedded, 1862.

—. *Patriotism, Philanthropy, and Religion: An Address before the American Colonization Society, January 16, 1977*. Washington, D.C.: Not Provided, 1877.

—. "Practical Theology: An Inaugural Discourse." In *Discourses at the Inauguration of the Rev. Alexander T. McGill, D.D., as Professor of Pastoral Theology* [sic]*, Church Government, and the Composition and Delivery of Sermons in the Theological Seminary at Princeton, N.J., Delivered at Princeton, September 12, 1854, Before the Directors of the Seminary*. Philadelphia: C. Sherman, 1854.

—. "Sinful but not Forsaken: A Sermon Preached in the Presbyterian Church, Fifth Avenue and Nineteenth Street, New York on the Day of National Fasting, January 4, 1861." New York: Fifth Avenue Presbyterian Church, 1861.

"McGill, Alexander Taggart." In *The National Cyclopædia of American Biography*, no author provided. New York: James T. White, 1904.

A Memorial of Mrs. Margaret Breckinridge. Philadelphia, PA: W.C. Martien, 1839. Special Collections, Princeton Theological Seminary Library.

Meyer, Ingrid and Barbara Chaapel. "Years of Courage: Looking Back—and Forward—to Women at Princeton." *inSpire*, Princeton Theological Seminary (Spring 1997): 12-6.

Miller, Samuel. *A Brief Retrospect of the Eighteenth Century*, vol. 1 and 2. Bristol, England: Thoemmes, 2001.

—. "Introductory Lecture." Samuel Miller papers, box 2, file 1.

—. "Lectures on Ecclesiastical History." Samuel Miller papers, box 2, file 10.

—. *Life of Samuel Miller*. Volume 2. Philadelphia: Claxton, Remsen, and Haffelfinger, 1869.

—. "Sermon at the Opening of General Assembly, May 21, 1807." Samuel Miller papers, box 12, file 8.

—. "The Sermon Delivered at the Inauguration of the Rev. Archibald Alexander D.D. as Professor of Didactic and Polemic Theology in the Theological Seminary of the Presbyterian Church in the United States of America. To which are Added the Professor's Inaugural Address and the Charge to the Professor and Students." New York: Whiting and Watson, 1812.

Nichols, James Hastings. "Eulogy." *The Princeton Seminary Bulletin*, 2:1 (1978): 26-7.

Niebuhr, H. Richard, Daniel D. Williams and James Gustafson. *The Advancement of Theological Education*. New York: Harper and Brothers, 1957.

Niebuhr, H. Richard, Daniel D. Williams and James Gustafson. *The Purpose of the Church and Its Ministry*. New York: Harper and Brothers, 1956.

Noll, Mark. "Charles Hodge as an Expositor of the Spiritual Life." *Charles Hodge Revisited: A Critical Appraisal of His Life and Work*, edited by John Stewart and James Moorhead. Grand Rapids: Eerdmans, 2002.

—. *The Civil War as Theological Crisis*. Chapel Hill, NC: University of North Carolina, 2006.

—. "The Princeton Theology." In *Reformed Theology in America: A History of Its Modern Development*, edited by David Wells. Grand Rapids: Eerdmans, 1985.

—. Introduction to *The Way of Life*, by Charles Hodge. Carlisle, PA: Banner of Truth, 1978.

Nykamp, Delwain. "A Presbyterian Power Struggle: A Critical History of Communication Strategies Employed in the Struggle for Control of the Presbyterian Church, U.S.A., 1922-1926." Ph.D. diss., Northwestern University, 1974.

Osmer, Richard. *Practical Theology: An Introduction*. Grand Rapids: Eerdmans, 2008.

Osmer, Richard R. and Friedrich Schweizer. *Religious Education between Modernization and Globalization: New Perspectives on the United States and Germany.* Grand Rapids: Eerdmans, 2003.

Outhwaite, William. *New Philosophies of Social Science: Realism, Hermeneutics, and Critical Theology.* New York: St. Martin's Press, 1987.

Patton, Francis Landey. "Princeton Seminary and the Faith." In *The Centennial Celebration of the Theological Seminary of the Presbyterian Church in the United States of America.* Unpublished.

Paxton, William M. *Homiletics: Classification of Divisions.* Princeton, NJ: Princeton Theological Seminary, 1904.

The Presbyterian, January 15, 1925.

The Presbyterian Advance, January 22, 1925.

The Princeton Seminary Bulletin, 13:3 (1923).

The Princeton Seminary Bulletin, 34:1 (July 1940).

Putnam, Robert and David Campbell. *American Grace: How Religion Divides and Unites Us.* New York: Simon & Schuster, 2010.

Rieff, Philip. *The Triumph of the Therapeutic: Uses of Faith after Freud.* New York: Harper Torchbooks, 1966.

Scheuerman, William. "Globalization." *The Stanford Encyclopedia of Philosophy (Summer 2010 Edition).* Edited by Edward N. Zalta. URL = http://plato.stanford.edu/archives/sum2010/entries/globalization/. Accessed June 26, 2011.

Schleiermacher, Friedrich. *Brief Outline of Theology as a Field of Study: Revised Translation of the 1811 and 1830 Editions.* Translated by Terrence N. Tice, 3rd ed. Louisville, KY: Westminster John Knox Press, 2011.

Schneewind, Jerome B. "Scottish Common Sense Philosophy." In *The Cambridge Dictionary of Philosophy*, 2nd ed., ed. Robert Audi. New York: Cambridge, 1999.

Selden, William K. *Princeton Theological Seminary: A Narrative History, 1812-1992.* Princeton: Princeton University Press, 1992.

"Seward Hiltner (1909-1984)." *The Princeton Seminary Bulletin,* 7:1 (1986): 76-8.

Shults, F. Leron. "The Philosophic Turn to Relationality and the Responsibility of Practical Theology. In *Redemptive Transformation in Practical Theology: Essays in Honor of James E. Loder, Jr.,* edited by Dana R. Wright and John D. Kuentzel. Grand Rapids: Eerdmans, 2004: 325-46.

Smith, Christian. *What Is A Person? Rethinking Humanity, Social Life, and the Moral Good from the Person Up.* Chicago: University of Chicago Press, 2010.

Smith, Gerald Birney, Shirley Jackson Case, and D. D. Luckenbill. "Theological Scholarship at Princeton." *American Journal of Theology,* 17 (1913): 94-102.

Stokes, Allison. *Ministry after Freud*. New York: Pilgrim Press, 1985.

Tennent, Gilbert. "On the Dangers of an Unconverted Ministry." In *Sermons of the Log College*. Ligonier, PA: Soli Deo Gloria, 1993: 375-404.

Twyman, Alfred R. "The Harmonies of Struggle and Light: The African American Experience at PTS." *inSpire*, Princeton Theological Seminary (Summer 1998): 12-6.

U.S. Department of Education. *Digest of Statistics*. http://nces.ed.gov/programs/digest/d07/tables/dt07_258.asp. Accessed February, 2010.

Van Dyke, Henry. Letter to the Editor. *Philadelphia Public Ledger*, January 5, 1924. Reprinted in *The Presbyterian*, January 1924.

Van Til, Cornelius. "A Substitute for Christianity." *The Presbyterian Guardian*, 12:10 (February 10, 1943): 35.

Vokuil, Dennis. *From Liberalism to Neo-orthodoxy: The History of a Theological Transition, 1925-1935*. Cambridge: Cambridge University Press, 1974.

Warfield, Benjamin B. *Notes on Certain Proposed Readjustments of the Curriculum*. Princeton: Privately printed, 1914.

—. "Memorial Discourse, Delivered by Appointment of the Faculty of Princeton Theological Seminary, in Miller Chapel, on the Twenty-Fourth of February, 1905, by the Rev. Benjamin B. Warfield." In *In Memoriam: William Miller Paxton, D.D., LL.D., 1824-1904: Funeral and Memorial Discourses with Appendixes and Notes*. New York: No Publisher, 1905.

—. *Perfectionism*. New York: Oxford University Press, 1931.

Weeks, William Earl. "War of 1812." In *Oxford Companion to United States History*, edited by Paul S. Boyer. New York: Oxford, 2001: 814-5.

Wheeler, Barbara G., Sharon L. Miller and Katarina Schuth. "Signs of the Times: Present and Future Theological Faculty." *Auburn Studies* 10 (February 2005). http://www.auburnseminary.org/sites/default/files/Signs%20of%20the%20Times.pdf.

Wikipedia, s.v. "Auburn Affirmation." Last modified June 1, 2011, http://en.wikipedia.org/wiki/Auburn_Affirmation.

Witherspoon, John. "Glorying in the Cross." In *The Works of the Rev. John Witherspoon* Vol. 1. Philadelphia: William Woodward, 1800.

Wood, Gordon S. *Empire of Liberty: A History of the Early Republic, 1789-1815*. New York: Oxford, 2009.

Wright, Dana R. "Are You There? Comedic Interrogation in the Life and Witness of James E. Loder." In *Redemptive Transformation in Practical Theology: Essays in Honor of James E. Loder, Jr.*, edited by Dana R. Wright and John D. Kuentzel. Grand Rapids: Eerdmans, 2004: 1-40.

—. "Elmer Homrighausen." In *Talbot School of Theology: Christian Educators*. http://www2.talbot.edu/ce20/educators/view.cfm?n=elmer_homrighausen.

—. "James E. Loder, Jr." *Talbot School of Theology: Christian Educators*. http://www2.talbot.edu/ce20/educators/view.cfm?n=james_loder

Wright, Dana R. and John D. Kuentzel, ed. *Redemptive Transformation in Practical Theology: Essays in Honor of James E. Loder, Jr.* Grand Rapids: Eerdmans, 2004.

Wuthnow, Robert. *The Restructuring of American Religion: Society and Faith Since World War II*. Princeton: Princeton University Press, 1988.

Index

Abolitionism 11, 27, 27n68, 29, 29n75, 30, 34-5, 66, 68
African Americans (see "blacks" and "slavery") xvii, 182-4, 182n8, 189
Afternoon conferences 62-3, 212
Alexander, Archibald xv-xvii, 1, 17n45, 21n61, 18n47, 57, 90n46, 207
   Biography 6
   Biblical Knowledge and 5-7
   Inaugural Lecture 2n1, 5-8
   Influence of 36-7, 38n20, 40, 43, 47-8, 50-3, 63, 66, 68, 70-1
   Pastoral Theology and 12, 14, 16, 17-22, 25-6, 30
   Revelation and 7-8
   Slavery and 26-9, 27n68, 28nn71 and 73, 30, 34, 66, 68
Alexander, James Waddell xvi, 27n68,
   Biography 36-7, 37nn15 and 16, 38nn17 and 20
   Practical Theology and 38-41, 40n27, 70-1
   Sacred Rhetoric and 52
   Church Government and 57
   Slavery, race and 64-6, 71-2
American Association of Practical Theology 135

Bailey, Mark 53-4
Barth, Karl xvi-xvii, 54n65, 105-6, 117, 119-20, 119n40, 122-3, 126, 132, 159-60, 166
Bartow, Charles xv, xvii, 121, 133, 138, 207, 210
   Biography 163-4
   God's Human Speech 164-76
   Performative nature of preaching and 165-76
   Threefold Word of God and 168-76
Beeners, W.J. 117, 134-5, 163-4, 164n67
Bible, Scripture
   adherence to 18, 21-2, 29-30, 33-4, 45-7, 58, 60, 70, 75, 86, 92, 98-9, 100-2, 113, 130, 203-4, 208
   English 81-2, 95, 102, 103n2
   historical nature of 77-8, 88-9, 124, 173
   interpretation of 2, 14-6, 58, 77-8, 106, 126, 167, 175
   knowledge of 1, 6-8, 94, 113
   performative nature of 166, 169-74, 176
   slavery and 66, 68-70, 72
   study of 5, 18, 45-6, 50, 84, 90, 93, 109, 144
   teaching 109, 118n37, 130, 169, 181
   Word of God and 123, 168
Blacks (see "race" and "slavery") 10, 27n68, 28n7329, 37, 64-71
Boisen, Anton 113-4, 114n28, 140, 142n15, 143, 143n17
Breckinridge, John xvi, 23n63, 30, 36, 36n14, 57, 60
   biography 23-6
   mission and 23-4, 26
   practical theology and 12, 18
   slavery and 29
   wife's death and 24-5
Breckinridge, Margaret Miller 23-6
Brown and May Study 81-3
Brown, Sally 184-99
Browning, Don 135-7, 152, 152n44

Calvin, John 44, 91, 99, 143n22, 172
Calvinism 75n7, 79, 86n38, 93,
Catechizing, catechisms (see "Teaching") 21-2, 45-6, 51, 93, 100-1

Cherry, Conrad 83-4, 84n36, 112-3, 117
Christian social science 60-1, 71
Church xi, xvi, 2-5, 7-8, 10, 13-4, 21-2, 24, 33, 38, 40-1, 44-7, 50, 57-60, 62, 73-5, 77, 80, 97-8, 107-8, 111, 122-30, 145, 168-9, 171-2, 174-5, 181-3, 186, 195-9, 203, 205, 212
   slavery and, 26-7, 66-70
   society and xii, 44, 83, 85-6, 91-2, 95-6, 100-1, 113, 122-6
Church history, ecclesiastical history 5, 13-5, 22, 31, 37-9, 42, 44, 50, 52, 59-60, 83-4, 93, 97, 124, 144, 167, 191, 197, 206
Civil War 10-1, 26, 31-5, 64-72
Clerical paradigm, clericalism xiv, 9, 11, 18, 61, 194
Clinical Pastoral Education 109, 113-7, 139-40
College of New Jersey ("Princeton University) 1, 23, 37, 52, 64, 74
Columbia Theological Seminary 42, 66
Colonization movement 10, 28-9, 66-8, 70-2
Community 62-3, 212
Context xii-xiv, xvii, 4, 5, 10, 19, 22, 72, 100-2, 116, 116n33, 122-4, 126, 132, 133, 137, 143, 153-4, 165, 168-9, 172, 174, 176, 178, 184, 187-91, 204-6, 208-12
Curriculum
   Conflict over 79-83, 94-5, 98
   Explicit, implicit 193-4
   Initial Vision of 3-7
   Influence of CPE upon 116-7
   Overview of late nineteenth century version 51-64
   Practical Character of xiii, 10-4, 185-91, 205
   Reform of xv, 79-83, 85, 94-5, 106-13, 196-8, 207-8
   Shape of xii, xv-xvi, 135, 137, 177, 185, 190, 193-4, 206-7, 209
   Westminster Theological Seminary's 92-3

Deacons 19, 59
Dean, Kenda 184-99
Denominationalism, decline of 137-8, 177-9, 199, 211
Department of Practical Theology xiii-xvi, xv n3, 108, 116-7, 137-42, 147, 149, 164, 178-85, 195-201, 203-212
Dewey, John Stewart 84n36, 85, 115, 122, 144n23
Diversity xi, xvii, 82, 95, 137, 177-85, 205, 210-212
Doctor of Ministry 135, 141, 149, 183
Dykstra, Craig 138n5, 178-9

Ecclesiology
Practical 22, 42-3, 45, 57-60, 198
Ecumenism xvii, 76, 78, 96-8, 100, 102, 106-9, 111, 113, 117, 131, 136, 179
Edinburgh World Missionary Conference 96
Education (see "Teaching") xi, xiv, xvi, 1, 3-5, 8-10, 19, 45, 61-3, 68, 81-6, 90, 92-3, 96, 100-2, 137-8, 145-6, 147n32, 149, 177, 179, 181, 193-4, 196-200, 208-9
Elders 19-21, 58-9
Elocution 52-6
Emancipation 64-71
Erdman, Charles xv-xvi
   Biography 93-5
   Practical Theology and 94-102
   Reformed Evangelical 92, 95-6, 98, 100, 102
   Spirituality and 96-8
   Trinitarianism and 97

Evangelical 8, 21, 34, 39, 41, 45, 61, 66-71, 75-6, 78, 83, 86, 92-6, 98, 100, 105, 107, 117, 119, 124, 127, 177
Evangelism 22, 28-9, 66-71, 126, 127n68, 128-31, 145, 147n32
Experience, experimental knowledge xv, 3, 5, 12-4, 17-8, 26-7, 39, 42, 47, 52, 57, 59, 63, 81, 88, 90, 93, 99, 101-2, 109, 114, 122-3, 128, 131, 142, 150-1, 162, 170-1, 173, 175, 189, 204, 207-8, 210

Farley, Edward xiv, xiv n2, 11n28, 43n36, 62n92, 83n34, 178, 194
Field education 63, 82, 108, 112, 116, 180, 193, 207-8
Fifth Avenue Presbyterian Church (New York City) 31, 38
First Presbyterian Church (New York City) 2, 48
First Presbyterian Church (Princeton) 73-4
First Presbyterian Church of Color (Witherspoon Street Presbyterian Church [Princeton]) 64, 37n16
Five point doctrinal Declaration 78, 92, 104

Gardner, Freda xvii, 180-1, 183n14
General Assembly 1-2, 5-6, 13, 22-3, 37, 42, 44, 48, 53, 57, 66-9, 77-8, 80, 88, 104-6, 109, 181-3
German Idealism 14-7, 17n46, 40-1, 40n27, 61, 83
Gillespie, Thomas 134, 138-9, 176
Globalization 35-6, 36n12, 136-7, 210-2
Gospel 4, 7, 10, 20-1, 24, 28, 33, 40-1, 44, 47, 50-1, 58, 74-5, 91, 113, 123, 125-6, 128-30, 145-6, 168, 176, 196, 207, 211
Government, church (see "Ecclesiology, practical") 2, 5, 22, 31, 36, 42-4, 52, 57-60, 71
Gradualism 27, 30, 34, 65-6, 68, 72, 204
Green, William Henry 42, 54, 57, 80
Gross, Nancy 164, 164n68, 184, 185-200

Hanson, Geddes W. xvii, 183-4
Harper, William Rainey 84
Hawkins, Edler Garnett xvii, 182-3, 182n8
Hiltner, Seward xv-xvii, 115-6, 121, 132, 133, 138-9, 143n17 166-7, 176, 178, 204, 206-7, 210
  Biography 139-42, 140nn8, 10 and 11, 141n13
  Contribution of Practical Theology and 142-4, 143n22, 144n24
  Perspectival Model of Practical Theology 139-147, 142n15, 147n32, 206-7
  Relationship with James Loder 133-5, 138-9, 149, 153
Hodge, Charles xv, 14-7, 26-7, 27n68, 37-8, 40, 42, 57-8, 79-81, 86, 89, 90n46, 92, 92n53, 106, 111
Holy Spirit 3, 8, 14, 39, 94, 96-8, 100-2, 122-5, 131, 149, 151, 154, 156-7, 159-62, 168-72, 178, 203
Homiletics 20, 45, 48-56, 48n51, 54n65, 56, 59-60, 71, 75n7, 93-5, 99, 106, 164, 166-7, 184, 189, 192, 206
Homrighausen, Elmer xv-xvii, 204, 207
  Attack by Samuel Craig and Cornelius Van Til 105-6
  Biography 103-6, 117-9

Christian Nurture and evangelism 126-31
Critique of the Religious Education Movement 121-3
Karl Barth and 105-6, 117, 119-20, 122-3, 126, 131
Justin Martyr and 119, 124-6,
Practical Theology and 120-1, 123-31
Theology of the Church and 123-6
Theological Liberalism and 104-6, 119-20, 123
Theological Assumptions 119-26
Humanism, humanist xvi, 5, 22, 29, 30, 47, 70, 121, 203
Hunsinger, Deborah 184-200
Hunter, Rodney 142-3, 142n15, 143n17, 144nn23 and 28, 145n29

Illumination, divine 7-8, 162
Immigration 9, 22, 35, 76
Indifferentism, doctrinal 75, 79, 92
Interdisciplinarity, Interdisciplinary Thinking 46-7, 52, 61, 71, 115-6, 121, 132, 137, 143n22, 146, 149, 151-2, 154, 157-60, 165-6, 166n75, 187, 205-6, 209

Jesus Christ 3, 7, 12-4, 16, 20-1, 24, 29, 39, 41, 44, 92, 96, 100-1, 113, 123, 125, 127-9, 143, 151, 155-7, 159-62, 168-72, 174-6, 186, 190, 196-7, 203, 207, 212

Kant, Immanuel 16-7, 40, 122
Kelly Study 81, 112n25
Keswick Holiness Movement 94, 94n57, 97
Kidd, Robert 53
Knowledge 5-8, 12-4, 17, 19-21, 39, 45, 89-90, 99, 102, 143n22, 144, 147n32, 155, 160-1, 166-7, 204, 206

biblical 1, 6, 29
"doctrinal" 13-4
"experimental" or practical 13-4
fundamental 142, 145, 167
"head" 90
human 7, 160, 169
of God 6, 8, 67, 90
of Scripture 6, 8
theological 5, 116, 142-3, 145, 166-7, 204, 207
specialized 83-5

Learning xv, 2-8, 3n3, 12-3, 18-9, 21-2, 40n27, 47, 50, 52, 60, 62, 107, 128, 130, 150, 187, 189, 195, 201, 207-9, 212
community 62-4, 212
Liberalism, theological 41, 73-5, 75n7, 77-9, 83-92, 96, 98, 100, 102, 104-6, 113, 115, 119-20, 123
Liberation Theology 136, 181, 210
Liberia 10, 29, 68-9
Liturgics 38, 45, 58, 60, 62-3, 90, 95, 99, 109, 146n30, 164-5, 206, 209
Loder, James E. xv-xvii, 121, 176, 178, 187, 203
Biography 148-51, 148n33
Constructive Framework of practical theology 156-63
Fundamental Practical Theology 151-6, 152nn43 and 44
generative problematic of practical theology 152-5, 152n44, 160
Relationality 157-163, 203, 207
Relationship with Seward Hiltner 133-5, 138-9, 149, 153
Transformational Paradigm of practical theology 150-1, 157, 160, 162
Logic-centered vs. Operation centered fields 144-5

Luther, Martin 44, 99, 119n39

Machen, J. Gresham xvii, 73-80, 82, 85-7, 89n45, 92nn53 and 56, 96, 98, 99, 102, 104, 106, 131
  Apologetics and 90-1
  Biography 87-8
  Practical Theology and 89-92
  Science and 89
  Theological Education and 92-3
  "van Dyke" incident 73-7
Mackay, John 103, 105-9, 111-2, 117
Macleod, Donald 117, 134-5, 163
McCord, James I. 117, 134, 138-9, 176
McGill, Alexander Taggart xiii-xiv, xvi, 11-2, 36-7, 205-6
  Biography 41-2
  Church government and 57-9
  Practical theology and 43-8, 70-2
  Sacred Rhetoric and 54-5
  "Sinful but Not Forsaken" 31-4
  Slavery and 66-70
Milledoler, Philip 1, 5-6, 8
Miller, Samuel xv, xvii, 34, 36, 207,
  Biography 2, 23
  Influence of 37-8, 38n20, 40, 43, 45, 47-8, 50-3, 57-8, 63, 68, 70-1
  Practical theology and 12-4, 18, 22, 30
  Sermon at the Inauguration 1-5
  Slavery and 26-30, 68
Ministry xiv, 1-6, 10, 11n28, 18-22, 26, 29-30, 38, 42, 44, 46-8, 50, 51, 53, 62, 71, 81-2, 94, 96, 100, 112-5, 120, 123-4, 131-2, 142-3, 143n17, 145, 147, 167, 172, 176, 182-4, 189, 194, 197-8, 205-7, 209
  education 25, 84, 101-2, 127, 134-5, 145, 147n32, 149, 185, 187, 199, 200, 206, 209
  youth 9, 21, 101, 129, 139, 146, 190
Mission xvi, 10, 22-6, 39, 45, 51, 60-3, 61n89, 70-1, 76, 75n7, 81, 91, 96-8, 100, 106-7, 110, 113, 117, 127, 130-1, 136, 138, 206
  of the church 33, 75, 75n7, 93, 96-8, 100-2, 122-6, 130, 136, 210
  of PTS 107, 138-9, 203
Modernist/fundamentalist Conflict 17n46, 74, 76-7, 79, 86
Moorhead, James 27, 27n68, 28n73,

Native Americans 35
New Discussion of Practical Theology 135-7, 210-1
Niebuhr/Gustafson/Williams Study 109-113

Old School/New School Presbyterians 33, 42, 87, 93-4
Oral communication, speech xv, 45, 51-6, 55n65, 110, 135, 139, 146, 163-4, 164n67, 167-9, 172, 189-90, 192, 195, 206-7
Orthodoxy (see "Reformed") xvi, 5, 15, 20, 34, 39-41, 73-5, 75n7, 83, 85-6, 88-9, 92-6, 98, 100, 102, 105-6, 112-3, 115, 117, 123, 130-1

Pastor, pastorate xiii-xvi, 1, 5, 8, 11-13, 11n28, 18-23, 28, 38-40, 45-8, 50, 52, 56-8, 61-4, 70, 75, 80, 95-7, 99-101, 107, 116, 138, 146, 165, 178-9, 184, 188, 190, 195, 197, 199, 207, 209, 211-2
Pastoral care and counseling xiv-xv, 26, 42, 51, 60, 100, 103, 114-6, 124, 127, 127n68, 135, 138, 184-6, 188, 195, 200, 206, 206n1, 209

Pastoral theology xiii-xv, 6, 11-2, 18-9, 22-4, 26, 29, 43-5, 51, 53, 56, 60-2, 71, 100, 100n82, 111, 114-5, 116n32, 117, 135-6, 142n15, 147n32, 187, 205-6, 206n1

Patriarchs (Alexander, Miller, Breckinridge) xvi, 11n28, 17-8, 26, 29, 34, 36-9, 43, 50-1, 53, 70-1, 205-6, 212

Patton, Francis Landey 54, 79, 90

Paxton, William Miller xvi, 12, 36-7, 57
  Biography 48-9
  Church government and 59-60
  Sacred Rhetoric and 54-7
  Slavery and 64, 70-1
  Technical excellence and 49-51

Peabody, S.G. 53-4

Perkins, Theodore E. 54

Perspectival Practical Theology 139-147, 142n15, 147n32

Piaget, Jean 133-4, 159

Piety 2, 4, 8, 15, 18-9, 26, 29, 32, 39, 40-1, 50, 90n46, 203

Piety and learning 1, 4-5, 8, 13, 40-1, 50, 70, 89-90, 90n46, 107, 131, 203

Pluralism 76, 87, 91, 174, 210

Polity (see "Government, church.") 2, 5, 22, 43, 45, 51, 58-60, 111, 209

Practical theology (see "Department of Practical Theology") xi-xvii, 11-2, 11n28, 16-8, 22-30, 31, 34, 36, 38-9, 42-5, 43n34, 75n7, 81-5, 84n36, 90-5, 98-102, 103-4, 109, 112-3, 117, 120-1, 125, 131-2, 134-9, 136n3, 138n5, 141-7, 142n15, 146n30, 147n32, 149-157, 160-72, 176, 177-9, 178n2, 184-7, 191-201, 203-212

Generative problematic of 152-5, 152n44, 160

Practice, wise 3, 60

Practitioner(s) 46-9, 194

Praxis 136-7, 165, 200

Prayer 8, 13, 34, 38, 45, 62, 90, 101, 104, 156, 175, 188, 193, 212
  Concert of 63
  Daily 62-3

Presbyterian Church, Presbyterian, Presbyterianism (see "First Presbyterian of") xiii, 1, 2, 17n46, 22-4, 31, 33, 36, 42-4, 57, 66-7, 69, 74-8, 75n7, 86-8, 91-3, 102, 104, 106, 108-9, 138, 179, 181, 199

Presbyterian Particularism 91, 91n51

Princeton Theological Seminary
  Conflict at xiv, xvi, 77-83, 131
  Curriculum xii-xiii, xv-xvi, 3-7, 10-4, 51-64, 79-83, 85, 94-5, 98, 106-13, 116-7, 135, 137, 177, 185-91, 193-4, 196-8, 205-9
  Founding of 1-8
  Future of 185-201, 203-212
  PhD Program 108, 138, 141, 149, 164, 179, 185-7, 201, 206n1
  Providence, divine 25, 33-4, 38, 67-70

Race 34-5, 64-72, 137, 179, 182, 184, 188, 204-5, 210

Reason 7-8, 66, 210

Reconstruction 34, 66, 69-70

Reconstructing theology and piety 11n28, 17, 207, 211-2

Reformed tradition, Reformed xvi-xvii, 5-6, 20, 40, 75n7, 83, 85-6, 88, 91-102, 105-7, 111-3, 117, 125, 130-1, 165, 168, 179, 203-4

Religious Education Movement xiv, 84-5, 101, 104, 115, 121-3, 131-2

Revelation 7, 17-8, 22, 27, 29-30, 44, 58, 66, 70-1, 92-3, 101-2, 122-3, 126, 128, 143, 156, 171, 186, 203-5, 208

Revivalism, revival 15, 18, 18n47, 22, 29, 33-4, 41, 61, 104

Sacred rhetoric 51-7

Scottish Common Sense philosophy xiv, 16-7, 17nn44 and 46, 40, 86-7, 86n38, 89, 92n56

Second Vatican Council (Vatican II), 136

Sin 16, 20-1, 31-4, 89-90, 94, 113, 123, 155, 161-2, 172, 187

Slavery 10-1, 26-30, 27n68, 33-5, 64-71, 204, 211

Smith, Henry W. 54

Society xi-xii, 14, 26-30, 32, 34, 39, 44, 47, 64, 70-1, 85-6, 95, 100, 102, 115-6, 125, 203, 209-10, 212

Stevenson, Ross 78-82, 104,

Sunday Schools, Sabbath schools 21, 28, 28n71, 38, 45, 63, 73,

Teaching (see "Ministry, teaching") xv-xvi, 3, 5, 11, 16, 20-22, 24-6, 28, 32, 37, 45-7, 49, 50-2, 56-60, 63, 77, 93, 116, 127-32, 137-8, 146, 150, 153, 156, 165, 175, 180, 182-4, 186-9, 191-5, 201, 207, 211-2

   Religious Education Movement and xiv, 84-5, 101, 104, 115, 121-3, 131-2

   Slaves and 28, 67-8

Tennent College of Christian Education 109

Theology 31-4, 75, 77-9, 83, 85, 89-92, 95-8, 104-7, 123-6, 156-63, 168-76

Theological Education 1-26, 51-63, 81-3, 86, 92-3, 100-2, 107-117, 126-31, 135-7, 140-1, 165-7, 177-9, 185-201, 203-212

   Professional Model of 83-5

Theological encyclopedia 61-2, 61n91, 62n92, 83, 98, 117, 144n24, 147n32, 197, 208-9

Theory and practice xii-xiii, xvi, 3, 11, 18, 23-4, 44-7, 51, 53, 63-4, 66, 71, 81-2, 84-5, 102, 137, 141, 153-4, 157, 166-7, 176, 184-5, 188, 191-5, 197, 203-212

Theory (intellectual frameworks) 127, 46-8

Thornwell, James 42, 87, 91,

Tillich, Paul 112, 115, 149

Transformational paradigm of practical theology 150-1, 157, 160, 162

Union Theological Seminary (New York) 48, 50, 77, 84, 93, 105, 112-3

University of Chicago Divinity School 77, 81, 84, 84n36, 104-5, 108, 112, 119, 124, 139-40, 204

Van Dyke, Henry 73-7, 104

Vinet, Alexandre 54, 54n65, 99

Warfield, Benjamin Breckinridge (B.B.) 49, 54, 56, 77, 79-82, 88, 90, 94n57, 106, 131,

Western Theological Seminary (Allegheny, PA) xvii, 17n46, 80, 92-3, 92n56, 106

Westminster Confession, documents 5, 106, 113,

Westminster Confessional Standards 75, 78, 92,

Wisdom xiv, 3, 5, 7, 12, 16, 116, 130

Witherspoon, John 2, 3n3, 5

Wyckoff, Campbell 104n3, 117, 134, 138n5

International Practical Theology
edited by Prof. Dr. Chris Hermans (Nijmegen), Prof. Dr. Maureen Junker-Kenny (Dublin),
Prof. Dr. Richard Osmer (Princeton), Prof. Dr. Friedrich Schweitzer (Tübingen),
Prof. Dr. Hans-Georg Ziebertz (Würzburg) in cooperation with the International Academy of
Practical Theology (IAPT), represented by Bonnie Miller-McLemore (President) and
Jean-Guy Nadeau (Vice President)

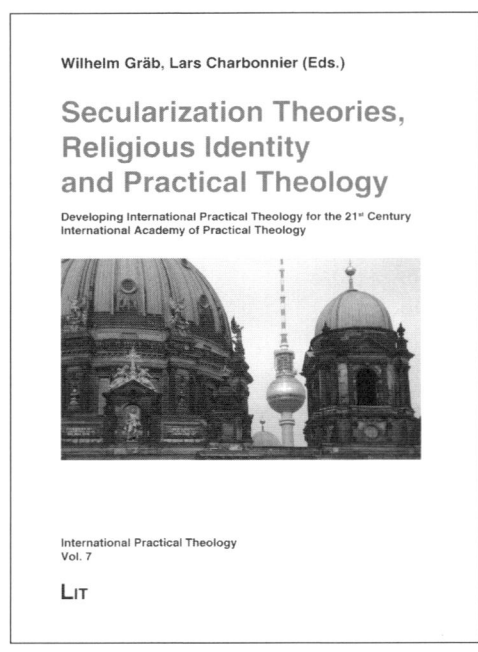

Wilhelm Gräb; Lars Charbonnier (Eds.)
Secularization Theories, Religious Identity and Practical Theology
Developing international Practical Theology for the 21st Century. International Academy of Practical Theology Berlin 2007
This volume represents the proceedings of the 2007 meeting of the International Academy of Practical Theology, which was held in Berlin (GER) on the theme of "secularization theories, religious identity and practical theology". This volume offers a wide variety of perspectives on the relationship between (practical) theology and sociology, psychology, education and culture, featuring papers from some of the world's leading practical theologians. They include subjects as "creating space within the dynamics of interculturality: the impact of religious and cultural transformations in post-apartheid South Africa", "redefining children's spirituality", "educating for religious identity in a secularizing world" and "Europe – a post-secular society". In this diversity of subjects, the common trend in international practical theological research regarding theories on secularization and religious identity in the globalized world is represented in this volume. Therefore, this book will be of interest not only to theological educators and students, but also to all those interested in the analysis of religion in its various phenomena at the beginning of the 21st century.
Bd. 7, 2009, 424 S., 39,90 €, br., ISBN 978-3-8258-0798-6

LIT Verlag Berlin – Münster – Wien – Zürich – London
Auslieferung Deutschland / Österreich: siehe Impressumsseite

Mechteld Jansen; Hijme Stoffels (Eds.)
A Moving God
Immigrant Churches in the Netherlands
This volume focuses on Christian immigrants and their churches in the Netherlands, with a special emphasis on the Amsterdam area. Many immigrants join one of the new immigrant churches that have originated in recent decades, while others attend Dutch Roman Catholic or Protestant congregations with a special ministry to immigrants. Immigrant churches form an exciting and multifaceted phenomenon in the Netherlands, just as they do in other parts of Europe and in North America. This volume is a joint effort of practical theologians and social scientists from VU University Amsterdam.
Bd. 8, 2008, 248 S., 24,90 €, br., ISBN 978-3-8258-0802-0

LIT Verlag Berlin – Münster – Wien – Zürich – London
Auslieferung Deutschland / Österreich: siehe Impressumsseite

Hans-Georg Ziebertz; Ulrich Riegel (Eds.)
Europe: secular or post-secular?
Religion is back on the agenda. Western societies are searching for an adequate understanding of religion. Media move religion into focus as a resource of significance in modern societies, but also as a source of tension and conflict. Politics is testing how to manage religious pluralism. Education is developing concepts of interreligious dialogue in order to promote a better intercultural understanding. The book discusses if the concept post-secularity allows a suitable understanding of the public presence of religion.
Ulrich Riegel ist Professor für Religionspädagogik im Seminar für Katholische Theologie an der Universität Siegen)
Bd. 9, 2008, 216 S., 19,90 €, br., ISBN 978-3-8258-1578-3

LIT Verlag Berlin – Münster – Wien – Zürich – London
Auslieferung Deutschland / Österreich: siehe Impressumsseite

Hans-Georg Ziebertz; William K Kay; Ulrich Riegel (Eds.)
Youth in Europe III
An international Empirical Study about the Impact of Religion on Life Orientation. With a preface by Silviu E. Rogobete
This book draws upon empirical data collected from 10,000 adolescent young people in 10 European countries. The first volume of this project was about young people's lifeperspectives and the second about their religious attitudes and practices. The current and final volume of this cross-cultural study connects both research dimensions. The analyses make clear that the influence of religion on values, life-orientation and politics differs strongly between different groups within Christianity and between Christians, Jews and Muslims. Many findings contain obvious surprises because they refute mainstream opinion on many topics. This book gives detailed and new insights in the public relevance of the religiosity of young people across Europe. All three volumes together are indispensable for scholars who work in public, religious and educational contexts. Ulrich Riegel ist Professor für Religionspädagogik im Seminar für Katholische Theologie an der Universität Siegen)
Bd. 10, 2009, 272 S., 19,90 €, br., ISBN 978-3-8258-1579-0

LIT Verlag Berlin – Münster – Wien – Zürich – London
Auslieferung Deutschland / Österreich: siehe Impressumsseite

Hans-Georg Ziebertz; Ulrich Riegel (Eds.)
How Teachers in Europe Teach Religion
An International Empirical Study
In 2007 about 3500 teachers in 16 European countries participated at a cross-cultural study "Teaching Religion in a multicultural Europe". The empirical survey researches existing teaching procedures in religion and theology. The book presents the results which are different approaches, strategies and ways of thinking when it comes to teaching religion in a multicultural context. This research was stimulated by the TRES Network (Teaching Religion in a multicultural European Society) which has been selected and approved by the EU Commission for a Socrates thematic network. Ulrich Riegel ist Professor für Religionspädagogik im Seminar für Katholische Theologie an der Universität Siegen)
Bd. 12, 2009, 408 S., 34,90 €, br., ISBN 978-3-643-10043-6

LIT Verlag Berlin – Münster – Wien – Zürich – London
Auslieferung Deutschland / Österreich: siehe Impressumsseite

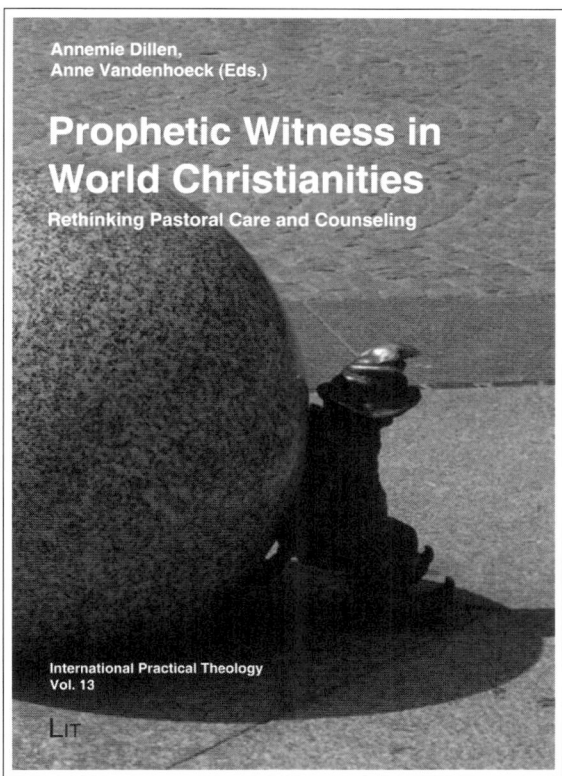

Annemie Dillen; Anne Vandenhoeck (Eds.)
Prophetic Witness in World Christianities
Rethinking Pastoral Care and Counseling
Prophets have a reputation of changing the relation between people and God for the better. Christianity has a long history of prophets who direct the faithful towards more justice and righteousness. What can Christians learn from prophets for daily life, for contemporary theology and pastoral care? This book undertakes the endeavor to look at prophetic acting from a biblical, pastoral and ethical perspective. The contributions of both, pastoral theologians and pastors from around the globe, make this study a unique exercise to keep the prophetic perspective in theological reflection and pastoral practice.
Bd. 13, 2011, 248 S., 24,90 €, br., ISBN 978-3-643-90041-8

LIT Verlag Berlin – Münster – Wien – Zürich – London
Auslieferung Deutschland / Österreich: siehe Impressumsseite

Edward Foley (Ed.)

RELIGION, DIVERSITY AND CONFLICT

International Practical Theology

L<small>IT</small>

Edward Foley (Ed.)
Religion, Diversity and Conflict
While religion can be a source of healing, peace and reconciliation, it can also be at least a trigger if not an underlying cause for conflict between peoples of varying beliefs. With that awareness, the International Academy of Practical Theology convened its 2007 meeting around the theme of "Religion, Diversity and Conflict." From the multiple seminars, lectures and studies presented at that meeting, a selection was chosen for this volume. Representing contributions from four continents, and drawing upon perspectives from African Traditional Religions, Judaism, Islam and Christianity this volume offers a rich introduction to the problems and promises of religion in dialogue with 21st century diversity. With contributions from leading figures in the field across a range of methods, Religion, Diversity and Conflict also serves as a varitable primer on the field of practical theology.
Bd. 15, 2011, 312 S., 29,90 €, br., ISBN 978-3-643-90086-9

L<small>IT</small> Verlag Berlin – Münster – Wien – Zürich – London
Auslieferung Deutschland / Österreich: siehe Impressumsseite